THE SCOTTISH CONNECTION

THE
SCOTTISH
CONNECTION

The Rise of
English Literary Study
in Early America

FRANKLIN E. COURT

SYRACUSE UNIVERSITY PRESS

First Edition 2001
01 02 03 04 05   6 5 4 3 2 1

The paper used in this publication meets the minimum requirements of American National Standard for
Information Sciences—Permanence of Paper for Printed Library Materials, ANSI Z39.48–1984.∞™

Library of Congress Cataloging-in-Publication Data
Court, Franklin E., 1939-
     The Scottish connection : the rise of English literary study in early America /
     Franklin E. Court.—1st ed.
          p. cm.
     Includes bibliographical references (p.) and index.
     ISBN 0-8156-2882-X (alk. paper)—ISBN 0-8156-2917-6 (pbk.: alk. paper)
     1. English literature—Study and teaching (Higher)—United States—History. 2. English
literature—Study and teaching—United States—History—19th century. 3. English
literature—History and criticism—Theory, etc. 4. Criticism—United States—History—19th
century. 5. United States—Civilization—Scottish influences. 6. English
literature—Appreciation—United States. 7. United States—Intellectual life—19th century.
8. English literature—Appreciation—Scotland. 9. Criticism—Scotland—History. 10.
Scotland—Intellectual life. I. Title.
PR51.U5 C68 2001
820.71173—dc21   00-059521

Contents

Illustrations

Franklin E. Court, professor emeritus of English at Northern Illinois University, is the author of *Institutionalizing English Literature: The Culture and Politics of Literary Study, 1750–1900.*

Acknowledgments

This book grew out of an essay called "The Early Impact of Scottish Literary Teaching in North America" that I contributed to Robert Crawford's edition of essays, *The Scottish Invention of English Literature* (1998). I am indebted to Professor Crawford for inviting me to participate in the 1995 symposium, the Scottish Invention of English Literature, held at St. Andrews University in Scotland. The exchange of ideas at the symposium encouraged me to continue with my part of the project. I am also grateful to the Folger Institute for providing me at the time with a travel grant to Scotland.

I am again deeply indebted to those helpful librarians who make the task of research a joy. Particular acknowledgment must go to the librarians and staff at the Library of Congress, the British Library, the Scottish National Library, the University of Edinburgh Library, the Huntington Library, the archives at the College of Charleston, the Bentley Historical Library at the University of Michigan, Founders Library at Northern Illinois University, and, most particularly, Chicago's Newberry Library, where I found archival material that was available nowhere else, and both Memorial Library and the Wisconsin Historical Library on the campus of the University of Wisconsin, Madison.

For their patient assistance with the pesky business of illustrations, I wish to thank Elizabeth Gombosi, Harvard University Art Museums; Denise Pulford, Hunterian Museum and Art Gallery at the University of Glasgow; Jane Schroeder, Special Collections at Dickinson College; Beverly Bach, Campus Archives at Miami University in Ohio, who also encouraged me to extend the section on William Holmes McGuffey; and Sarita Oertling at the Moody Medical Library, University of Texas in Galveston, whose Scottish connections in both culinary and musical dimensions run deep.

Thanks again to Jesse Lamb, Dylan Fleugh, and Jacob Reich for their expert computer help, and to Brian Sage for discussing the issues with me on our many journeys between Illinois and Wisconsin. Thanks also to Jenifer Warren, my beloved daughter, for her unflagging interest in my academic projects over these many years. As usual, I am deeply grateful to *La Belle Dame,* Abigail Loomis, my live-in reference librarian, who continues to assist me with my research and to encourage me in my writing pursuits.

THE SCOTTISH CONNECTION

I

Scotland and the
Rise of Literary Criticism

The direction of language study in American colleges underwent a
monumental transition during the course of the eighteenth century
from a concentration on classical rhetoric to a concentration on English
rhetoric. By the end of the century, however, the study of English rhetoric
had evolved into a broader study that included oratory and disputation.
The new approach, which linked the study of moral philosophy directly
with rhetoric, created a course emphasis that both Jonathan Maxcy and Edward Tyrell Channing in the early years of the nineteenth century referred
to as "philosophical criticism."

Maxcy was the president, in sequence, of Union College (Schenectady,
New York); Rhode Island College, later Brown University; and the College
of South Carolina, later the University of South Carolina. Channing was
the Boylston Professor of Oratory and Rhetoric at Harvard University in
the early years of the nineteenth century. Addressing the subject of "philosophical criticism," Maxcy observed in an 1817 lecture to seniors at South
Carolina that his teaching objective was to "unfold" the principles that he
associated with the combined study of "rhetoric and philosophical criticism" (Maxcy 1844, 397). Around the same time, Channing observed in a
lecture to his Harvard seniors on the "general view of rhetoric" that he
could not see "how a liberal and philosophic rhetoric can overlook any
form of composition, any use of language that aims at power over the
heart" (E. T. Channing 1968, 34). *Philosophy* is the key word here. Out of
the combination of moral philosophy with rhetoric, oratory, and classical
literary criticism, vernacular literary study in North America was born. The
driving force behind the new "philosophical rhetoric" was the dominating

1

influence of eighteenth-century Scottish moral philosophy and Scottish or, more specifically, Scots-Irish Presbyterianism on all phases of colonial higher education in the United States. To say that colonial America went to school on the Scots is hardly an exaggeration.

The formative impact of Scotland, the Scottish rhetorical tradition, and Scottish moral philosophy on the history of English literary studies in North America extends from the early eighteenth century to the mid–nineteenth century. From the mid-nineteenth century onward, other influences, particularly philology from continental Europe, were paramount. During the early colonial years, however, the Scottish educational system, owing to reforms that favored the separation of education from government control, was more in tune with life as lived and idealized in America than any other European educational system.

For one thing, Scottish education in the eighteenth century, at least in theory, purported to be democratic. The system guaranteed as much as possible that all Scottish children had some means of education available to them. Scottish "little schools" were designed to provide an early opportunity for the populace to learn to read, write, and count. Scottish and Scots-Irish Presbyterian academies played prominent roles in the education of prospective ministers and laymen seeking careers in business and the professions. Eighteenth-century Scottish universities made their courses accessible to a large number of students from a variety of backgrounds. Caste, particularly where the Presbyterian influence was present, appears not to have been as much of a deterrent to educational opportunity as it was, for instance, in England.

One salient reason for the promotion of democratic education in Scotland was the widespread desire among educated Scots for a respectable degree of English literacy among the Scottish populace. When John Ramsay of Ochertype (1736–1814) in his memoir *Scotland and Scotsmen in the Eighteenth Century* was attempting to account for the Scottish revival of letters in the eighteenth century, he cited particularly the desire of the Scots to read and imitate the best English authors (Robbins 1954, 234–35). Caroline Robbins, writing about the impact of Scotland's Francis Hutcheson on political developments in the American colonies, notes that accounts of the rise of interest in English literature in eighteenth-century Scotland consistently stressed the link between reading and the Scottish "love of conversation." She cites, as an example, President Duncan Forbes (1685–1747) of Culloden, who reserved Sunday evenings for meetings with his friends in order to exchange views about English literature (1954, 235).

The desire for increased English literacy was also at the basis of Lord Henry Brougham's and Thomas Campbell's efforts to establish a college in London in the early nineteenth century. Both Brougham and Campbell, of course, were Scots. University College, London University, which opened in 1828, owed its inception largely to their efforts. Brougham, who was named Lord Chancellor in 1830, promoted the study of English literature at University College in an effort to encourage national literacy. He hoped to propagate a national reading campaign that would educate the British populace about the complexities of politics and political reform. A university course emphasizing "good" reading, that is, instructional reading in English as an end in itself, would add academic legitimacy to the campaign to promote the habit nationally. Educators and reformers who would carry the "gospel" of literacy to the masses could also be trained in the new institution. Campbell, who is remembered more for his poetry than his politics, believed that, because literature was primarily a social phenomenon, its future depended on a literate populace (Court 1992, 42–46).

Campbell, however, also envisioned literacy and literature as nationalizing forces that could eventually assist in uniting the Scots, a lesson in unity that was not lost on American colonists. Most educated Scots in the eighteenth century realized that English was the language of power, both political and economic, and they encouraged its study. There is no clear evidence, incidentally, given the preference for education in English, that educated Scots or Scottish educators in the eighteenth century were opposed to bilingualism, especially in the Highlands, or that they ever intended for the formal study of English to render Scots Gaelic obsolete.

The Scottish educational system also was evolving during the eighteenth century, the time of the Scottish Enlightenment, in the direction of curriculum expansion and a recognition of the value of utility as an educational objective. As we shall see, both developments, especially the promise of an educational system promoting utilitarian ideals, appealed to practical-minded North American educators. Oxford and Cambridge continued to emphasize classical education and to enroll an elite minority of aristocratic young men whose families were part of the establishment that guided and controlled the British Empire. Eighteenth-century Scottish universities, on the other hand, had developed in the direction of expanding the curriculum to make it appeal across class barriers and to include, among other innovative studies, the teaching of English as well as other modern vernacular languages.

Theoretically, the early difference between the old and the new rested on whether the focus of higher education should be "classical," with a concentration on the study of Greek, Latin, and Hebrew, or what was termed at the time "philosophical." The term *philosophical* carried a meaning that eighteenth-century scholars associated with ancient school texts such as Cicero's *De Oratore* where the word was used specifically to suggest the mastery of all knowledge, either "by scientific investigation or by the methods of dialectic," as Cicero informed Quintus. "For indeed," Cicero advised, " 'philosophy' " is "the creator and mother, as it were, of all the reputable arts" (Cicero 1942, 9). As this study argues, in the history of the development of vernacular literary study in the United States, the term is most appropriate; from approximately the 1740s onward, expanding interest in the formal study of moral philosophy, combined frequently with courses in rhetoric, provided the foundation from which English and American literary study as autonomous disciplines eventually would emerge. Course offerings in moral philosophy encouraged and augmented training in the art of oratory which, as some literary historians have suggested, produced the first academic effort in North America to combine general principles of an all-inclusive literary criticism with an appreciation of vernacular literature, English and American.[1] The "philosophical" approach to higher

1. Gerald Graff, writing about the rise of oratory in American colleges in *Professing Literature: An Institutional History,* suggests that by the mid-nineteenth century "the oratorical culture . . . pervaded the college and linked the classical courses with . . . courses in English rhetoric and elocution, with . . . literary and debating societies, and with the literary culture outside" (1987, 35). The present study suggests that the oratorical culture actually began to influence the development of English studies in the United States much earlier than the period suggested by Graff. Robert Scholes, in his recent study *The Rise and Fall of English,* also suggests that the link between the tradition of belletristic oratory and the progress of literary study at Yale and Brown began in the late eighteenth century (1998, 1–28). For more insight into the connection among oratory, literary criticism, and the developing appreciation of English and American literature in the United States, see also Kermit Vanderbilt, *American Literature and the Academy: The Roots, Growth, and Maturity of a Profession* (esp. 29–48); Richard Ohmann, *English in America: A Radical View of the Profession*; Andrew Hook, *Scotland and America, 1750–1835*; Robert Crawford, *Devolving English Literature* (esp. 176–215); and Gregory Clark and S. Michael Halloran, eds., *Oratorical Culture in Nineteenth-Century America: Transformations in the Theory and Practice of Rhetoric.*

education also stressed a knowledge of general principles that automatically favored the study of the humanities. Scots in the eighteenth century, as the anthropologist George Stocking observes, "tended to see progress as grounded in the passional nature of man, and in the conditions of social and economic life" (1987, 16); thus, it follows that subjects that addressed humanity's passions and their link to economic progress would fare particularly well in the new progressive curriculum. Literary study was just such a subject.

Hutcheson, Smith, and Blair

The driving force behind Scottish curricular changes was the dominating influence on all phases of eighteenth-century Scottish life of the work of the Scottish "moral sense theorists." Two major schools of moral philosophy existed in eighteenth-century Britain. One was initially inspired by Thomas Hobbes; the other by Anthony Ashley Cooper, Lord Shaftesbury. In the view of Hobbes, author of *Elements of Law,* written in 1640, and *Leviathan,* published in 1651, humans acted primarily from motives of self-concern and selfishness. To Shaftesbury, who wrote *Inquiry Concerning Virtue* in 1699 and published it in *Characteristics of Men, Manners, Opinions, and Times* in 1711, humans acted primarily out of feelings of charity, love, and compassion. The moral sense and the sense of beauty, Shaftesbury maintained, were mutually interdependent.

Although Shaftesbury pushed his vision of humanity's innate moral sense to optimistic extremes, both he and Francis Hutcheson, the prominent Scottish moral philosopher who followed him, envisioned humans as essentially productive and virtuous, capable of acting from motives of sympathetic benevolence and selflessness. In all cases, however, for both Shaftesbury and Hutcheson, humans were motivated primarily by feelings rather than by reason. In this perspective, reason was conceived of as a lesser force, activated principally by the affective consciousness. Cultivating one's intrinsic sense of sympathy, consequently, as Adam Smith would later argue in *The Theory of Moral Sentiments* (1759), was essential to the performance of good actions.

In 1725, Hutcheson published *An Inquiry into the Origin of Our Ideas of Beauty and Virtue; in Two Treatises.* The book, cited by Ian Simpson Ross in his splendid biography of Adam Smith as the first work to be published in Britain that dealt specifically with aesthetics (1995, 50), promoted

Shaftesbury's claim that humans have an innate sense of beauty analogous to the moral sense. As Ross notes, the idea formed the basis of a developing set of arguments that linked aesthetics directly to morals, by specifying an "Author of Nature" who had blessed us with "strong Affections to be the Springs of each virtuous Action" (1995, 50). The idea that there was a benevolent Author of Nature behind virtuous human actions also appealed to the sensibilities of many eighteenth-century writers, rhetoricians as well as philosophers, including Adam Smith, who, according to Ross, explored the idea in detail in his *Theory of Moral Sentiments*. The value of virtuous actions was also at the heart of the desire to work for the common good and became an essential part of utilitarian thought, summed up in Hutcheson's famous phrase from the *Inquiry* that the "best" action is that "which accomplishes the *greatest happiness* for the *greatest Numbers*" (1725, 2: 164). William Robert Scott, in a 1966 biography of Hutcheson, was one of the first to observe that Hutcheson's "intense interest in the elevation of life" and "his passion for the improvement and advancement of mankind" actually made him a pioneer of utilitarianism as John Stuart Mill understood it (1966, 2).

Hutcheson's role as a precursor of utilitarianism is important in the context of the history of literary study in the United States, because embedded in the connection between the desire for virtuous actions and utilitarianism is the desire to be a good citizen as well as a virtuous person.[2] To be socially useful, then, was also to be virtuous. Terry Eagleton, in an essay on Hutcheson, observes that "in an age of empiricism, abstract ideas are no longer any very sound basis in which to lodge our sense of human community; so Hutcheson's creaturely ethics . . . turn the other way, back to the very senses which seem the source of all our conceptual uncertainty, and discover in this sensuous substratum the source of our social sympathies" (1995, 119). Education, it was believed, could enhance the socializing process by teaching individuals to understand, as Mill would later argue in *On Liberty*, that in acting for the common good they were also promoting personal gratification. For Hutcheson, like Mill, subjective morality was intimately related to the sense of beauty. Although Hutcheson distinguished several internal senses to explain various human experiences, he, like Lord Kames, Adam

2. For some informative, though controversial, insights into the extent of Hutcheson's influence in the United States, see Chapter 12 of Garry Wills, *Inventing America: Jefferson's Declaration of Independence*.

Francis Hutcheson. Portrait by Allan Ramsey. Courtesy of the Hunterian Art Gallery, University of Glasgow.

Smith, Thomas Reid, Hugh Blair, George Turnbull, William Barron, and the other influential eighteenth-century Scottish men of letters who followed him, built on the romantic premise of the intimate connection between beauty and personal virtue. Consequently, these writers promoted their individual conceptions of the manner in which ethics complemented aesthetics.

An interest in combining ethics with aesthetics led naturally to a preoccupation with the moral sense theory, represented first in Scotland by Hutcheson and, to a lesser degree, by his most illustrious pupil, Adam

Smith, who, while a student at Glasgow University, attended Hutcheson's moral philosophy lectures from 1738 to 1740. Hutcheson was Glasgow's professor of moral philosophy from 1730 to 1746. Against Hobbes's contention that humans acted from motives of selfishness and egotism, Scottish moral sense theorists, following Shaftesbury, Hutcheson, and, to a degree, David Hume, argued that the "moral sense" disposes us to the approvals and disapprovals, the pleasures and pains, that we feel. They maintained that humans comprehend moral values and virtue through this innate sense or sentiment, and they insisted on the importance of the "social nature" of humanity as one normal way to experience approval. Accordingly, the presence of a moral sense, therefore, depended primarily on feelings (Copleston 1963, 48f.).

Hutcheson's courses at Glasgow University extended the scope of the study of moral philosophy to include contemporary social and cultural issues. Hutcheson was particularly keen on teaching the works of Cicero, particularly Cicero's *De Officiis* from which he borrowed heavily for the *Inquiry*. He promoted, consequently, a predictable classical brand of Ciceronian humanism that linked a variety of academic subjects, including the study of rhetoric and belles lettres, with practical social concerns.[3] Because Ciceronian humanism traditionally emphasized civic responsibility and the value of civic discourse, it also, by extension, encouraged the formation of debating societies and the classroom practice of disputation. The practice in turn was at the center of what literary historians call the "oratorical tradition," a naggingly ill-defined academic and critical phenomenon that, as this study argues, greatly influenced the development of English language study in the late-eighteenth- and early-nineteenth-century United States. It also promoted the art of politics, given that oratory and statesmanship were considered complementary entities in the promotion of government.

Hutcheson wanted to be remembered as a teacher. He was instrumental in establishing an academy supported by Presbyterian dissenters in Dublin in 1721–22 designed for, among other academic pursuits, the promotion of philosophical inquiry (Scott 1966, 23–26). In the preface to his major Latin work, the *Compend,* he acknowledged publishing his writings princi-

---

3. For an insightful discussion of Hutcheson's Ciceronian humanism, see Thomas P. Miller, "John Witherspoon," in *Eighteenth-Century British and American Rhetorics and Rhetoricians.*

pally with the academic marketplace in mind.[4] Though some of his students found his religious liberalism distasteful, most remembered him fondly and admired his teaching techniques. If nothing else, he was innovative and exciting, and he lectured in English.

Hutcheson also dealt openly in his lectures with controversial questions of politics, particularly civic humanism and religious liberty; and, in an effort that foreshadowed later attempts by Adam Smith and others to combine literary study with the formation of moral character, he insisted that moral philosophy be taught didactically in order to have a practical and realizable ethical effect on the students (Scott 1966, 64–77). He is also said to have required his students to write individual abstracts and abridgements, in English, of essays from popular English language sources such as the *Spectator* and the *Guardian*. Adam Smith, Lord Kames, Thomas Reid, Hugh Blair, and other eighteenth-century promoters of Scottish rhetoric and moral philosophy admittedly learned much from him. He was the preeminent teacher who also listed among his many famous students Alexander Carlyle, James Wodrow, James Moor, Archdeacon Francis Blackburne, Joseph Priestley, Thomas Brand Hollis, John Witherspoon, and Francis Alison. Witherspoon, though he was critical of Hutcheson's theology,[5] nevertheless promoted the Hutchesonian link between ethics and aesthetics in early efforts to teach vernacular literature, when serving as the first president of the College of New Jersey, later Princeton University. Alison in 1756 was named the first vice provost of the College of Philadelphia, which in 1791 became the University of Pennsylvania. He also figured prominently in early efforts to promote university English literary study.

Hutcheson provided Adam Smith, when Smith was a student at Glasgow University, with a background in philosophy that, as both Ross and Eagleton suggest, formed the basis for Smith's moral philosophy and, eventually, his entire system of economics (Ross 1995, xviii, 48–59; Eagleton 1995, 119). Ross points out that Smith, while at the university, saw how free trade with expanding North American and Caribbean markets was creating wealth. As Ross puts it, "economic protection" offered by the British government at the time temporarily favored Glasgow merchants

4. In the preface, Hutcheson states that he published the *Compend* specifically "for those who study at universities" (1747, i-ii).

5. Witherspoon, a staunch Evangelical, satirized Hutcheson's liberal theology. He was particularly critical of Hutcheson's low-key, academic approach to preaching.

and manufacturers, but "free trade [that] extended beyond the British empire was a vision" that offered them unlimited promise (1995, xviii-xix). The thought of cross-Atlantic markets and trade extending beyond the boundaries of the British Empire also inspired young Smith, who essentially favored increasing the markets. His concern for capitalizing on the potential for new markets, unexplored economic investments, the division of labor, and the possibility of creating an educated labor force for the first time in history, would eventually link the progressive vision of business-minded Americans with his economic theories, particularly as outlined in *Wealth of Nations*, in a way that the young Glasgow student in the waning years of the 1730s could never have anticipated.[6]

While a student at Oxford from 1740 to 1746, Smith studied, largely on his own, moral and political philosophy and the ancient and modern languages. He also worked at translations, mainly from the French, in order to improve his English style. After Smith had returned to Edinburgh from Oxford, Henry Home, Lord Kames, a lawyer and later a judge, approached him in 1748 with a request to deliver a series of public lectures on rhetoric and belles lettres. Kames was acutely aware of the necessity among aspiring Scottish professionals for formal training in English. Although he thought the Scots should develop a facility with English at least as proficient as that of their neighbors to the south, his chief concern was for the linguistic effectiveness of Scottish legal advocates under the British-Scottish union. He wanted to broaden the preparatory program for the study of law by creating a liberal arts curriculum that included belles lettres and criticism, mathematics, physics, and natural history. Proficiency in English was essential to the education of Scottish lawyers defending, particularly, Scottish interests in the English metropolitan arena. At Kames's suggestion, Smith constructed a series of lectures that included discussions of authors and literary selections taken particularly from English literature. As a result, for the first time in the history of higher education in Britain, a formal course was offered that was devoted to the study of the works of English authors as something other than simple illustrations of rhetorical or grammatical principles.

As I have argued elsewhere, Smith was by nature a commonsense his-

6. For an informative discussion of Adam Smith's position on potential economic opportunities in North America, see Andrew S. Skinner's article "Adam Smith and America: The Political Economy of Conflict," in *Scotland and America in the Age of Enlightenment*.

toricist, who believed, in anticipation of Hegel, that civilization was advancing in an orderly, evolutionary fashion (Court 1992, 19–20). Education was increasingly recognized as a political necessity in the process. Smith envisioned the formal study of English literature as a possible corrective for ethical deficiencies that he thought inherent in the implementation of free-market economic and social theories. The study of English literature provided a wide-ranging method for teaching conduct, not as a measure of "polite learning" necessarily but as a way to transcend class-based distinctions of refinement and to promote citizenship, particularly among the lower classes. His principal social objective, detailed in *Wealth of Nations,* was to discredit the prevailing economic system in order to underscore what he stoically believed was the unfitness of European governments to direct industrial growth. He wanted to eclipse the old, centrally controlled mercantile system, a royalist caste system based on political favor and government patronage, excessive taxation, restricted land ownership, and the accumulation of vast amounts of money for the military. In its place, he promoted a progressive system based on ideals of equality and democracy that advocated a utilitarian rather than an aesthetic vision of education. He wanted a well-educated, commercial ruling class sensitive to the responsibilities of leadership. The immediate need, one that proves to have been particularly applicable to the United States and Canada during the post-Revolutionary War era, was for sympathetic leaders who would be ethical and trustworthy as well as educated—sober, prudent men who, as active borrowers, investors, and managers in a free world market, could be trusted to promote the interests of the market fairly and equitably and to practice high standards of political behavior (Court 1992, 21). From Smith's perspective, the study of English literature provided training in the formation of the "moral sense," which was, as Stocking notes, an amalgam of "the instinct of personal rights" and Smith's doctrine of "sympathy" (1987, 131).

Smith recognized what many Americans in positions of leadership in the late eighteenth century also recognized, and that was the potential power of the free market, particularly in the "new world," as a promising mechanism for political control, one that was in direct opposition to the "old world," aristocratic order of caste and government by preferment. The dilemma that faced these "new world" economists, however, and which was also an ongoing concern of Scottish Enlightenment philosophers, was how passion and a desire for beauty could be reconciled with morality in order to advance the continuing viability of practical, utilitarian ethics without succumbing totally to the restraining metaphysical axioms of standard religious dogma.

Smith delivered the Edinburgh lectures between 1748 and 1751. Arthur Applebee, in his pioneering work on the history of English teaching, says the occasion was the "first time that literary criticism had been dealt with in a separate course of lectures" (1974, 8). John Stevenson, Edinburgh University's professor of logic from 1730 to 1755, repeatedly read at random in class from the works of contemporary English authors and devoted approximately one-third of his class time to literary analysis. But Smith's lectures, as Applebee observes, were likely the first to deal extensively with English literary criticism.

There is no record of exactly what Smith said in his Edinburgh lectures or where he delivered them. We do know that Hugh Blair, who was a student at Edinburgh University at the time, attended them. After Smith was appointed to the Chair of Logic and Moral Philosophy at Glasgow in 1751–52, he put together another course on English rhetoric and literary criticism. Ross suggests that he likely "fell back on the rhetoric material presented at Edinburgh" (1995, 87). Ross also notes, as this study argues, that the historical record shows that Smith's innovative approach to the study of rhetoric and belles lettres was widely imitated throughout Scotland and North America in the years following Smith's appointment (1995, xx).

During his years as a professor, from 1751 to 1764, Smith's thoughts on literary criticism matured in parallel to his work on ethics and economics. The philosophical rationale behind his case for the formal study of English literature was closely connected to his thoughts on "sympathy" and his argument for the education of the "good man" (the "good bourgeois") and "studious observer," which he eventually developed in *The Theory of Moral Sentiments,* published in 1759. Smith's thoughts on literary education found their context in his theory of a self-regulating free market that eventually would link the self-interest of his students with the public interest. The exercise was based largely on a contemporary conception of "civic humanism" that can be traced directly to Cicero's works on civic duty. Students, it was believed, would learn to share experiences and feelings over time through a process of associative, imitative identification that naturally approved good acts and deplored evil ones. *The Theory of Moral Sentiments* provided the philosophical foundation for the formalized study of biographical models and characters in literary texts as examples of both ethical and unethical behavior. Literary analysis made the appropriation possible, for the study of character, as it still does, required close textual examination and interpretation.

Smith's hypothetical eighteenth-century student was "economic man" in miniature, undergoing a rite of passage into the soon-to-be-realized political certainties of industrial society. American educators supported the concept, even if they had no immediate familiarity with Smith's works. Smith had little interest in doctrines of taste as a way of distinguishing merit. His influence on the development of the discipline in North America was embedded in arguments for the immediate utility of literary study, not primarily as a measure of polite learning or as a way to acquire "taste," but as a practical way to further one's facility with the language, to improve character and conduct, and, consequently, to improve the body politic.

His lectures, though technically not published until recent times,[7] may have been distributed by enterprising students, because the practice of copying and selling class lectures was prevalent at the time. An extant copy of the lectures was discovered among holdings in the library of the Forbes-Leith family of Whitehaugh in Aberdeenshire. They may have been left with the family by a hired tutor who was either one of Smith's former students or had acquired the lectures from another student. As Ross suggests, another possibility is that they may have belonged to Thomas Reid, Smith's successor in the Chair of Moral Philosophy at Glasgow. Reid came from Aberdeenshire and could have passed them on (1995, 124). Smith's lectures, consequently, may have made their way to the North American colonies even before the official publication of any of his works in North America. Henry May, in his study of *The Enlightenment in America,* contends that the Scottish authors exerted their greatest influence during the 1790s. Kames, Reid, Dugald Stewart, and James Beattie, in particular, sold well in the United States during that time. May also asserts that by the 1790s "the standard curriculum in American colleges" was modeled after Scottish sources with the study of "moral philosophy . . . central to the curriculum" (1976, 346–47). Smith's reputation had been ongoing, because he was well known in America as a moral philosopher even before the

7. Smith's *Lectures on Rhetoric and Belles Lettres,* edited by John M. Lothian, was first published in 1963. In 1983, J. C. Bryce published another edition.

Revolution (May 1976, 349). Actual documentation of Smith's connection with American university studies, however, dates initially from the 1825 publication of George Jardine's *Outlines of Philosophical Education, illustrated by the Method of Teaching the Logic Class in the University of Glasgow.* Jardine, professor of logic at Glasgow, was one of Smith's students in the 1760s, and shared Smith's thoughts on how the course should be taught. Jardine's book, which was highly influential in North American universities in the nineteenth century, incorporates, as Ross suggests, "the legacy of Smith's reformulation of rhetoric and its integration into university studies" (1995, 131).[8]

By far the most influential eighteenth-century Scottish rhetorician, in both England and North America, was the Reverend Hugh Blair, who, in 1762, was made Regius Professor of Rhetoric and Belles Lettres at Edinburgh University. A lengthy volume of his sermons and an edition of Shakespeare had appeared as early as 1753. His most notable contribution to the development of English literary study, however, was his famous forty-four-volume edition of *The British Poets,* the first uniform edition of British poets ever published in the British Isles. The lectures in Blair's *Lectures on Rhetoric and Belles Lettres* were enormously popular throughout North America. Although they were not published formally until 1783, they were available and circulated earlier in the form of student notes. By the end of the nineteenth century, his *Lectures,* in one form or another (often abridged in the United States), had appeared in more than fifty editions.

In both Scotland and the United States, the study of rhetoric was traditionally linked with morality. Blair's lectures, consequently, served a dual purpose. They were used to teach rhetoric but they also promoted a conception of language that emphasized the moral value of the study of aesthetics. At Yale, Blair's *Lectures* was introduced into the curriculum in 1785. Harvard adopted the text in 1788. In 1783, the College of Rhode Island had adopted Lord Kames's *Elements of Criticism,* but by 1803, both Kames and Blair were required (Hook 1975, 76). Between 1800 and 1835, Blair's *Lectures* was being taught at Amherst, Columbia, Middle-

---

8. Ross cites for support William Charvat's *The Origins of American Critical Thought* (esp. Chapter 3); see also Edward P. J. Corbett, *Classical Rhetoric for the Modern Student* (esp. 563–68); and Henry E. May, *The Enlightenment in America* (esp. 346–50).

bury, North Carolina, Pennsylvania, Hamilton, Williams, and Wesleyan (Charvat 1936, 31–32).

Andrew Hook suggests that, in spite of the popularity of Blair's *Lectures* as a text, its effects in the United States and in Scotland, "from the point of view of potential, native, linguistic vitality, were probably slightly debilitating." Hook argues that the study of Blair and other Scottish rhetoricians in North America may have been largely responsible for promoting and sustaining a genteel tradition in American letters that emphasized elegance and correctness at the expense of works of a vernacular character. "One might go so far as to say," Hook writes, that, to that extent, "the study of rhetoric in schools and colleges impeded the development of a native American literary idiom" (1975, 82). Hook's point is hard to dispute, but the role of teaching rhetoric in the history of literary study in North America may have been less formative than he thinks.

Courses in rhetoric, even in North American colleges, generally included literary selections as examples illustrating various grammatical and rhetorical principles. Attempts were also generally made to define the characteristics of various literary genres as potential composition assignments for student writing. But the meager literary efforts of the rhetoricians, almost without exception (including Blair), grew primarily out of a concern for English as a language, with a clear concentration on grammar and principles of style, thought, and correct expression. Units on literary taste in most rhetoric texts, including Blair's, concentrated on encouraging students to identify and use figures of speech in order to stimulate their minds, as Charlotte Downey observed, to a recognition of the significance of using figures of speech to point out resemblances and relations (Newman 1995, 15). The development of English and American literary studies, as independent, self-contained academic disciplines, clearly owed a debt to the rhetoricians who first introduced literary criticism and vernacular literary selections into their courses of study. But a greater debt, one that shaped the direction literary study would take as it developed in the nineteenth century, was owed to moral philosophy. Literary study, as it was developing, was employed principally for something other than the promotion of taste and the study of the language; it was used "philosophically" and "critically" to promote morality and religion, and eventually to improve techniques of persuasive disputation in courses in oratory.

The Ulster Enlightenment: The Scots-Irish

Many of the themes that the Scottish moral philosophers promoted were themes that, in turn, had a decisive impact on educational developments in North America, where Scottish immigrants helped to disseminate their teachings. Scottish immigration to the American colonies increased considerably after 1700. Most of the immigrants were, like Hutcheson himself, Scots-Irish from Ulster. James G. Leyburn estimates that well over two hundred thousand Scots-Irish left Ulster for North America between 1700 and 1776 (1962, 180). According to Ian Graham, most of the immigration directly from Scotland occurred during a short twelve-year period between 1763 and 1775 (1956, 189). Consequently, most American colleges with a discernible Scottish connection founded before 1776 trace the connection to the Scots-Irish and, in almost all instances, to Scots-Irish Presbyterians from Ulster.

The Scots-Irish carried two very important principles with them when they left Ulster: One was an insatiable desire for independence, especially from exploitive government control; the other was a traditional concern for community education embodied in the figures of their Presbyterian ministers, most of whom were graduates of Scotland's universities. As Douglas Sloan suggests in *The Scottish Enlightenment and the American College Ideal,* had the Scots-Irish "not brought with them their Presbyterian ministers," their contributions "to American higher education in the colonial period would doubtless have been slight" (1971, 37). Traditionally, in Presbyterian communities, the minister was the intellectual and cultural source of knowledge. Most of the Ulster-born ministers who immigrated were products of education first in academies similar to Francis Hutcheson's Dublin academy, usually run by resident ministers. When they went on to college, they usually attended Scottish universities. Sloan notes that of the twenty-six ministers on record with the Presbytery of Philadelphia before 1717, twelve had finished their education at Glasgow University, four at Edinburgh (1971, 41).

In order to preserve educational standards similar to those practiced in Scotland and Ulster, the Presbytery of Philadelphia early in the eighteenth century decided that young men from the colonies who desired to become ministers should have proper educational opportunities available to them in the colonies and should, in all areas of study, measure up to the level of competence demanded by the Scottish and Scots-Irish examining boards.

A show of competence in theology and the liberal arts was of particular concern. The three existing American colleges—Harvard, founded in 1636, William and Mary in 1693, and Yale in 1701—made no special provisions for the education of the Presbyterian ministry. Consequently, there was increasing sentiment among Presbyterians, especially in the early decades of the eighteenth century when Scots-Irish immigration was at its highest, for the establishment of a college in North America that would educate Presbyterian ministers. As a result, in 1746, the College of New Jersey, later, Princeton, was established by Presbyterian ministers and supportive community leaders as a legally chartered liberal arts college that would educate ministers and other men interested in the professions but would require no religious tests or demonstrations of religious allegiance for either admission or graduation.

Remarkably, the College of New Jersey was the first and only new liberal arts college founded in North America following the opening of Yale, forty-five years earlier, in 1701. However, within eighteen years after the appearance of the College of New Jersey, three prominent American colleges were established, all of which had influential Scottish and Scots-Irish connections. They were: King's College, later, Columbia University, opening in 1754; the College of Philadelphia, later, the University of Pennsylvania, opening in 1756; and the College of Rhode Island, later, Brown University, opening in 1764.

Francis Alison's New London Academy, 1742

The first plausible date of consequence in the traceable history of English literary study in North America was 1742, the date when the Reverend Francis Alison, a Scots-Irish Presbyterian minister, appeared on record as combining the teaching of English grammar, composition, and literature at his academy at New London, Maryland, in an effort to preserve "Old Side" Presbyterianism (Sloan 1971, 75). Old Side Presbyterians were opposed to a growing revivalist faction in the colonial American Presbyterian Church that was promoting a type of "born-again" Evangelicalism that encouraged tent revivals, fire and brimstone pulpit oratory, and other highly emotional public displays of religious fervor. The revivalists were called New Siders. Old Siders accused them of being anti-intellectual and of promoting religious fanaticism. New Siders, most of whom were New England-based and listed Jonathan Edwards and George Whitefield among their supporters, promoted an open, freer ecclesiastical organization than the Old Siders wanted, one that would enable ministers to capitalize on highly emotional religious conversions and the appeal to inner "lights" wherever and whenever the opportunity arose.

New Siders were opposed to what they deemed a "dead church" and to a moribund classical educational system that they believed supported it. The issue was political; the concern was power and control of the Presbyterian Church in North America. New Siders wanted reform, so they proposed the establishment of a series of colleges throughout dedicated to the propagation of new revivalist theology. These new schools were to be called Log Colleges, after William Tennent's famous Log College which opened in 1735 at Neshaminy, north of Philadelphia. Tennent, a New Sider, was an outspoken Scot, a 1695 graduate of Edinburgh University, who was at first a Presbyterian minister but became an ordained Anglican minister in 1704. After he immigrated in 1718, he denounced his Anglicanism and was reinstated in the Presbyterian ministry. His Log College was increasingly viewed as offensive to the more conservative Old Siders, most of whom were recent Scots-Irish immigrants from Ulster who feared a deterioration of doctrine and central discipline if the New Siders gained ecclesiastical control. The very idea of a series of Log Colleges scattered around the land dedicated to the education of revivalist ministers repulsed and threatened them (Sloan 1971, 42–60).

Alison, an Old Sider who graduated from Edinburgh University in 1732, came under the influence of Francis Hutcheson at some crucial point in his youth. Their friendship was close enough to enable Alison in 1746 to write freely to Hutcheson for advice on the course of study and on books that he could use in the New London Academy. As a result of his progressive educational designs, Alison devised a curriculum that, he thought, went well beyond what he believed was the Log Colleges' concentration on religion and theology. Alison was only partially correct in his assumption. Other subjects, including some that for the time were experimental, actually were taught in New Sider Log Colleges. Divinity studies formed only the core of the Log College curriculum.

Alison's advanced course of study, however, ranged more broadly. For one thing, he taught composition and critically examined student themes. He also adopted Hutcheson's practice of requiring his students to write, in English, abstracts and abridgements of essays from various English literary sources. He particularly liked to have students in his moral philosophy course draft English abridgements of Hutcheson's *Short Introduction to Moral Philosophy*. Consequently, one must conclude that, because Alison's students studied critical readings of essays with accompanying classroom written exercises based on the readings, and because those written exercises were in turn evaluated by the instructor, his classes were involved, at however elementary a level, in the critical study of English literature.

Alison also used a technique borrowed from John Stevenson, professor of logic and metaphysics at Edinburgh, who may have been the first to introduce young Alison to the critical study of modern literature. The technique involved comparing classical authors with modern French and English authors (Sloan 1971, 76). Alison also taught, as Matthew Wilson, one of his students, recalled, "a *course of philosophy, instrumental, natural and moral*" (Sellers 1973, 20–21). Alison's moral philosophy course was indebted to Hutcheson, from whom he drew the principle that philosophical teaching of any kind should concentrate more on feelings than on a priori reason as a guide to ethical conduct (Norton 1976, 1562–65). He also acquired from Hutcheson the belief that recognition of the virtuous affections was akin to a sense of taste. Like Hutcheson, Alison promoted a civic humanism that envisioned society and the bonds of social commitment as a learning stage for the observation of proper human conduct. Sloan contends that Alison actually was responsible for introducing Hutcheson's theories to America (1971, 88). Alison's moral philosophy course was essentially the first of a long line of similar courses that would remain at the core of the liberal arts curriculum of Presbyterian-dominated colleges in the United States and Canada until well into the early half of the nineteenth century.

The College of Philadelphia, 1756

When Alison left New London for the Philadelphia Academy in 1752, he took his curriculum with him. In 1756, the Philadelphia Academy became the College of Philadelphia; in 1791, it would become the University of Pennsylvania. There, in 1756, another Scottish immigrant to the colonies, William Smith, would be provost; Alison, of Scots-Irish descent, would be vice provost. Although the new college had no official church connection, Alison continued to promote his Old Side Presbyterianism. Smith, an Anglican, worked to have an Anglican bishop seated in the colonies, a prospect that Alison translated into the dreaded possibility that the College of Philadelphia could eventually become an Anglican institution, a possibility which Alison found unacceptable.

From 1743 to 1747, while Alison had been overseeing the New London Academy, William Smith had been enrolled as a student at Aberdeen's King's College where he likely studied with Thomas Reid, a leading force in Scottish academic reform. Smith came to America as a tutor in 1751. By 1753, he had published a pamphlet describing an imaginary college, titled *A General Idea of the College of Mirania* (Pryde 1957, 24, 30). The pamphlet generated enough interest that on May 31, 1754, an advertisement appeared in the *New York Gazette* outlining a course of study planned for the newly conceived King's College (later Columbia University), which was based on Smith's pamphlet. The course of study was never realized at Columbia, but it would be at the center of the College of Philadelphia's experimental curriculum.

The plan was heavily indebted to David Fordyce's *Dialogues concerning Education,* published in 1745, and to the curriculum reforms at Aberdeen that were inspired by Fordyce (Diamond 1990, 122). Smith's professors at Aberdeen had been acutely aware of the need to use education to refine the moral sense of pupils, enabling them subsequently to become "good and useful citizens" (Diamond 1990, 122). As Peter J. Diamond points out, "[George] Turnbull's *Principles of Moral Philosophy* (1740) and *Observations upon Liberal Education* (1742), Fordyce's *Dialogues* and *Elements of Moral Philosophy* (1754), and Alexander Gerard's *Plan of Education in the Marischal College and University of Aberdeen* (1755) all testify to the broadly Hutchesonian temper of Aberdeen's educationists" (1990, 122–23). Fordyce's lectures and writings particularly promoted Hutcheson's moral sense philosophy. Gerard and Turnbull were less influential because they resisted the antirationalist, Hutchesonian conclusion that morality ultimately is grounded in feeling. Yet, they all promoted the technique, reminiscent of both Hutcheson and Adam Smith, of teaching by examples taken from history and nature. Diamond quotes Turnbull as saying that "true philosophy teaches the order of nature, and the order of human life." Otherwise, "how abstruse, how abstract, dry and laborious will lectures [in moral philosophy] be, till youth have been led by real examples to the knowledge of moral facts and their causes" (Diamond 1990, 123).

The study of natural philosophy, as Turnbull conceived it, advanced from a Ciceronian perspective, focusing on the order and goodness inherent in nature but now expanded to include an acknowledgment of the harmony of man and nature in a grand God-ordained scheme. William Smith, like Hutcheson and Adam Smith, promoted an educational vision of Ciceronian humanism grounded in the desire to produce students who would be good citizens. Smith also advocated capitalizing on the opportunity to educate future patriots, even though, as an Anglican, he supported British loyalism rather than American independence when hostilities developed.[9]

The 1753 pamphlet on the *College of Mirania* included a detailed outline of Smith's ideal course of study. The course was designed to realize the philosophical principle at the center of Scottish commonsense education, a design intended to produce, as Smith observed in the pamphlet, quoting Adam Smith, "a succession of sober, virtuous, industrious citizens" (Snow 1907, 60). Louis Franklin Snow, in his invaluable study of early curricula in American colleges, calls the pamphlet the "first comprehensive plan of a college course developed logically" in the North American colonies (1907, 60). In the pamphlet, Smith addressed the issue of offering courses in English literary study. He argued that the study of polite literature not only taught students to write well and rendered "life comfortable," but also contributed "highly to the cement of society and the tranquillity of the state." The argument was based on the contention that a college education should be a preparation for citizenship, an argument that was also a primary tenet of Scottish Enlightenment thinking.

The imaginary Miranians, the pamphlet continued, "greatly condemn the practice of neglecting the mother tongue, and embarrassing a young student, by obliging him to speak or compose in a dead language" (Snow 1907, 64). Significantly, the writings on moral philosophy of Francis Hutcheson were recommended for study in the third year. In the fourth year, students were to link their previous studies to the actual business of life. Smith writes:

You may observe that what has been chiefly aimed at, in the foregoing classes, is to teach youth to think well, that is, closely and justly. When this is attained it is a noble basis, but would, however, be useless without its superstructure; without teaching them to call forth and avail themselves of their thoughts, in writing, speaking, acting and living well. To make youth masters of the first two, viz., writing and speaking well, nothing contributes so much as being capable to relish what has been well written or spoken by others. Hence, the

9. For more on Smith as an educator and British patriot, see Albert Frank Gegenheimer, *William Smith, Educator and Churchman, 1727–1803.*

proper studies of this class are rhetoric and poetry, from which arise criticism
and composition. (Snow 1907, 63)

William Smith was a practical-minded educator, a product of Scottish
empiricism, and, like Alison, an educational visionary for his time. Shortly
after the *College of Mirania* appeared, he had an opportunity to test his
ideal course of study in a real college. In the early 1750s, Smith had aligned
himself with Alison at the academy in Philadelphia. Together they proposed to the academy's Board of Trustees that a College of Philadelphia be
established that could grant degrees. In 1755, a college charter was
drafted. Smith was to be the provost; Alison, vice provost (Sloan 1971,
82–83). On April 13, 1756, the board approved a course of study that, according to Snow, remained virtually the same at the nascent University of
Pennsylvania throughout most of the colonial period (1907, 67). William
Riley Parker, in a pioneering 1967 *College English* article on the origin of
English departments in North America, notes that a teacher named
Ebenezer Kinnersley headed a so-called English School that, in 1755, was
associated with the College of Philadelphia. Kinnersley, according to
Parker, was given the title "professor of the English Tongue and Oratory"
when the college opened. Kinnersley, about whom little is known, remained at the college until 1773 when he resigned. Parker calls him "probably our first college professor of English in any sense" (1967, 342). Parker
may be right, but there appears to be no extant record of exactly what Kinnersley taught. What is certain is that, although Kinnersley may have been
the professor of "English . . . and Oratory" at the College of Philadelphia,
the course of study that was followed was essentially the work of William
Smith and Francis Alison.

Smith's and Alison's course of study was designed with practical objectives in mind. Consequently, the study of the classical languages was subordinated to more utilitarian concerns, and it eliminated "any special aim
toward theology as a profession" (Snow 1907, 72). The course design covered three years; moral philosophy was introduced in the second year.
Moral philosophy continued into the third year with afternoons set aside
for composition and declamation on moral and ethical topics. Smith noted
in the outline of his program, "composition . . . cannot well be begun at an
earlier period in the plan. The knowledge of Mathematics is not more necessary, as an introduction to natural philosophy, than an acquaintance with
the best ancient and modern writers, especially the critics, is to just compo-

sition; and besides this, the topics or materials are to be supplied, in a good measure from moral and natural philosophy" (Snow 1907, 72 n. 1).

For study during "private hours," Smith included in the course outline a lengthy list of authors with instructions that the ideal students in his ideal college would "neither at college, nor afterwards, rest satisfied with a general knowledge, as is to be acquired from the public lectures and exercises." The hope was that "for the acquisition of solid wisdom," they would, randomly during the three years, "accomplish themselves still further" through private study. As a guide to their private reading, he included in a separate section in his outline a wide "choice of approved writers in the various branches of literature." These books, he added, were not intended to be consulted only occasionally; they were to be read in order to accomplish the completion of "the whole" of their education.

The list included, among a wide selection of religious, classical and scientific titles and authors, popular offerings from English literature but, mainly, works of literary criticism. Specifically, he listed essays from Joseph Addison's and Richard Steele's *Spectator* and Samuel Johnson's *Rambler* ("for improvement of style and knowledge of life"), John Dryden's *Essays and Prefaces,* and Joseph Spence's *Essay on Pope's Odyssey.* The list also included the dramatic works of Sir William Davenant, poet laureate from 1638 to 1668. The students were also advised to read Hutcheson's *Works,* John Locke's *Essay on Human Understanding,* Richard Hooker's *Ecclesiastical Polity,* and the works of Sir Francis Bacon (Snow 1907, 70–71). In essence, the course outline that Smith laid before the Board of Trustees of the College of Philadelphia in 1756 may well have been the first in colonial America to include authors and titles that later would be considered standard reading in surveys of English literary criticism.

Charles Janeway Stille, who later would also serve as provost at the University of Pennsylvania, writing in his 1869 biography of Smith, claimed that Smith's curriculum formed the basis of the "present American College System," and that "it may be safely affirmed that in 1756 no such comprehensive scheme of education existed in any college in the American colonies" (Snow 1907, 73). Beyond his formative role in the creation of the College of Philadelphia, Smith's influence on the development of early American college courses remains problematic. Indisputable, however, is the fact that his ideal course of study bore roots that were distinctly Scottish, with an emphasis on philosophical and literary criticism. His pedagogical vision owed much to his years as a student at Aberdeen. In fact, Smith's ideal course outline is strikingly similar to a revised course of study introduced by request at Aberdeen in 1753 by Alexander Gerard (Pittock 1998, 121–23).

In 1795, the recently named University of Pennsylvania modified Smith's *College of Mirania* design by instituting, for the first time in American university history, an arrangement of schools on the campus similar to what we now call colleges. Significantly, one of the designated schools was labeled "Philosophical." The published "Report of the Committee for the arrangement of the Schools" noted that when a class "is admitted into the Philosophical schools they shall apply themselves to the farther prosecution of Mathematics and classical learning, and to the study of philosophy, for . . . two years, after which . . . they shall be admitted to the degree of Bachelor of Arts" (Snow 1907, 135). The course of study at Pennsylvania for the second year notably included in what was termed the Moral Philosophy Department, the study of ethics, economics, politics, logic, and rhetoric. Required reading included Cicero's *Offices* and Longinus's *On the Sublime*.

Within fifteen years, in 1811, the duties of the professor of moral philosophy at the University of Pennsylvania included, along with teaching logic and moral philosophy, instruction in belles lettres and the "English language generally." During the sophomore year, the moral philosophy professor taught rhetoric, grammar, logic, and declamation in English. The required texts were Longinus, Quintilian, Cicero's *De Oratore* and Horace's *Art of Poetry*. The teaching focus was on criticism. All of the required texts, classical or modern, the class notes advised, were to be taught "critically" (Snow 1907, 136–37). By 1820, sophomores were studying Hugh Blair's *Lectures* and Homer's *Iliad*. By 1826, the moral philosophy professor was charged with instructing sophomores in English composition and in "rhetoric and criticism." The professor taught juniors logic, grammar, composition, moral philosophy, and forensics. He taught seniors natural and political law, metaphysics, and "composition and forensics" (Snow 1907, 141).

The University of Pennsylvania by the 1820s had established a pattern for the development of English language study that would be copied by other American universities. Requiring subjects taken from individual specialized schools or colleges, including separate programs for the classics, history, and philosophy, was revolutionary. The innovation initiated the eventual movement toward uniformity of course requirements in other American colleges. By 1842, Francis Wayland, the president of Brown, would observe that studies in all northern colleges were now so similar that "students, in good standing in one institution, find little difficulty in being admitted to any other" (Wayland 1842, 35).

Teaching "Criticism" at Columbia, 1784, and William and Mary, 1776

One college in particular that followed the University of Pennsylvania's lead was Columbia. Established in New York in 1754 as King's College, by 1785, one year after becoming Columbia College, the school offered a course of study that included many of the reforms that originally had appeared in William Smith's 1754 pamphlet on the *College of Mirania*. Regularly scheduled lectures were offered in English composition and in subjects appearing for the first time in an American college, specifically, courses in "Universal Grammar," "the Rise and Progress of Language," and a course in literary criticism listed as the "Rise and Progress of the Written Character and Criticism."

The subjects, appropriately, were under the direction of the professor of rhetoric and moral philosophy. Seniors concentrated on moral philosophy with lectures three times a week. The senior courses on the "Rise and Progress of Language" and on the "Rise and Progress of the Written Character and Criticism" required the reading of Cicero's *De Oratore,* Quintilian (likely the *Institutio Oratoria*), Longinus's *On the Sublime,* and other relevant titles in literary criticism chosen by the professors of rhetoric and moral philosophy.

By 1811, Columbia was making allowances strictly for the study of criticism. Although its freshmen and sophomores were still studying rhetoric, grammar, and composition under the rubric "rhetoric and belles lettres," using Blair's *Lectures* and John Holmes's and John Sterling's *A System of Rhetoric,* both juniors and seniors were studying courses designated specifically as "criticism," using, as Snow points out, a variety of selected classical and modern literary works. In the junior year, the professor of languages required Cicero's *De Oratore,* Quintilian, and Longinus, along with Terence, Horace's *Satires,* and Sophocles (1907, 105–6), among others. By 1821, Columbia's course for juniors would be called "Principles of Taste and Criticism." It was described as a "course of criticism—including the classical works—ancient and modern" and was taught in conjunction with the "Theory and Practice of English Composition." Columbia's juniors in

1821 also had the option of studying a general history of European literature and a "Critical History of English Literature." The senior class of 1821 concentrated on philosophy, moral philosophy, and political economy.

Initially, William and Mary College was an Episcopalian institution founded by James Blair, a Scot who was educated at Marischal College, Aberdeen. Blair emigrated to the colonies in 1685. In 1691, he went to England to petition for a college in Virginia, and it was chartered in Williamsburg, Virginia, in 1693 as William and Mary College. Blair was named president for life, and until his death in 1743, the curriculum at William and Mary remained largely classical and traditionally Episcopalian (Pryde 1957, 9–16). By 1776, however, William and Mary had adopted a curriculum similar to William Smith's course of study at the College of Philadelphia. Exactly how influential Smith was in the development of William and Mary's curriculum remains unclear, however.[10]

There is also the possibility that Thomas Jefferson, who first proposed the use of the elective system of courses, may have been the primary agent behind the college's curricular reforms. If so, Jefferson's reforms also bear a distinct Scottish connection; they were probably inspired by his earlier association, while a student at William and Mary, with a progressive Scottish professor named William Small, who, like James Blair, was also a graduate, but in 1775, of Aberdeen's Marischal College. Jefferson entered William and Mary in 1760 at age seventeen, and studied with Small, who taught mathematics and natural philosophy, from 1760 to 1762. Jefferson cited Small as "the first who ever gave . . . regular lectures in Ethics, Rhetoric, and Belles Lettres" at William and Mary (Sloan 1971, 246). The extent to which William Small's rather than William Smith's influence shaped Jefferson's reforms at William and Mary in 1779, which included designating a particular professor to teach the course that then combined the study of ethics with belles lettres, can only be conjectured. As Sloan observes, however, "Jefferson's proposals," regardless of where they originated, were similar to programs in other American colleges at the time "that had similar links to the Scottish universities" (1971, 247).

10. Smith's great-grandson, Horace Wemyss Smith, in the *Life and Correspondence of Rev. William Smith, D.D.*, observed that James Madison, an older cousin of the American president of the same name, who in 1776 was president of the College of William and Mary, chose Smith's course of study for use in the college. Thomas Harrison Montgomery, in *History of the University of Pennsylvania,* however, disputes the accuracy of the claim (1900, 263).

Jefferson's influence on curricular reform and his debt to Scottish educational principles are well understood, but his specific role in the development of English literary study is less clear. He was a steadfast student of the classics. In 1812, he wrote to John Adams, "I have given up newspapers in exchange for Tacitus and Thucydides . . . and I find myself much the happier" (Bruce 1920, 1: 29–30). Philip Bruce, in his history of the University of Virginia, observes that it was "remarkable how slightly" Jefferson "depended for recreation on the variety and beauty of the literature of his own language" (1920, 1: 30). The lasting impression that Jefferson made on the character of the University of Virginia is revealed in the development of the university's school of languages. But Jefferson's only concession to an English chair, to which he was relatively indifferent, was what Bruce calls "a barren school of Anglo-Saxon" (1920, 1: 30). Consequently, the University of Virginia throughout the nineteenth century never made a serious commitment to the study of English or American literature. Bruce could write as late as 1920 that "as a fructifying force in the field of even Southern literature, the institution has not gained the reputation which it has won in all the other departments of mental culture and practical efficiency" (30).

New Side Revivalism and Literary Study
at the College of New Jersey, 1759–1779

In 1752, the year Francis Alison left New London to head the Philadelphia Academy and William Smith was in the final stages of drafting *A General Idea of the College of Mirania,* Samuel Davies, a practicing Scottish Presbyterian minister living in Virginia acknowledged in popular print the important educational link that he envisioned between literary study, civic morality, and public service in the colonies. Davies, who at the time was a poet of religious verse of some slight renown and who traveled in Scotland raising money for American education, valued good reading and desired to share the benefits of fine literature with his congregation. The congregation was poor, so Davies wrote to his friends abroad requesting books. When the books arrived, they were circulated among the churchgoers. Davies commented in a collection of verse that he published in 1752, titled *Miscellaneous Poems Chiefly on Divine Subjects,* on the promising potential for the use of literature as a teaching tool to impart lessons to the masses and to improve public morality. The masses "may not accurately discern the fairest charms of Poetry," he observed, "yet they generally are pleased with the Consonance of final Syllables, proportioned Numbers, etc. So they are more ready to receive and retain those things which are conveyed into their Minds in their Form than in heavy and tiresome Prose" (Sloan 1971, 54).

What Davies, a Presbyterian New Sider, was addressing in 1752 was the romantic concept of using English literature, especially English poetry, to assist people to understand what New Side revivalists, inspired by the Hutchesonian defense of emotion rather than reason as a preferred guide to truth, promoted as the rational, eminently sensible nature of the conversion experience. Literature was respectable and could appeal to the masses on the level of emotions and feelings without seeming excessive. Samuel Blair, another Scottish-bred minister and a New Side leader, observed that he had made a special effort to convince his congregation that the conversion experience did not involve just "visions, dreams, or immediate inspirations," but a rational comprehension of the value of emotions and feelings in the acceptance of religious ideals (Trinterud 1949, 79f.). The argument, of course, in all respects, was essentially Hutchesonian.

Davies, an astute social reformer, recognized the ways that literature could be used publicly to teach ethics and morality. The objective—raising the public moral consciousness—complemented the New Side revivalist conception of Presbyterianism. English literature, according to this vision, should be read for more than just improving one's taste, writing, or declamatory style. New Side ministers, consequently, felt just as comfortable alluding to Pope, Addison, George Whitefield, and Thomas Prince in their sermons as they did to Horace, Plato, Tacitus, and Cicero. According to Sloan, they were always prepared "to abandon classical and genteel literary canons of taste when the occasion demanded" (1971, 50–51). Consequently, the psychology of conversion developed by New Side Presbyterians was deliberately related to other avenues of learning. For Davies and other New Side ministers, farmers and common folk were not only fully able to enjoy the excitement of literature as one of those avenues of learning but also entitled to it by nature.

Davies's sentiments were at the basis of college reforms that associated literary study with practical moral and political objectives. For a period from 1759 to 1761, Davies was the president of the infant College of New Jersey, in 1896 to be officially known as Princeton. The college had been founded in Princeton, New Jersey, in 1746 on the model of Tennent's Log College by a small group of New England Presbyterian clergymen who felt the need for a college in the middle colonies that would train evangelical ministers to accommodate the increasing influx of settlers and immigrants, mostly Scots-Irish, to the area (Collins 1914, 3–5). In an address to the class of 1760, Davies urged the graduates to "imbibe and cherish a publick spirit"; not to live for themselves, but to plan joyously to serve their generation and their expanding nation.[11] New Siders assumed that the ideal of public service, i.e., working for that action "which procures the greatest happiness for the greatest numbers," as Hutcheson initially put it, was what a converted Evangelical Christian naturally would pursue. True virtue, consequently, involved civic humanism and the practice of benevolent good will toward others.

The College of New Jersey eventually became the experimental college model in the United States for the trying out of Presbyterian New Side educational principles, just as Old Side Presbyterian principles prevailed for the most part, in spite of its claim of nonsectarianism, at the College of Philadelphia. Aaron Burr, a New Sider, served as head of the College of New Jersey from 1748 to 1757. Jonathan Edwards, his successor and a New Side sympathizer, died a brief six weeks after following Burr in the position. Edwards's successor, none other than Samuel Davies, was president for two years, dying of tuberculosis in 1761. In 1761, Samuel Finley left his position as head of the Nottingham Academy in Pennsylvania in order to assume the presidency of the new college. Finley was a Scots-Irish Presbyterian minister who had emigrated to Philadelphia in 1743 and in 1744 founded the Nottingham Academy on the Pennsylvania-Maryland border (Dunaway 1944, 222–23).

At Nottingham, in addition to the usual fare of Greek and Latin, Finley had put special emphasis on the study of English and had encouraged as much instruction in belles lettres as was reasonably possible. Once at the helm of the College of New Jersey, Finley revised the curriculum, perhaps feeling the influence of Francis Alison at the College of Philadelphia, in order to give greater importance to the study of English and English literature. Students read Shakespeare, Addison, Milton, and other modern writers. During their last two years students were required to take part in public disputations in both Latin and English. In 1763, Finley established an English Department designed to teach "young lads to write well, to cipher,

11. Davies's *Religion and Public Spirit; a Valedictory Address to the Senior Class, Delivered in Nassau Hall, September 21, 1760* was published in 1761.

and to pronounce and read the English tongue with accuracy and precision." Eventually, the English Department was deemed an "inconven-
ience" and classes were ordered held outside the college (Collins 1914,
60–61).

Finley's successor in 1768 was the Reverend John Witherspoon. David
Daiches calls Witherspoon "the single most influential educator in America in his time" (1991, 167). Witherspoon was also a Scottish Presbyterian
minister. Although committed to neither New Side nor Old Side factions
in the American church, he was the favorite choice of the New Siders. He
appears to have made a very favorable impression on Samuel Davies and
Gilbert Tennent, William Tennent's son, when Davies and Tennent visited
Scotland in 1753 in an effort to raise funds for education (Sloan 1971,
104). Like the New Side, Witherspoon sympathized with the importance
of civic commitment and the conversion experience, but, like the Old
Side, he also supported the conservative controlling center of the church
establishment.

While a student at Edinburgh University, Witherspoon had studied literary criticism, classical and modern, with John Stevenson, professor of
logic and metaphysics. Stevenson had included in his classes the reading of
Cicero and Quintilian, as primary classical sources in literary criticism, but
he also included modern selections, Bacon and Locke particularly (Pryde
1957, 30–32). Witherspoon was predisposed toward Ciceronian humanism. He believed that good citizens automatically serve the common interest.[12] But Witherspoon also felt the influence of Francis Hutcheson's
teachings while a student in Scotland. With Hutcheson, he promoted the
belief in the existence of an innate moral sense and in the essential goodness
and "good sense" of ordinary citizens. Also following Hutcheson, he believed that morality was a matter of the heart as well as the mind.[13] Consequently, he was a staunch supporter of the rights of the commonality and in
1776 was the only prominent colonial academic to sign the Declaration of

12. For a helpful summary perspective on this particular point, see Thomas P. Miller's
"John Witherspoon," in *Eighteenth-Century British and American Rhetorics and Rhetori-
cians*; see also Miller's essay "Witherspoon, Blair and the Rhetoric of Civic Humanism," in
Scotland and America in the Age of the Enlightenment.

13. Ned C. Landsman, in his essay "Witherspoon and the Problem of Provincial Identity,"
notes that, although Witherspoon shared most of "Hutcheson's Whiggish political ideals"
which formed "the basis of his own lectures on moral philosophy," he consciously dissociated
himself from Hutcheson's utilitarian ethical bent (1990, 37).

Independence (Diamond 1990, 128). He placed great emphasis on the role of education in the formation of civic character and encouraged his students to address the practicalities of public discourse by focusing on practical ethical and political issues. Like Hugh Blair and other Scottish and American rhetoricians, Witherspoon identified rhetoric with the propagation of democratic ideals, but he singularly linked the study of rhetoric directly with practical politics and with oratory—i.e., public disputation.

Invited to take the presidency of the College of New Jersey in 1766, Witherspoon refused, but was subsequently persuaded to take the position partly through the urging of Benjamin Rush, a College of New Jersey graduate and a key figure in the founding of Dickinson College (Pryde 1957, 30). In 1768, Witherspoon finally left Scotland to take up the duties. From the outset, like Finley before him, he insisted on the educational value of English studies. Before he left Scotland, he arranged for more than three hundred books to be sent to the college's library. Included among them were works by Hutcheson, David Hume, Adam Ferguson, Adam Smith, and other contemporary Scottish authors (Sloan 1971, 110–11).

Witherspoon's *Lectures on Moral Philosophy,* published posthumously in 1800–1801, were actually his class lecture notes. In his classes, he used a teaching technique reminiscent of both John Stevenson and Hutcheson that involved a comparative reading of classic and modern authors. Because he systematically incorporated into his classroom analysis works by Shakespeare, Addison, Johnson, Hume, Pope, and Jonathan Swift, among others, an argument can be made, apropos of Daiches's claim, that Witherspoon was the first North American professor actually to teach a course that concentrated on English literary study, even though there was no course labeled "English literature."[14] Witherspoon taught moral philosophy, divinity, jurisprudence, civics, history, and literary criticism. His lectures on eloquence, particularly, show him to have been a teacher with an especially strong background in literary criticism. Sloan writes that he "cited name after name from the ancient authors . . . holding them as models that in many areas had never been surpassed." Yet, he paid equal attention to modern English writers in order to show his students that the ancients were not superhuman (1971, 133). He also instituted a system of prize competitions in declamation which lasted long after his time. His role

14. For an example of how Witherspoon incorporated English literary selections into his lectures, see his lecture on "Eloquence," in *Works,* vol. 7.

in the early development of the oratorical tradition in American letters, which is the focus of the next chapter, is paramount.

During Witherspoon's administration, the freshman year curriculum remained elementary and basically classical, but the sophomore year involved the study of the classics, mathematics, geography, and Witherspoon's own addition, the study of English grammar and composition. With this addition, as Varnum Collins suggests, Witherspoon's emphasis on English expression commenced. The junior year was devoted chiefly to science but was augmented by Witherspoon's lectures on history and "eloquence," or what might also be called "public oratory." The lectures on eloquence included the study of rhetoric, advanced English composition, style, and literary criticism. Collins reports that in the 1772 address to the graduates, Witherspoon noted that he had delivered his history and eloquence lectures twice, specifically so that the seniors would have the experience of hearing them twice (1914, 300). Seniors reviewed the classics, studied logic and natural philosophy, and heard lectures on ethics, politics, and government, which were delivered under the rubric "moral philosophy." Public oratory was always one of Witherspoon's major concerns; consequently, as Collins notes, his "insistence on the serious study of written and spoken English was plainly discernible in the public style of his graduates." A student named Ashbel Green observed of the curriculum in 1783 that since the War of Independence the junior and senior classes at the College of New Jersey had studied primarily mathematics, philosophy, belles lettres, literary criticism, and eloquence. French was also available as an extracurricular subject (1914, 301).

Witherspoon had learned much from Hutcheson and also from Thomas Reid, whom he knew personally. He is often credited with introducing Reid's theories on "philosophical realism" into North America (Pryde 1957, 33). Reid was Adam Smith's successor to the Chair of Moral Philosophy at Glasgow. He is usually remembered as the first serious moral philosopher to attack British empiricism's reliance on "ideas" as the true test of knowledge. The alternative to abstract ideas for Reid was the recognition of the place of the principles of common sense in the pursuit of knowledge—that is, original judgments or primary qualities based on self-evident, "realistic" truths which, as Reid argued, formed the foundation of all reasoning and all science. Belief in the existence of anything, therefore, was not gained by comparing ideas but depended in essence on the very nature of the perception (Copleston 1994, 364–68).

Following Reid, Witherspoon believed that the object of formal university study should be directed at learning more about the essential nature of mankind. Moral philosophy, for instance, benefitted more from the direct study of human nature than from the conceptual study of general principles. Hence, along with Hutcheson, he valued the usefulness, the utility, of academic subjects as they addressed and enhanced the common experience of all people. The test of utility, therefore, was applied to the college curriculum as an exercise in "common sense," if not in ethics. Witherspoon also posited, after both Hutcheson and Adam Smith, the ideal of the bourgeois gentleman—Smith's economic man—as a desired standard of conduct for his graduates. According to Sloan, Witherspoon's gentleman was "the man who, not by birth, but by virtue of his prudence, industry, and learning could provide leadership to a burgeoning and aggressive middle class" (1971, 137).

Witherspoon's successor at the College of New Jersey was his son-in-law, Samuel Stanhope Smith, who had graduated in 1769 from the college. In 1779, Smith accepted the position as professor of moral philosophy and almost immediately took charge of the administration, owing to Witherspoon's commitment at the time to the Continental Congress and to other duties which kept him away from the college. Although Witherspoon was officially head until his death in 1794, Smith, especially after Witherspoon started going blind and could no longer discharge his duties, assumed almost sole control of the school. But the Witherspoon curriculum, with its courses on English study and on literary criticism, was preserved for at least fifty years after his death (Collins 1914, 302). Smith resigned the office of president in 1811.

A student entering the College of New Jersey in 1803, during Smith's presidency, would have been expected to recite from memory well over one hundred pages of rules of English grammar, all of which were studied privately (Snow 1907, 117). Of the teaching assignments, one track of lectures involved mathematics, natural philosophy, astronomy, chemistry, and natural history; the other track combined the teaching of logic, history, belles lettres, and moral and political science. By 1822, courses in English grammar were required of freshmen and sophomores. The course in belles lettres was restricted to seniors.

As William Charvat observes in his study of *The Origins of American Critical Thought, 1810–1835*, the College of New Jersey well into the nineteenth century harbored the greatest promoters of Scottish moral philosophy (1936, 35). Scottish moral philosophy was at the center of curricular developments in English study at the College of New Jersey. Courses in English taught students to write and to orate, but, as I have argued in this chapter, they were also intended to promote philosophical ideals in the service of morality and civic responsibility. Often, particularly as the century waned, the principal teaching technique by which these civic and moral objectives were promoted directly involved training in the critical skills that were fundamental to the study of oratory or public disputation, giving rise to a bona fide "oratorical tradition" in the history of late-eighteenth- and early-nineteenth-century American literary study. That is the focus of the next chapter.

2

Criticism and the Oratorical Tradition

English at Brown, South Carolina, Yale, and Harvard

> It is a position generally admitted, that eloquence will flourish, in every
> nation, in proportion as the government is free. The first governments
> instituted over men, were despotic monarchies. In these the people felt
> no interest.
>
> —Jonathan Maxcy, April 8, 1817

From the outset, many schools in colonial America, especially on the frontier, conducted lessons orally, inadvertently promoting the art of public speaking. Whether this was intended or not, colonial educators often had no choice but to promote vocal forms of learning, because schoolbooks were scarce and, in some areas, simply nonexistent. Also, oral examinations, literally by default, were the best way, because usually the only way, to measure student progress. As a result, students involuntarily learned to declaim; the exercises they completed, the themes they wrote, were intended to be read aloud and critiqued aloud.

By the end of the eighteenth century, however, the study of oratory was universally recognized as a legitimate academic discipline, owing in large measure to a dramatic rise in parliamentary forms of government in the late eighteenth century which encouraged the training of public orators who, for the first time in European history, were not principally clergymen. Courses in oratory in American colleges increased. They were augmented, in most instances, by a parallel rise of interest in "criticism" as a science, a separate discipline that had gained, as Jonathan Maxcy at the College of South Carolina put it in 1802, increased respect and a reputation "as a support to morality" (1844, 335).

That literary criticism and oratory were taught in combination is not surprising. The earliest form of literary criticism, traced to ancient times and studied as a matter of course from at least the twelfth century by students of the classics, included discussions of both poetry and oratory considered together as subject matter. As J. H. Smith and E. W. Parks observe in their introduction to *The Great Critics,* among the ancients, Longinus and Quintilian in particular "interested themselves with the problems of the speaker, whose aim, in their opinion, was to persuade" (1951, xvi). Because persuading and pleasing were viewed as complementary accomplishments, oratorical criticism and criticism of poetry often took the same form. As a result, the great literary critics, from Aristotle to the Renaissance, when discussing the aesthetic nature of belles lettres, referred to it as "poetry"; when they discussed prose as a vehicle for persuasion or pleasure, they were inclined to call it "oratory" (1951, xvi).

Formal courses devoted to oratory in colonial America principally involved the teaching of public speaking, usually under the rubric "elocution"; but the course objectives almost always hinged on the widely held belief that the art of persuasion was, in fact, an acquired *critical* talent. Hence, the day-to-day study routine dealt with critical terminology, much of it literary and rhetorical. Class lectures focused on the use of special words. During the colonial era they were the catchwords of neoclassical literary criticism, such as *invention, wit, imitation, imagination, nature, taste, unity,* and *propriety*—all the concerns that an astute literary critic in the eighteenth century would have been expected to address. They were also the concerns that a student examining literary works critically for a classroom exercise would be expected to address. The increasing interest in the use of literary criticism to augment the formal study of oratory at the time was the shaping force behind the development of the "oratorical tradition," a late-eighteenth- and early-nineteenth-century cultural phenomenon that has received surprisingly little scholarly attention over the years from literary and cultural historians.

Essentially, as Gregory Clark and S. Michael Halloran contend in their summary introduction to a helpful collection of essays, *Oratorical Culture in Nineteenth-Century America,* the influence of the oratorical tradition in American higher education was short-lived (1993, 13), spanning a period from approximately the end of the eighteenth century to 1850. It was a time, however, that witnessed a steady, traceable increase in the introduction of college courses involving concentrated exercises in criticism, oral and written, taught in combination with lessons on various methods for acquiring proficiency in public speaking.

The immense success of Noah Webster's *An American Selection of Lessons in Reading and Speaking,* first published as a school reader in 1795, is tied directly to the oratorical tradition.[1] The declamatory practicality of its broad content and the fact that Webster chose to combine instruction in both reading and speaking largely accounts for its popularity. He chose selections for his anthology, as the full title indicated, purposely for their moral didacticism, their utility as patriotic set pieces, and their function as classroom examples of how an author could appeal to an audience on several emotional levels while addressing a variety of critical concerns. The objective, of course, was the complementary "oratorical" objective, that is, the desire to persuade and to give pleasure simultaneously. John Ward's *System of Oratory,* Thomas Sheridan's *A Course of Lectures on Elocution,* and William Enfield's *The Speaker; or, Miscellaneous pieces, selected from the best English writing* were popular early classroom textbooks used to teach oratory in the colonies. They included, as did Webster's *Lessons in Reading and Speaking,* ample lessons in patriotism and character building as well as a wide variety of literary examples elucidating, in essence, principles of literary criticism.

Ward's *System of Oratory* was used widely in early American universities. The text, originally published in two volumes, contains the complete course of lectures in oratory that Ward delivered at London's Gresham College. The lectures were published posthumously in 1759, the year after Ward died. In the final years of his teaching career, he had a fair copy of the lectures transcribed for the purpose of publication after his death. The published work, consequently, was the final drafts of lectures on oratory that Ward delivered and revised over a thirty-eight-year span from his initial appointment in 1720 to 1758. In their final form, they stand as a polished record of how a very distinguished educator taught oratory at the time. We can assume that the American teachers who used his text taught their oratory courses in much the same way.

---

1. The full title of Webster's text—*An American Selection of Lessons in Reading and Speaking. Calculated to Improve the Minds and Refine the Taste of Youth. And also to Instruct Them in the Geography, History, and Politics of the United States*—speaks directly to the book's broad-ranged focus and to its bias in favor of teaching civic responsibility.

Ward began his course by defining the "nature of oratory" as a subject. He maintained throughout his lectures that the education of a rhetorician was different from the education of an orator, because an orator, unlike a rhetorician, was essentially the end product of a far more specialized, well-ordered "system" or "discipline" (1759, 1: 16–17). As he explained it, the terms *rhetoric* and *oratory* can be used "promiscuously; but the case is not the same with respect to the words, *rhetorician* and *orator.*" A rhetorician was trained to use language technically and generally in order to promote arguments; an orator, however, was more specialized and concentrated particularly on "the art of speaking well upon any subject, in order to persuade" (1759, 1: 19). The orator, according to Ward, spoke from a position of "authority"; the rhetorician did not. Given this qualification, accordingly, oratory was a "discipline" that promoted "the study of eloquence" (1759, 1: 20). Rhetoric, as Ward observed, was not as specialized and too easily degenerated into sophistry (1759, 1: 17). The business of oratory then "is to teach us to *speak well,* which, as Cicero explains, is to speak *justly, methodically, floridly, and copiously.*" To speak "justly," Ward added, "a person must be master of his subject, that he may be able to say all that is proper."

In essence, Ward was suggesting that the accomplished orator must lay claim to a degree of wisdom and scholarly expertise in all the subjects addressed. Knowledge of the primary subject matter of a discourse, therefore, was more essential than the method of delivery. Hence, the accomplished eighteenth-century orator aspired to be a master of all knowledge; his preparation was content-oriented, unlike the emphasis of the rhetorician's preparation, which was form-oriented, given primarily to matters of grammar, style, and argument. "The *subject* of oratory," therefore, Ward concluded, was *"every thing"* (1759, 1: 25). Hence, one might say, with Francis Bacon, that the orator was one who presumed to "take all knowledge as his province."

Of primary importance in the training of an orator, in light of Ward's explanation, was the close, almost symbiotic, connection that eighteenth- and early-nineteenth-century educators envisioned between the formal study of oratory and the promotion of the humanities. The role that a sound knowledge of literary content played in the study of oratory at the time was also much easier to understand. For literary study not only provided written access to limitless branches of knowledge, it also provided orators with a ready source of elements of emotive "pleasure" with which

they could grace and improve their persuasive declamations. In "deliberative discourses," in particular, Ward suggested, where "we either advise to
a thing, or dissuade from it," the element of "pleasure" is most important,
given that "every one knows what an influence [pleasure] has upon the
generality of mankind" (1759, 1: 107, 111) For Quintilian, he continued,
"pleasure ought not of itself to be proposed, as a fit motive for action in serious discourses, but when it is designed to recommend something useful,"
one would be well-advised to engage "the pursuit of polite literature"
(1759, 1: 11).

By "polite literature," Ward meant primarily the writings of the ancients, but in volume two of the *Oratory,* in a chapter on the importance of
reading in the training of an orator, Ward elaborated on the general benefits of reading. Significantly, in this chapter, no classical writers were cited as
primary examples. He first observed that hearing an accomplished person
speak can have considerable influence on the making of an orator, but there
were, in addition, distinct advantages to be "gained by reading" (1759, 2:
397). By reading critically, he added, "persons are best capable of passing a
just sentiment upon any performance, and discovering all its real beauties,
or defects. The mind is then at leisure to examine in the most exact, and
critical manner, every thing relating either to the thought, language,
method, or whatever else may appear worthy of observation" (1759, 2:
398). Because reading critically was so important, he concluded, an orator
"should not be altogether a stranger to any of the polite arts, because he
must expect to have occasion some time or other to make use of them all"
(1759, 2: 399).

Ward advised that orators, in their academic preparation, should first
read the "best poets, because they abound in fine thoughts, beautiful turns
of expression, strong images, and lively descriptions" (1759, 2: 399). Aspiring orators also were advised to read historians, Ward added, because
"by history we are not only informed of matters of fact, but likewise of the
springs of human actions, the manner in which they were conducted, and
likewise their events" (1759, 2: 401). A third group of authors orators
were advised to read were the philosophers. The reading assignments,
Ward recommended, were to be accompanied by written exercises. Cicero,
he noted, called the combination of writing and reading *"the best manner of
eloquence"* (1759, 2: 405).

The most exemplary kind of reading encouraged excellence through
imitation. Ward devoted an entire chapter to "Imitation, and Who are to

be imitated." He noted that "the most celebrated writers among the antients copied after those, who went before them, and in a great measure acquired that reputation, which they have so justly gained in their several ways, by their examples." He added, however, that the like might also be shown "in some of the best of our modern authors" (1759, 2: 411–12). Imitation, he advised, was not mere copying, and, hence, the employment of the critical faculty was essential to distinguishing the difference (1759, 2: 414). Imitation, therefore, of modern authors as well as of the ancients was an integral part of Ward's system.

The core of the oratory curriculum, wherever it was offered between 1770 and 1820, was geared principally to the works of Cicero, Quintilian, and Longinus. Almost all courses in oratory, as Ward's lectures and extant required reading lists for eighteenth-century colleges in Europe and North America made clear, almost by rote, required the reading of Cicero's *De Oratore* (i.e., *The Making of an Orator*), Quintilian's *Institutio Oratoria* (i.e., *On the Training of an Orator*), and Longinus's *On the Sublime*. William Richardson, a student of Adam Smith's at Glasgow, for instance, writing in 1803, recalled gratefully Smith's frequent digressions into Cicero and the subject of criticism. The digressions occurred, Richardson noted, "with much display of learning and knowledge, in his occasional explanations of those philosophical works of Cicero, which are also a very useful and important subject of examination in the class of Moral Philosophy" (Ross 1995, 126).

The rise of the oratorical tradition in the United States in the later eighteenth century, and its connection to the notion that oratory could prepare citizens and statesmen to assume the grave responsibility of directing the new nation, are developments largely owed to Scotland and Scottish educators. The practice in early eighteenth-century Scottish universities of combining traditional classical rhetoric with oratory, moral philosophy, and exercises in literary criticism provided a model that appeared in American colleges as early as the 1770s. At that time American colleges began to experiment with directions in language study that departed from traditional classical rhetoric courses and moved toward courses that promised to be more declamatory, practical, and current in scope. Clark and Halloran contend that the oratorical tradition from approximately the turn of the century involved more than the limited, ivory-towered world of academe. American politics and society in general, they suggest, "were informed by a discourse inherited from the Revolutionary period," one based essentially on classical Roman models. In principle, the discourse promoted civic virtue, that is, the classical concept of *sensus communis,* which was based on the idea that the moral authority of a community generates from public consensus rather than individual conviction (1993, 1–2). What we now call "literature," they argue, was actually the offspring of both a civic and an academic oratorical culture bent on passing on "the established values of the culture" and promoting *sensus communis* by providing a "common ground upon which arguments about . . . particularized current issues could be conducted" (1993, 2).

The association of civic virtue, classical Roman democracy, and the practice of the "art" of oratory was what young Charles Thompson, for instance, had in mind in 1769 when he delivered the valedictory address at the first commencement of the College of Rhode Island (which in 1804 became Brown University). The title of Thompson's address was the "Oratorical Art." Referring to Rome as "this land of liberty," he observed that the "arts and sciences," dependent on the liberty of free expression, could "flourish in no other soil" (Guild 1897, 105). Oratory itself he defined as an "irresistible energy accompanying truth," which could only be properly delivered by "men thoroughly acquainted with the human heart" and the "passions of human nature." Hence, he maintained, the art of oratory, because it was so closely connected "with every branch of polite erudition . . . as the collected force and perfection of them all," was "the mistress of the arts" (Guild 1897, 103).

Promoting the reading of literary works in courses in oratory, especially modern literary works written in English, was yet one more manifestation of the connection between oratory and polite learning. Modern literary works enhanced the polemical process by making available classroom texts that either directed students to some kind of oral or written critical evaluation of pressing current social and political issues or, at least, dramatized the conflicts. As Gerald Graff notes in *Professing Literature,* as one would expect, early exercises in elocution in American schools, often with the fate of the republic in mind, were purposely designed for prospective lawyers, politicians, and legislators, who were destined to serve the cause of liberty and free expression (1987, 43).

The study of oratory in the United States after the Revolutionary War, consequently, was thought to be particularly important in the preparation of citizen statesmen and other political officials who were destined to guide the new nation. Good citizens were knowledgeable citizens. Webster's

American Selection of Lessons in Reading and Speaking was not the only text that linked the study of oratory directly to the promotion of democracy and American patriotism. In the post Revolutionary War era, oratory was viewed increasingly, therefore, as a promising course of general study for the preparation of citizen statesmen and prospective legislators.

The study of oratory, given the nature of its critical exercises and the wide breadth of its reading assignments, inadvertently brought many students into contact with English and American classics for the first time, creating, as Graff suggests, a link between "technical analysis" and an appreciation of those classics (1987, 43).[2] What Graff refers to as "technical analysis" might also be viewed more broadly as criticism—that is, in the sense that any formal, studied oral or written judgment of a literary work, especially in an academic setting, can be called "criticism." In fact, colonial students of the classics in the late eighteenth century would have conceived the meaning of the word *critic* in terms of the ancient Greek word *kritikos,* which, according to René Wellek, specifically meant "a judge of literature." The Latin equivalent, *criticus,* though rare in classical Latin, is found, quite appropriately as Wellek notes, "in Cicero and was used of Longinus by Hieron in his *Epistolae.*" Wellek also suggests that *criticus* was a much higher term than *grammaticus,* and that "the *criticus* was also concerned with the interpretation of texts and words." The extensive classroom study, both in Europe and in the United States, of classical rhetoricians such as Cicero, Quintilian, and Longinus and of classical philosophers such as Aristotle was based largely on their availability as sources for the study of Greek, Latin, and classical principles of rhetoric. It was also based in part on their significance as fundamental literary critics promoting the virtues of civic humanism and aesthetic refinement (Wellek 1963, 22–23).

The oratorical tradition advanced the combination of declamatory eloquence, a wide scholarly breadth of subject matter, and the critical acumen of a trained textual critic. Because, as Ward put it in the *Oratory,* "the greater part of mankind are swayed by authority, rather than arguments," it followed logically that the orator must demonstrate "the character of wisdom" in order to gain the respect and trust of the audience (1759, 1: 143). Teaching students to acquire "the character of wisdom" in the promotion of civic virtue was the task that challenged burgeoning universities in

2. On this point, see also Arthur Applebee, *Tradition and Reform in the Teaching of English: A History* (1974, 3–4).

North America at the time. Among the foremost was the College of Rhode Island.

Oratory and Criticism at Brown, 1764, and Union College, 1795

In 1762, James Manning, a language specialist from Elizabethtown, New Jersey, graduated with honors from the College of New Jersey. Manning excelled especially in the fields of rhetoric, eloquence, moral philosophy, and the classics (Guild 1897, 31). In 1763, he was licensed to preach and was appointed to the pastorate of the Baptist Church in Warren, Rhode Island. That same year, he proposed that a college be established in Warren. His efforts were successful, and in 1764 a charter for the College of Rhode Island was obtained from the colonial legislature. In 1804, it was renamed Brown University. When the College of Rhode Island opened in 1765, Manning was the obvious choice for president. He was also officially appointed professor of languages (Maxcy 1844, 33). In 1770, the college, whose enrollment until then had not exceeded thirty students, was relocated at Providence, a larger and more promising town. Manning remained president until his death in 1791.

The course of study at the College of Rhode Island under Manning in 1783, one modeled largely on Manning's alma mater, the College of New Jersey, was described as follows: "The President and Tutors, according to their judgments, shall teach and instruct the several Classes in the learned languages and in the Liberal Arts and Sciences, together with the vernacular tongus" (Bronson 1971, 103). First-year students studied Latin and Greek classical authors and the New Testament in Greek. Second-year students studied Cicero's *De Oratore*, Caesar's *Commentaries*, Homer's *Iliad*, and Longinus's *On the Sublime*. They also studied geography, Robert Lowth's *English Grammar* and *Rhetoric*, Ward's *System of Oratory*, Sheridan's *A Course of Lectures on Elocution*, Lord Kames's *Elements of Criticism*, and Watts's and Duncan's *Logic*. Hutcheson's *Moral Philosophy* was taught in the third year, along with astronomy, mathematics, and Benjamin Martins's *Philosophia Britannica*. Fourth-year students studied history, Locke's *Essay on Human Understanding*, John Kennedy's *Complete System of Astronomical Chronology*, and Lord Bolingbroke on history, with a review of the languages, arts, and sciences studied in the preceding years (Guild 1897, 355–56). Every student in the college had to present an oration at two o'clock on the last Wednesday afternoon in every month.

Freshmen and sophomores could choose a piece; juniors and seniors had to write their own (Guild 1897, 356).

The 1783 College of Rhode Island curriculum was Manning's design. What is particularly noteworthy is the limited number of assigned works in Latin and Greek when compared with assigned works written in English. Throughout the four years of their studies, students were also urged to compose their themes in English rather than in Latin. Manning's 1783 Rhode Island curriculum was a harbinger of the increasing influence of oratory as a subject in American colleges—language study that would eventually link the study of oratory with experimental exercises in literary criticism. Manning actually was the first teacher at the College of Rhode Island to offer rhetoric courses that required simultaneously the study of oratory and English composition. As early as 1774, according to Walter C. Bronson, regular student declamations, many committed to memory, were given high priority in the list of required college activities (1971, 105).

Manning, in his role as college president and professor of languages, also oversaw the development of the library. In 1783, although works by Thomas Hobbes, Blaise Pascal, John Bunyan, John Milton, and some *Spectator* essays were available, most of the library's approximately five hundred volumes were theological or classical in nature, a circumstance that deeply troubled Manning. Within a year, however, he had raised enough money to expand the collection to more than two thousand books. Among the purchases were titles in English literature by Joseph Addison, Edmund Burke, John Gay, James Thomson, Edward Young, Daniel Defoe, Alexander Pope, Colley Cibber, William Congreve, Samuel Johnson, Thomas Otway, James Macpherson's "Ossian," David Hume, Jonathan Swift, Oliver Goldsmith, and John Dryden. Students were encouraged to take advantage of the availability of all the newly purchased books. In fact, college policy mandated that students would have free access to the new books; books in the original collection, mostly classical and theological works, on the other hand, were to be handled only by the college librarian (Bronson 1971, 110).

Manning openly promoted the study of English literature by assigning reading selections written in English in his rhetoric, composition, and oratory courses, but it was Jonathan Maxcy, Manning's successor as college president, who first specifically combined the teaching of oratory with belles lettres. Maxcy, a 1787 College of Rhode Island graduate, succeeded Manning in 1792. From 1787 to 1791, Maxcy had served the college as a tutor. He remained as president until 1802, when he left Rhode Island to assume the presidency of Union College in Schenectady, New York, where he continued to promote English studies, oratory, and elements of criticism (Raymond 1907, 1: 88, 109).

In 1793, however, the College of Rhode Island, under Maxcy's direction, moved Lord Kames's *Elements of Criticism* from the second to the third year. Sheridan's *A Course of Lectures on Elocution* was moved to the freshman year to be studied as a prerequisite for more advanced courses in oratory, and, significantly, a separate subject called simply "criticism" was instituted. Noah Webster's *An American Selection of Lessons in Reading and Speaking* was also added to the reading list for first-year students, and Cicero's *De Oratore* was combined with Longinus's *On the Sublime* for the sophomore year (Snow 1907, 111). Under Maxcy's administration, the College of Rhode Island began to acquire a reputation as a center for the study of oratory, belles lettres, literary criticism, and moral philosophy.

Maxcy's efforts to promote the combination of oratory and literary study at Rhode Island eventually were responsible for the institution in 1804 of a formal Chair of Oratory and Belles Lettres. It was the first endowed chair at the newly designated Brown University. By 1823, the course of study at Brown included, among the list of usual classical selections, Hugh Blair's *Lectures on Rhetoric and Belles Lettres,* Lord Kames's *Criticism,* Levi Hedge's *Logic,* William Paley's *Moral Philosophy* and his *Evidences,* George Campbell's *Philosophy of Rhetoric,* Dugald Stewart's *Philosophy of the Human Mind,* and Bishop Joseph Butler's *Analogy.* Bronson notes that in those early years, according to one student, Brown's students were expected to memorize whole sections from Blair, Kames, Stewart, and Hedge (1971, 167).

By 1827, the oratorical tradition was in full play at Brown. Freshmen continued to read Sheridan's *Lectures on Elocution* as a prerequisite to more advanced courses in oratory. Sophomores read Cicero's *De Oratore* and Longinus's *On the Sublime,* but now added both Blair's *Lectures* and Kames's *Elements of Criticism.* Juniors studied Paley's *Moral Philosophy* and *Natural Theology,* but now with Campbell's *Philosophy of Rhetoric.* "Criticism" continued to be listed as a separate and distinct subject assigned to the professor who taught natural philosophy (Snow 1907, 122).

In 1827, Francis Wayland, who was a graduate of Union College, became the fourth president of Brown University, a position he would hold until 1855. Wayland had been a student at Union College during the presidency of the legendary Eliphalet Nott, about whom I will have more to say. In 1854, Wayland delivered a commemorative address at Union College on Nott's fiftieth anniversary as president. The address, titled *The Education Demanded by the People of the United States,* was topically critical. Theodore R. Crane, in an "Introduction" to a published version of the address, noted that Wayland was "committed to popularizing higher education," and that immediately after his 1827 arrival in Providence to assume the presidency of Brown, he proposed to establish "a course of study in modern languages and English literature and science" (Wayland 1854, 9). Crane also noted that Wayland was committed to the "educational economics of Adam Smith" and that he looked to the Scottish universities, rather than to Oxford or Cambridge, as models (Wayland 1854, 11–12).

During Wayland's presidency at Brown, regular courses in the modern languages were added. Wayland's academic specialties, not surprisingly, were moral philosophy and political economy; he published textbooks in both fields. And his academic connections, as noted by Crane, were primarily Scottish. James Robert Boyd, a Presbyterian clergyman and the author of several popular textbooks, including *Elements of Rhetoric and Literary Criticism,* a text used extensively in American schools and colleges from 1844 to 1876, cited Wayland as a key source for his publications on moral philosophy (I will have more to say about Boyd in Chapter 4). Both Boyd and Wayland were also greatly inspired by Thomas Chalmers, the Scottish Presbyterian divine who was instrumental in the formation in 1843 of the Free Church of Scotland. In 1864, Wayland published *A Memoir of the Christian Labors . . . of Thomas Chalmers.*

It took time, but eventually, in 1876, the formal study of English literature as an autonomous subject offered for credit was added to the Brown curriculum. Literary study at Brown owed its development to the earlier combined study of oratory and criticism. After 1850, the study of criticism became increasingly more concentrated on literature written in English. Although elocution and declamation eventually were subordinated to rhetorical exercises taught under the rubric of "rhetoric," the courses still included occasional critical exegeses of literary selections written in English. By the 1870s, literary selections were being taught autonomously with the primary objective being the improvement of conduct and the promotion of civic humanism. The evolving concentration on the study of English and American literature as a force for improving morality and promoting nationalism eventually would be responsible for the surge of interest in literary history that dominated English literary study into the early years of the twentieth century.

As at Brown, the history of Union College in Schenectady, New York, was closely connected with the College of New Jersey and with Scottish moral philosophy. John Blair Smith, brother of Samuel Stanhope Smith and the first president of Union College when it was instituted in 1795, had graduated in 1773 from the College of New Jersey where he had studied under John Witherspoon. Smith had been the president of Hampden-Sydney College in Virginia from 1779 to 1789, and from 1791 to 1795, the pastor of the Third Presbyterian Church of Philadelphia. In 1799, Smith resigned as president of Union College to resume his duties as pastor of the church (Raymond 1907, 1: 60–68).

During Smith's presidency, students at Union College spent the first year studying languages; the second studying history and belles lettres; the third, mathematics; and the fourth, almost solely on the study of philosophy (Raymond 1907, 1: 43). Students entering the college had to be able to render into English Caesar's *Commentaries,* four orations of Cicero, Virgil's *Eclogues,* the first book of the *Iliad,* and three of the biblical Evangelists in the original. They also had to be able to explain the grammar and syntax of English, Latin, and Greek (Raymond 1907, 1: 53).

In 1802, when Jonathan Maxcy was elected to Union College's presidency, a new and elaborate system of college rules and regulations was adopted by the trustees. The system revised entrance requirements so that proficiency in English grammar and arithmetic was required for admission, along with demonstration of the ability to "read, construe and parce, at least six books of Virgil's *Eneid,* four orations in Cicero, and the four Evangelists in Greek" (Raymond 1907, 1: 83). Freshmen now studied Latin, Greek, and English, in addition to arithmetic and Sheridan's *Lectures on Elocution.* Oratory was introduced as a core subject. Along with a concentration of courses in mathematics and science, sophomores studied Blair's *Lectures* and "such parts of eminent authors in the learned languages as the Officers in College shall prescribe." Juniors studied elements of criticism and natural and moral philosophy. Seniors studied ancient and modern history, Locke's *Essay on Human Understanding,* and Stewart's *Elements of the Philosophy of the Human Mind,* and were responsible for reviewing Virgil, Cicero, and Horace and the application of principles of criticism. Sophomores, juniors, and seniors were required to write English compositions and declaim publicly "in the English language every Saturday morning." In addition, "subjects for disputation" were assigned to the classes "by their respective instructors" as often as the instructors judged proper (Raymond 1907, 1: 86). In order for the students to improve their proficiency in the art of public oratory, they committed pieces to memory, many of them literary, which were subsequently delivered publicly in an assembly every Wednesday afternoon. Andrew Raymond, the college historian, notes that, while at Union College, Maxcy himself paid particular attention to "English composition and to extemporaneous speaking" (1907, 1: 109).

Maxcy's successor at Union College was the legendary Dr. Eliphalet Nott, who was elected on August 24, 1804, the year that Maxcy left to become president of the newly instituted College of South Carolina. Nott was a graduate of the College of Rhode Island and had been a trustee of Union College before being named its president. He would remain president for sixty-two years until his death in 1866. His was a career that was, Raymond judged in 1907, "without a parallel in the American educational world" (1: 134). Indeed, Nott was a nineteenth-century American legend; "stories abounded illustrating his wit and his wisdom in the class-room; his understanding of human nature, especially student nature . . . his generosity in all his relations with 'his sons,' as he called his students."

In addition to his notable personal qualities, his educational policies were experimental and widely respected. He was a pragmatist, in sympathy with progressive, commonsense developments in education, particularly in the promotion of what Raymond refers to as the "spirit of scientific enquiry" which was shaping American universities in the early years of the nineteenth century (1907, 1: 155). To make his students "men of action," as Nott put it, was his admitted object. In order to realize his hope, he promoted science but he also believed that "books, philosophy, literary culture, even . . . scholastic logic" would help to make them even stronger and more successful (Raymond 1907, 1: 156).

With these progressive objectives in mind, he proposed in 1828 the blanket substitution of the study of modern languages for ancient languages, a revolutionary step. His efforts were widely criticized but the criticism served to enlist support from many Americans and American educators, in particular, who thought he was right. The immediate result, according to Raymond, was "a large increase in patronage and a widespread conviction that Union was a college for the times" (Raymond 1907, 1: 156). When new college buildings were erected in 1814, Nott arranged for the construction of separate rooms for the campus literary societies, the

Philomathean Society and the Adelphic Society. The major purpose of the societies was to encourage, as their charters designated, "the acquirement of literary knowledge, the promotion of virtue and the cultivation of social harmony and friendship" (Raymond 1907, 1: 156). The literary exercises they engaged in included public declamations, compositions, and literary criticism, often in the form of open critical readings of English literary selections, all of which was heartily supported by Nott.

Nott's use of the works of Lord Kames is of particular interest here because it speaks to a direct Scottish influence, although one that was put to a rather unorthodox use. The book on which Nott based "his formal teachings on the conduct of life" was Kames's *Elements of Criticism*. He taught it to the seniors, and used *Elements of Criticism* as a type of source book for lectures on "the fine art of living" which usually ended up having far more to do with Nott's perceptions and personal advice about life than anything necessarily associated with either Kames or *Elements*.

The Union College library owns a student notebook, cited in Raymond's history, that contains notes based on Nott's idiosyncratic lectures on Kames. The notebook, titled "Instructions Delivered to the Senior Class in Union College . . . in 1828–29, by the Rev. Eliphalet Nott," was copied from class notes taken by two students, William Soul and Henry Baldwin. Nott's advice to his students, cited in the notebook, was that they "read but few books and that they keep re-reading them until the knowledge in them had been transformed into power" (Raymond 1907, 1: 208). With Kames and other Scottish commonsense philosophers, he believed in the Hutchesonian contention that people were governed less by reason than by feelings. "The recognition of this truth he rightly considered fundamental in education," Raymond suggests. Nott is quoted as saying, "Man seldom acts from reason. You might enumerate in your own mind in a moment all the acts you have done from reason in a year." Hence, Raymond adds, Nott recognized "that the education of the feelings is the most important, as it is the most difficult, part of education" (1907, 1: 208–9). Nott's Romantic interest in promoting the "education of the feelings" helps also to account for his sustained promotion of literary study at Union College during his long tenure as president.

Frederick W. Seward, Union College class of 1849, said of Nott's class in "the fine art of living" that the study, one of "prime importance," was known around Union College simply as "Kames." It was a regular afternoon lecture session to the seniors but in Nott's hands it had become, according to Seward, "a comprehensive study of human nature, ranging over the whole field of physical, moral and intellectual philosophy, and applied to practical use in business, politics and religion." Seward added that all graduates of that period remembered "their 'Kames' with interest and pleasure." Many clergymen, authors, lawyers, and statesmen, Seward noted, found that Nott and Kames had given them solutions to "some of the most perplexing problems of . . . life" (Raymond 1907, 1: 269–70).

"Criticism" and Jonathan Maxcy at South Carolina

Jonathan Maxcy, Nott's predecessor, resigned the Union College presidency in 1804. In July of that year he assumed the presidency of the College of South Carolina in Columbia, which had been originally chartered in 1801.[3] Maxcy, too, was influenced by the Scottish philosophers, especially Lord Kames. He combined his administrative duties while at South Carolina with the teaching of belles lettres, criticism, and metaphysics, after a fashion reminiscent of Kames, Campbell, and other Scottish commonsense philosophers. He actually assumed the title of professor of belles lettres, criticism, and metaphysics. Maxcy's intention, according to Patrick Scott, was "to emphasize esthetics as an element of general philosophy, in the style of Kames . . . Campbell and the Scottish school, rather than occupy himself with rhetoric as it traditionally had been taught" (1983, 23).

"Criticism," as Maxcy had defined it in 1802 in his commencement ad-

---

3. The College of South Carolina was not the earliest college chartered in South Carolina. Neither was it the first to offer courses in English oratory and rhetoric. The College of Charleston traces its history from 1762, when the old Charles Town Library Society first advertised for a professor of "English Rhetoric or Oratory" and for a professor of "Natural and Experimental Philosophy." Charleston appears to have been a college in name only, however, until 1789 when it finally opened formally for classes. William Mason, from Harvard, was the first professor of English language and belles lettres. The college also had Scottish connections. Dr. George Buist, a Presbyterian minister, a native Scot, and a graduate of Edinburgh University, was elected principal in 1805. Under Buist the curriculum was enlarged and included courses in "English grammar, and Exercises in Public Speaking," "Translations into Latin of passages from English Authors," as well as the more traditional course in "Rhetorick and Belles Lettres" (Easterby 1935, 32–54). When Jasper Adams, an 1815 graduate of Brown, became principal in 1824, he stressed the importance of an "English course of studies." According to J. H. Easterby, Adams actually had implemented a plan for the improvement of the curriculum that Buist unsuccessfully had advocated as early as 1806 (1935, 81–82).

dress to the College of Rhode Island graduates, respected "all the productions of genius in the fine arts" and taught students "to distinguish what is defective, what is decent and proper, grand, sublime and beautiful." Those who studied criticism as a science, Maxcy believed, would find the same feelings "springing up" as were otherwise excited by precepts learned in the study of moral philosophy (1844, 335). Two years later, in 1804, in his "Introductory Lecture, to a Course on the Philosophical Principles of Rhetoric and Criticism" delivered to seniors at the College of South Carolina, Maxcy formally designated "rhetoric" as a complementary combination of oratory and criticism directed at instruction in "the art of speaking, so as to convince and persuade" (1844, 397). By 1804, according to Clark and Halloran, oratory was becoming increasingly important as the forensic means through which general knowledge (Nott's lessons on the "conduct of life") and shared principles of community conduct were being conveyed (1993, 23). Public debates and oratorical presentations were becoming increasingly popular nationwide as a form of entertainment that drew large audiences and helped to forge a spirit of community in the American populace. In his 1802 College of Rhode Island commencement address, Maxcy had recognized Hugh Blair on the importance of the combination of language study and conduct and then went on to attest to the value of the combined study of oratory and criticism as a "rational science" that "occupies a middle status between the higher senses and the intellect." In a clear recognition of the pedagogical relationship between literary criticism, in particular, and the Hutchesonian emphasis on feeling and emotions as a check on reason in the process of promoting enlightened discourse, he added that the virtue of "criticism" was that it united "sentiment and reason," and that it enlivened and improved both (1844, 333–35).

Maxcy recognized that one of the surest ways simultaneously to appeal to emotion, to promote pleasure, and to encourage reasoned, critical evaluation was through the careful study of literary selections. A true Hutchesonian, Maxcy believed that sound critical judgment depended on understanding "the inmost recesses of the heart" and the passions as well as the "innumerable modifications in the innumerable and ever varying circumstances and characters of men" (1844, 398).

Maxcy's impact on the progress of the oratorical tradition in the early nineteenth century, one that by 1804 envisioned academic courses in "criticism" as the ideal synthesis of moral philosophy, oratory, and literary study, was significant. Criticism or, more to the point, "philosophical criticism," for Maxcy, applied "scientific principles to the productions of art and genius, with a view to ascertain the beauties and defects of the latter, and to adjust their intrinsic and comparative merits" (1844, 398–99). The study of criticism, he argued, provided students with valuable self-knowledge. The study, in other words, improved conduct and enhanced character building. The argument recalls the line of thought advocated by Adam Smith and other Scottish moral philosophers and rhetoricians on the study of rhetoric and belles lettres as ultimately a way to improve morality and conduct. For Maxcy, like the Scottish moralists, combining the study of philosophy with literature enlarged one's "knowledge of mind." As he put it, to study language, "as a philosopher does," was to study "the powers, laws, and operations of the mind" (1844, 401). Maxcy knew that one of the strengths of a philosophically based assessment of literature was its promotion of a vision of criticism that examined states of mind as well as rhetorical or stylistic measures. As he observed:

> While investigating the philosophical principles of Rhetoric and Criticism, we are occupied with mental phenomena. These are proper subjects of observation, and contain in them, the principles of all our knowledge of mind, as much as the appearances of the visible world contain the principles of all our knowledge of matter. Hence, Criticism assumes a scientific form, and rests on a basis not less certain, than that of natural philosophy. (1844, 403)

Like Adam Smith, Kames, and Campbell, Maxcy thought that courses involving the critical study of literary texts had the potential to serve as pivotal connecting points for other courses in the curriculum. "Words" themselves, he asserted, "distributed into their various kinds," were to be understood as "objects of high consideration and subjects of critical scrutiny." Criticism, from Aristotle's time, had always involved "a deep and thorough search into the principles of good writing." Aristotle had "reduced criticism to a scientific form, and presented its principles in such an alliance with philosophy," he thought, "that we can call it by no better name than philosophical criticism" (1844, 404–5). Philosophical criticism, at the time, had opened numerous fields of inquiry, he added, for rhetoricians, grammarians, orators, logicians, and moralists. By blending the study of philosophy with the arts, he continued, one might reasonably expect that all of the "intellectual powers" would now more completely evolve (1844, 405–6).

Combining the study of philosophy with oratory and literary criticism directly influenced the design of Maxcy's curriculum at South Carolina, but the idea was also very much in the air at the time and helped to promote major curricular changes in language study in other American colleges. To the extent to which Maxcy connected philosophy, oratory, and literary criticism, as Scott observes, his curriculum was "absolutely representative of its period" (1983, 23). In 1816, Maxcy circulated a pamphlet among his South Carolina students titled *A Course of Historical and Miscellaneous Reading,* which listed useful supplementary reading. For the junior and senior classes, he listed titles designed particularly to complement the reading for his courses on "the study of Rhetorick, Criticism, and the Philosophy of the Human Mind" (Scott 1983, 24). Among the titles were the works of Cicero, Quintilian, and Longinus. But he also listed Campbell's *Philosophy of Rhetoric,* Charles Rollin on belles lettres, Burke on the sublime; Johnson's *Lives of the Poets,* the preface to his *Dictionary,* and his prefaces to Shakespeare; John Walker on elocution, Joseph Warton on Pope, Addison on Milton, Pope's preface to Homer, and Joseph Priestley's lectures on oratory. Of the twenty-eight titles recommended for upperclassmen, ten were written by Scots (Scott 1983, 24). Important also is the frequency with which actual works of literary criticism were cited in the list—e.g., Johnson's prefaces, his *Lives of the Poets,* Pope on Homer, Warton on Pope, and Addison on Milton, as well as the works of Cicero, Quintilian, and Longinus, who represented the best of classical literary criticism to Maxcy.

The list was clearly intended to encourage upperclassmen, once they had completed their basic courses in the classics, to study a wider spectrum of subjects geared to critical readings of literary texts. The list, along with Maxcy's encouragement of secondary research for the writing assignments based on topics drawn from current affairs, suggests that Maxcy likely was working to provide students with an education geared to modern practical objectives. It is certain that Maxcy, like the Scottish moral philosophers, clearly understood the pedagogical value of philosophy and belles lettres in shaping character as well as intellect. He also consciously promoted a philosophical approach to oratory as the formal study of persuasion and pleasure, or what Maxcy called "passion." In a passage in his "Introductory

Lecture" to the South Carolina senior class on the importance of attending to the emotions and feelings, he observed that the study of oratory had suffered in "modern times," because of "the neglect of the language of fancy and passions." Language, he added:

> is limited to words, either written or spoken. Language thus understood would probably answer every purpose, did man possess no power but intellect. This however is far from being the case. He possesses fancy and passions . . . [which] are furnished by nature with a language peculiar to themselves; a language which without art or study instantly expresses all . . . impulses, movements and modifications. On this language depends all that is forcible, affecting and sublime in oratory.—Words are sufficient to convey what are called ideas, but are absolutely incapable of expressing our internal feelings, sentiments and passions. (1844, 408)

Clark and Halloran argue that a major transformation in the oratorical tradition in the United States took place as the century progressed, so that by the late 1820s—specifically, by 1828, when Andrew Jackson defeated John Quincy Adams for the presidency—the importance of public discourse as an educational vehicle and the collectivist assumptions about moral conduct upon which it had been based went into a visible decline. Adams, the loser, represented the centralized and patrician leadership of a classically educated elite; Jackson, the winner, promoted decentralization and democratic principles that celebrated individual expression and secularism rather than traditional prescriptive religion. Jackson also promoted a vision of trust in the judgment of the commonality. The shift was essentially from morality and conduct viewed as public or institutional concerns to a vision of spiritual authority as predominantly a matter of private, emotive, individual concern (1993, 13).

Clark and Halloran may be correct in their assumptions, given that the oratorical tradition that extended into the middle years of the century did seem to undergo a transformation in the public world, but in the academic world, at universities like Brown, Union College, and South Carolina, which continued to promote the combined study of oratory and literature with moral philosophy, the transformations are not as clearly visible. In fact, what seems apparent in the universities is that literature studied under the ever-expanding umbrella of "criticism" began to emerge as a separate, autonomous discourse, as it did clearly at Brown by the 1870s; the role of the study of oratory in the course combination eventually diminished. In time, oratory as a subject, especially after the Civil War, was reduced to little more than classroom exercises in public speaking.

"Criticism" and the "Oratorical Tradition" at Yale

Jonathan Maxcy died in 1820, too soon to realize the degree of influence the oratorical tradition would exert on American higher education in the first half of the century. The interest in oratory, what Spiller's *Literary History of the United States* refers to as a "national habit," influential particularly during the fifty years before the Civil War, was swept along by a ferment of literary experimentation that characterized the first half of the nineteenth century (1963, 542). By the 1820s colleges and universities were taking up the challenge of preparing graduates for new opportunities, many in the literary worlds of journalism and publishing.

By the 1820s, Yale and Harvard had shifted academic priorities away from the old preoccupation with divinity and had begun to offer subjects that covered a much wider spectrum of learning. One important change was the gradual introduction of courses in criticism into a curriculum intended to accommodate public needs (Snow 1907, 119–23). Yale, founded in 1701 to promote the arts and sciences, originally had envisioned its mission as twofold: The first was the education of the ministry, but the second was an acknowledged commitment to preparing students "for Publick employment" (Kelly 1974, 8). In 1731, the Anglican divine George Berkeley, who had settled for a time on a farm in Rhode Island, gave Yale the deed to his ninety-six-acre farm in gratitude for its successful role in educating clergymen. In 1733, he gave the college another gift that may have been, in some respects, more farsighted and, hence, more valuable. That was a gift of 880 books for the college library, which increased its collection by half. Included among the books, mostly theological selections, were also volumes of English literature (Kelly 1974, 40). Works by Spenser, Shakespeare, Ben Jonson, Abraham Cowley, Samuel Butler, Milton, and Dryden, among others, were consequently accessible to Yale's students for the first time. As a result, in 1733 Yale had one of the best collections of English literature in North America.

In 1731, the Yale curriculum involved standard classical courses, i.e., Latin, Greek, Hebrew, logic, mathematics, and so forth. In 1740, Thomas Clap, who was president from 1740 until 1766, introduced courses on moral philosophy and history. By 1750, some forensic debates were conducted in English. Naphtali Daggett, who replaced Clap as president in 1766, encouraged the introduction of English grammar and English literary selections into the curriculum, but there was little interest in promoting actual courses in modern literature until the arrival of Timothy Dwight.

In 1771, Timothy Dwight, whose grandfather was Jonathan Edwards, was made a tutor at Yale. Dwight was a 1769 Yale graduate. There is no solid evidence suggesting that he had ever read Francis Hutcheson but Charles Cuningham, in his biography of Dwight, records the following entry taken from Dwight's college memorandum book for 1768: "All the labour of men is to promote their happiness. And the notion of doing good is entirely explained by contributions to the happiness of ourselves and fellow creatures" (1942, 29). The entry reads like a paraphrase of Hutcheson's "greatest happiness" claim. At the very least, it was a conscious affirmation of Hutcheson's romantic contention that one's moral sense was improved by choosing to work for the benefit of the community. Like Hutcheson and the other Scottish moral sense theorists, Dwight also maintained that philosophy or "ideas" alone could not produce truth. Philosophy left the mind informed but not necessarily wiser. As Cuningham notes, Dwight consequently emphasized the value of personal emotions, the experience of pleasure, and social experience in the pursuit of virtue (1942, 137).

Even though Dwight was, by persuasion, a Congregationalist, he was sympathetic with Scottish Enlightenment thinking and with Scottish Presbyterianism. He appreciated particularly the wide range of theological views that Scottish Presbyterianism accommodated. Sloan points out that the reconciliation between religion and the progressive spirit of the times that Scottish moral philosophy and Scottish Presbyterianism encouraged appealed to a wide ecclesiastical spectrum of colonial American theologians (1971, 238). Dwight actually made little distinction between Congregational and Presbyterian, leaning most of the time more decidedly in the direction of Old Side Presbyterianism (Cuningham 1942, 126). The increasing movement of people, especially European immigrants, into the frontier also possibly influenced his attitude; to theologically conservative Congregationalists like Dwight, Presbyterianism appeared to have a more solid organizational control than other colonial religions. As a practicing minister in Greenfield Hill, Connecticut, in 1787, Dwight had been asked by an association of ministers to help draw up a plan to unite Presbyterians throughout the United States, an effort that appears eventually to have succeeded (Cuningham 1942, 128).

Dwight's religious convictions considerably shaped his dedication to teaching. While tutoring at Yale in the 1770s, in an attempt to interest his students in reading and evaluating English literature, he took measures that testify to that dedication. Voluntarily, after hours, he offered courses in which he lectured on matters of style and composition. He had acquired a knowledge on his own, as an undergraduate, of the arts of rhetorical criticism and oratory. When he became a tutor, he and his young associates scheduled private meetings during which they took turns openly declaiming on a variety of subjects. He also had studied John Ward's *System of Oratory* on his own. As a Yale tutor, he instituted a similar activity for his students. The students declaimed and he and the others in the class critiqued the presentations. They also read and criticized the written papers, but providing constructive criticism orally appears to have been the primary object of the exercise. Cuningham says of Dwight that, having lived through the economic instability of the Revolutionary War, he saw the need for a solid financial base for the new nation. He also believed in putting men "who managed their private affairs successfully, in charge of public affairs" (1942, 341). Thinking critically about issues raised in a classroom, along with developing the ability to address those issues with conviction and clarity, improved the nation's prospects for a more promising commercial future.

Dwight, like Joseph Howe and John Trumbull, his fellow tutors at Yale, shared the opinion that the greatest weakness in Yale's curriculum in the 1770s was the neglect of belles lettres in the English studies program (Cuningham 1942, 36). Consequently, from the time Dwight and Trumbull were hired "every effort was unanimously made" to teach style and elocution (Snow 1907, 53 n. 1). In 1776, as the direct result of the voluntary tutoring in English by Dwight, Howe, and Trumbull, a petition was presented to the Yale Corporation requesting that the senior class be permitted to hire Dwight to instruct them in rhetoric, history, and belles lettres (Kingsley 1879, 1: 99). The corporation grudgingly acceded to the request, but refused to fund the course and required that every student enrolling get parental approval. In spite of the corporation's misgivings, the course was offered and Dwight taught it. Dwight stayed on at Yale as a tutor until 1777, at which time he entered the Revolutionary army as a chaplain. In 1783, he took over the parish of Greenfield Hill, located near New York and close to his beloved Yale. In 1795, he returned to Yale as its president.

From 1778 to 1795, Ezra Stiles had been Yale's president. Stiles, who graduated from Yale in 1746, was able to change the curriculum slightly in favor of English studies in the 1780s. He moved English grammar into the freshman year, and he permitted the sophomores to study English literature. In 1792, the Connecticut General Assembly formally recognized the curriculum changes and acknowledged that they were implemented "so as the better to accommodate the Education of the Undergraduates to the present State of Literature" (Kelly 1974, 109).

As Stiles's successor at Yale from 1795 to 1817, Dwight made even more significant changes. He helped to establish the Connecticut Academy of Arts and Sciences and he succeeded finally in shifting the language emphasis from classical Latin to English (Cuningham 1942, 237). During his tenure seniors were required to study rhetoric in combination with ethics, logic, metaphysics, and the history of civil society. Dwight was the teacher. For the rhetoric course, he used Blair's *Lectures*, but, as Cuningham notes, he examined Blair's principles "freely," allowing the discussion of whatever questions arose to develop organically (1942, 243).

James L. Kingsley, Yale's professor of languages during Dwight's presidency, taught biblical criticism and courses in English composition. Criticism was his academic forte. He was well published as a literary critic and as a historian. Thomas A. Thacher in a commemorative portrait of Kingsley writes of Kingsley's "genuine relish" for English literature. "He was familiar with the best English writers in prose and verse," Thacher adds, "enjoying a kind of personal acquaintance with Addison . . . Johnson . . . Milton, and Shakspeare . . . from his habit of giving a personal existence to the writers" (1852, 45–46). Kingsley's "feel" for English literature both colored and augmented his classes.

The efforts of Stiles, Dwight, Kingsley, and other early promoters of English studies greatly advanced the oratorical tradition at Yale. In 1828, they succeeded in gaining an influential formal public acknowledgment of the link between the critical reading of literary selections in English and the formal study of oratory. Then President Jeremiah Day claimed in the famous Yale Report of 1828 to the Connecticut General Assembly, part two of which was authored by Kingsley, that by reading English authors, the Yale students were learning "the powers of the language" in which they "speak and write." In this reading, students were also learning, Day added, "that eloquence and solid learning should go together; that he who has accumulated the richest treasures of thought, should possess the highest powers of oratory." He also warned of the danger of concentrating strictly on rhetorical matters of grammar, style, and argument in the English classes. "Of what use is a display of rhetorical elegance," he observed, "from one who knows a little or nothing which is worth communicating" (Kelly 1974, 163).

The Yale Report was a timely document attesting to a developing trend in higher education in the United States that, by the 1820s, as Spiller suggests, was encouraging the use of both English and American literary selections in the teaching of humanistic principles in courses in oratory and criticism (1963, 228). The effort remained visibly indebted to the work of earlier Scottish moral philosophers and rhetoricians. In 1824, in a course called "rhetoric and oratory," Yale's students read Cicero's *De Oratore* in combination with Homer's *Iliad* for the first term. Seniors read Blair's *Lectures on Rhetoric* during the first term and Dugald Stewart's *Philosophy of the Human Mind* in the second term, along with Paley's *Natural Theology*. Paley's *Moral Philosophy* was required of seniors during the third term. As early as 1824, the majority of texts read by the seniors at Yale were written in English.

Harvard and E. T. Channing

The link between the oratorical tradition and Scottish moral philosophy during the last quarter of the eighteenth century and the early decades of the nineteenth century becomes even more evident when one considers the early history of Harvard College (later Harvard University). Harvard, North America's first college, was founded in 1636. The Harvard curriculum before the 1770s changed little. It required the study of Greek, Latin, and Hebrew and offered subjects designed mainly to prepare young men for the ministry. By the 1780s, however, under the influence of the Scottish Enlightenment, progressive changes began to occur.

In the beginning, Harvard was English to the core. The Harvards, its founding family, were Puritans, although support for the college came from no particular church, Anglican or otherwise. Throughout the seventeenth century, English traditions dominated and the college retained an almost medieval program of study. Students were admitted who could read, according to the college catalog, a "classicall Latine Author *extempore,* and make and speake true Latine in Verse and Prose, *Suo ut aiunt Marte;* And decline perfectly the Paradigm's of *Nounes* and *Verbes* in the *Greek* tongue" (Morison 1995, 433). They studied grammar, Hebrew *"and the Easterne tongues,"* rhetoric, logic, some arithmetic, and some natural and moral philosophy. The education of ministers was the primary purpose of the college; consequently, the curriculum concentrated on subjects related almost exclusively to divinity studies.

As late as the early 1780s, although innovative changes had been made in the curriculum, Harvard still made no allowance specifically for the study of English. But there was interest in offering English studies as a course of instruction that would encourage oratory and declamation in English. By 1786, the professor assigned to teach Hebrew, owing to a declining interest in the subject, was instructed to begin offering courses in English. By 1788, a committee formed to revise the method of instruction at the college approved the introduction of an abridgement of Hugh Blair's *Lectures* to the language course with the hope of encouraging the students to "proceed with the art of speaking and declaiming."[4] By 1791, professors were lecturing on the English language one afternoon per week. Students were examined yearly on elements of English grammar and rhetoric, and it appears that the examinations also involved some meager knowledge of belles lettres and English composition (Richardson 1878, 206, 268, 325). By 1797, separate texts, classical and English, dealing with matters related to English composition were being assigned (Snow 1907, 90).

With the appearance of Edward Tyrell Channing, however, as Boylston Professor of Oratory and Rhetoric in 1819, a position he would retain for thirty-two years, the influence of the Scottish philosophers became particularly evident at Harvard and so did a strong shift of emphasis in English studies to a concentration almost solely on literary criticism and oratory. From 1817 to 1819, E. T. Channing, William Ellery Channing's brother, had edited the *North American Review.* A collection published in 1856 under the title *Lectures Read to the Seniors in Harvard College* reveals the importance he attached to the combination of oratory and literary criticism and to the Scottish Enlightenment as a source. His debt to Scottish moral

4. J. Tarver suggests that abridgements of Blair's *Lectures* originated at Harvard in 1802 with the publication of Eliphalet Pearson's popular abridgement of the *Lectures* (1996, 54–67).

philosophy has prompted Charvat, for one, to single him out as "perhaps the most important individual of his time" in the dissemination of Scottish aesthetics (1936, 186).

Richard H. Dana Jr., Channing's cousin, in a "Biographical Notice" to the 1856 edition of the *Lectures* noted that, during his tenure at Harvard, Channing was very clear about the difference between the study of classical rhetoric for its own sake and the study of criticism (Channing 1856, xiii). Of course, Channing recognized the relationship between the study of rhetoric, including classical rhetoric, and criticism. However, he chose to link the study of oratory rather than rhetoric with classroom assignments in literary criticism (Tuman 1986, 344). Dana records that Channing had always been a "thoughtful student" of English literature who had read and taught at various times the works or excerpts from the works of Chaucer, Shakespeare, Milton, and Spenser. Among the "moderns," he taught selections from Burke, Johnson, Goldsmith, Fielding, Richardson, and Scott. He also promoted the works in English of prominent theologians such as Isaac Barrow, Jeremy Taylor, and Robert South. He was familiar with the publications of Young, Cowper, and Bunyan. He was also, according to Dana, "among the earliest to recognize the genius and influences . . . of Wordsworth, Coleridge, Byron, Southey, Campbell, and Lamb." Among American authors, he promoted the works of Irving, Cooper, Bryant, Longfellow, and Catharine Maria Sedgwick, a Massachusetts novelist who was famous at the time for her depiction of the simple virtues of American domesticity (Channing 1856, xiv-xv).

Channing appears, therefore, to have been as revolutionary a teacher as he was a critic. When he began his Harvard career in 1819, he opted to use the same texts for his rhetorical theory courses that his predecessors had used: i.e., freshmen read Robert Lowth's *English Grammar* and John Walker's *Rhetorical Grammar;* sophomores read Cicero's *De Oratore* and Blair's *Lectures* (Snow 1907, 126–27). A short seven years later, in 1827, however, he took the drastic step of postponing textbook study to the sophomore year, with the exception of two weeks of assigned reading for freshmen in Lowth's *Grammar.* Between 1827 and 1839, he systematically instituted a series of revolutionary changes in the rhetoric and oratory course that survived until his retirement in 1851. Essentially, he cut back all of the textbook reading in grammar and rhetoric so that sophomores spent only one term on Lowth's *Grammar,* Ebenezer Porter's *Analysis of Rhetorical Delivery,* and books two and three of George Campbell's *Philosophy of*

Edward Tyrell Channing. Portrait by George Peter Alexander Healy. Courtesy of the Harvard Portrait Collection, President and Fellows of Harvard College; gift of a large number of the alumni graduated since 1819 to Harvard College, 1852.

Rhetoric. Juniors studied Richard Whately's *Elements of Logic* for only one term; seniors studied Whately's *Elements of Rhetoric* also for one term (Channing 1968, xviii-xix).

What Channing seems to have decided, circa 1827, was that rules for studying rhetoric should be derived more from firsthand experiences and observations about life than from dogmatic textbook prescriptions. The principle, of course, is essentially Hutchesonian and Scottish. Instead of accepting prescriptive pronouncements on rhetoric and criticism, Channing, like the eighteenth-century Scottish commonsense philosophers he had studied, preferred to try to understand human nature and the art of living empirically, in the context of contemporary society. Consequently, he reduced textbook reading and, instead, encouraged his students to study the world around them. Because the ancient orators, Cicero and Quintilian, particularly, he thought, had actually studied the temper of their countrymen, modern orators would do well to follow their example. He urged his oratory students, consequently, to study not only the temper of their countrymen but also the temper of the times.

Channing may have been responding partially to the national debate that surfaced in the 1820s over the value of continuing to concentrate on the study of classical rhetoric and literature in American colleges. A controversial Amherst College report, dated 1826–27, was drafted in direct response to an increasingly popular claim that prevailing systems of classical education were inadequate to meet the contemporary needs and demands of American students. After a series of special meetings, the Amherst College faculty presented the Board of Trustees with a radical plan for altering the curriculum. The plan called for the implementation of a "parallel or equivalent course" for students enrolled for the four-year degree. In contrast to the old course of study, which devoted the bulk of its time to the ancient languages, the new course of study concentrated on modern languages and literature, especially literature in English. The report listed first among its recommendations that more prominence be given "to English literature, than which no subject has higher claims upon the American scholar, or can more richly reward his diligence" (Snow 1907, 158).

The report went on to emphasize particularly the value of the *critical* study of "admired classics" in English (Snow 1907, 158). The plan also recommended that modern languages, especially French and Spanish, and, if possible, German and Italian, "with particular attention to the literature" be substituted for the ancient languages; that experiments in mechanical philosophy be multiplied and varied; that chemistry and other kindred branches of physical sciences be geared more to the useful arts and trades, to the cultivation of the soil, and to domestic economy; that a course of lectures be devoted to labor-saving machines, to bridges, locks, and aqueducts, and to the different orders of architecture; that more time be devoted to natural history; that modern history be taught, especially the history of the Puritans, in connection with the civil and ecclesiastical history of the United States; that the U.S. constitution be included in the study of civil and political law; and that drawing and civil engineering be added. Common to both courses of study would be ancient history; geography; grammar; rhetoric and oratory; mathematics; natural, intellectual and moral philosophy; anatomy; political economy; and theology (Tyler 1873, 170–71).

The radically new course of study went into effect at Amherst during the 1827–28 academic year, with eighteen out of sixty-seven incoming freshmen opting for the "modern languages." But the new course was woefully ahead of its time, even for Amherst, and it did not succeed. Of the students entering for the 1828–29 year, so few registered for the new course that the program was scrapped. Inadequate staffing appears to have been at the surface among the reasons for the cancellation, but at the root was resistance to such a radically "modern" program of study from "old" faculty with a bias in favor of the traditional curriculum. William Seymour Tyler, an 1830 graduate of Amherst who was appointed professor of Latin, Greek, and Hebrew in 1836 and who wrote the original history of the college, observed of the "parallel" program, in retrospect, that it actually was "the favorite scheme of one of the Professors" and was never heartily supported by the rest of the faculty, who taught in it "with far less courage and enthusiasm" than they devoted to the old curriculum (1873, 173).

The Amherst College plan failed and the classical curriculum remained relatively unchanged right into the middle years of the century, a development that appears to have left Tyler, a classics professor, with no regrets. He seemed happy to report in his 1873 history of the college, regarding the early experiment: "Thus ended the first attempt to introduce the Modern Language and the Physical Sciences as an equivalent for the *time-honored system of classical culture in our American colleges*" (emphasis mine, 1873, 173). He also alluded to similar attempts, "intensified by the omission of the Mathematics as well as the Ancient Classics," occurring as late as the 1870s in other colleges around the nation. Of the result, he guardedly advised, only "time must determine" (1873, 174).

The 1827 Amherst experiment in the teaching of the modern languages failed. Developments at Harvard, however, especially in the promotion of English studies, appear to have had a quite different fate, owing largely to the efforts of E. T. Channing. By the 1820s, Channing was making noticeable strides to promote the teaching of English literature at Harvard. In a lecture titled "The Study of Our Own Language," he makes clear his contention that "mere grammar" could no longer be his sole concern. Accuracy with English, he argued, owed more to "familiarity with

English books and with good society" (1968, 218–19). To study the great writers who have mastered English, he added, "is the true way to establish a thoroughly native and a thoroughly scholar-like knowledge and employment of the language" (1968, 228). In a lecture on "literary tribunals," he observed that works of literary genius, "as in the elegant arts generally," must be studied long and patiently in order to isolate their strengths (1968, 156). In a lecture on forms of criticism, he acknowledged the existence of various kinds of criticism, including something as basic as the quiet and confidential criticism we receive from a friend or a teacher (1968, 166); but literary criticism, he insisted, needed to be studied as a separate discipline.

Nor was it to be confused with philology, Channing advised: "You know how common it is to publish the early English writers, and especially the poets, with notes and illustrations of various kinds," he remarked. Such extensive annotation, however, is little appreciated, he added, and for good reasons. Too often the explanations are "needless and ostentatious." It is bad enough, he said, to be required to move from the text to the notes incessantly, but to be required to read notes that lacked any real critical merit was intolerable (1968, 175). Literature, he added, should have "some effect upon our tempers, opinions and course of life." The literature that should be read and critically studied "should lead us to look as *Philosophers,* as Christians and as men of feeling upon those high exercises of the mind which pass under the general name of taste" (emphasis mine, 1968, 179).

Most of the changes in Channing's teaching during those early years involved a shift away from prescriptive textbooks on rhetoric and grammar in favor of a more open but critical study of current events in combination with randomly chosen works of literature. As he put it in a lecture titled "A Writer's Preparation," the "dull books and exercises of the rhetoric-class . . . had their work to do . . . and their effect has not perished, though they themselves . . . are now forgotten." What had become most important, he added, sounding very much like Union College's Eliphalet Nott, is the study of the conduct of everyday life (1968, 186, 189–90). Much of the shift in emphasis in Channing's pedagogy can be traced to the influence on his thinking, especially about rhetoric, oratory, and criticism, of the Scottish philosopher Thomas Reid, who also played a major role in John Witherspoon's revolutionary curricular reforms at the College of New Jersey (as has been described).

E. T. Channing and Thomas Reid

Dana documented the important effect of Reid on Channing's thinking and teaching (Channing 1856, xvi). According to Anderson and Braden, editors of a 1968 edition of Channing's *Lectures Read to the Seniors,* many of Reid's methods and conclusions were already evident in portions of the rhetoric of Blair, Campbell, and Whately, all of whom Channing taught. They add that Reid's theories and those of Dugald Stewart, Reid's Scottish disciple, "permeated the thinking of American academic communities, especially Harvard," during the late eighteenth and early nineteenth centuries (Channing 1968, xxi). Stewart's *Philosophy of the Human Mind,* for instance, was required reading by seniors in their course of study in intellectual philosophy during Channing's years at Harvard (Snow 1907, 127). Charvat notes that in 1829 the Reverend James Marsh wrote Samuel Coleridge and told him that "whereas American colleges formerly taught their students Locke, they now taught [Dugald] Stewart and [Thomas] Brown; and that furthermore it was Stewart's *History of Philosophy* which kept students away from German philosophy (1936, 34). Levi Hedge, who taught philosophy at Harvard from 1800 to 1832, was a specialist in Stewart, Brown, and Reid. Indeed, according to Charvat, the works of Stewart in particular were immensely popular in the waning years of the eighteenth century and the early nineteenth century, in both the United States and Scotland. While in Edinburgh, scores of young men flocked to the university just to hear them. Francis Wayland, for instance, recalled entering Union College in 1811 at the age of fifteen where he studied "Stewart on the mind" and Kames's *Elements,* and after "hearing the essays of older students on these and kindred topics," he was inspired and clung to the "vague notion that if I were older I could do the same thing" (1854, 4). Reid, of course, had a major influence on Stewart's psychological theories (Copleston 1994, 377).

Reid, as has been discussed, emphasized the value of open, unrestricted observation and experiment in the examination of sense experiences, in order to learn more about human nature. Included in the category of "senses" were memory, judgment, taste, habits, appetites, desires, and language, as well as senses of duty and moral obligation (Reid 1846, 1: xxii). Reid, always an empiricist, although he was the first to attack the British empiricist reliance on "ideas" as the only sure way to gain knowledge, conjectured that his experimental, commonsense methodology also could provide a basis for understanding and developing a critical appreciation of the fine and practical arts. He believed that the fundamental defining elements of poetry, music, painting, and the other fine arts existed unchanged throughout time. His point was that artistic excellence would always be recognized by good people with good hearts who had developed the ability to judge critically. Judgment, consequently, was an educational objective because it would enable one to recognize the qualities and virtues that *naturally* would please a person of good taste. Judging a work meant examining it scientifically; hence, the act became an exercise in criticism.

Channing's adoption and promotion of the need for a sound heart and a sense of good taste in making artistic judgments unquestionably reveals his debt to aesthetic principles promoted by Hutcheson, Reid, and other eighteenth-century Scottish moral sense theorists. This is essentially why Charvat made the sweeping observation that Channing was most important in the dissemination of Scottish thinking on aesthetics (1936, 186). Channing noted in an unpublished lecture that "the design of criticism is to examine the merits and tendencies of a work, to direct the public judgment, and to guide the future efforts of an author, to animate and encourage him by assuring him that his works are known, to inform him of the taste and wants of society" (1968, xlvi). Like Adam Smith, he thought that novels should be valued for the moral influence they could exert on readers by exhibiting truths and revealing strengths and flaws in character. He also believed that reading classic English and American authors could help to check corruptive, unwelcome changes in the English language. Following Reid, in an early pre-Romantic, eighteenth-century affirmation of the value of the psychological or expressive mode of judgment in literary analysis, he declared that the best critic was one who could isolate and reveal the secret of an author's genius so that other readers would also recognize the author's power. As he explained to his seniors in a lecture on "permanent literary fame," the ability to recognize and appreciate the "home character and experience of . . . writers," knowledge essential to the formation of any "great and commanding literature," was, to that degree, also essential to the eventual formation of a widely respected tradition of American literature (1968, 268).

Reid's pedagogical recommendation for developing the critical faculty in students was particularly appealing to early American educators because it promoted the revolutionary theory that "where you begin influences your ultimate destination" (Lehrer 1989, 288). Keith Lehrer, in his critical biography of Reid, explains, "If your method is to assume only the existence of the internal world of thought, you will be epistemologically limited to this internal world and be unable to attain knowledge of the external world. . . . Reid gave priority to our common-sense knowledge of the world." Accordingly, for Reid, "common-sense knowledge of the internal and external world is where we should begin" (1989, 288–89). Like any conscientious educator, then, Channing was especially concerned with "beginnings." He believed that the oral and written exercises in observation and expression that he was encouraging in his Harvard students would provide them with a solid, realistic "beginning" on their way to developing the ability to make mature, sound critical judgments. The effort would also provide for the eventual recognition and promotion of a respected and admired national literature.

Scattered throughout Channing's lectures and articles on literary criticism is abundant evidence of the impact of Reid and other Scottish philosophers on his teaching. He fully accepted Reid's commonsense belief that the study of human nature should form the basis for the study of criticism. In his lectures on literary criticism and principles of oratorical declamation he emphasized, after Hutcheson, Ciceronian or civic humanism by concentrating on social institutions and various social circumstances in which speech and language were evidently instrumental in the formation of humanistic judgments and decisions. Yet, though he believed that the best eloquence grew naturally out of its close connections with the institutions and the temper of the times, he warned constantly of the foolishness of thinking that contemporary oratory should do little more than simply replicate classical oratory. Channing, also a serious reader of Adam Smith, envisioned the patriot as basically an educated public servant, one of the multitude bound in sympathy to public service.

In a lecture to the seniors called "Deliberative Oratory," in a reaffirmation of the link he envisioned among the "modern" orator, the oratorical tradition, and society, he argued that the best oratory in the United States will grow "naturally out of our institutions and state of society" (1968, 77). "The picture may be ideal," he added, "or, at any rate, few orators may answer to it in the whole. . . . Still . . . it will be more just and more instructive . . . than one which gave you a sort of average estimate of modern oratory" (1968, 77). Channing, of course, was not talking about preparation for the bar as did the ancients or, necessarily, about preparation for the ministry as his immediate predecessors would have. He was referring primarily to the role of the orator in legislative state and national assemblies. In general, he added, the eloquence of the nation's deliberative assemblies is exactly what

> we should expect from their constitution or theory. . . . It is marked by a spirit of independence, or by a man's sense of this individual importance. . . . The independence . . . is dignified and unoppressive, and springs immediately from a becoming pride, and from a man's consciousness of his political privileges, and of his responsibility to himself as well as to others. He is not to bring his prejudices or his private interests with him, when he professes to act for a whole people. . . . He is not the creature of a king, of a set of ministers, or of his constituents. (1968, 77–78)

Moral checks upon one's self-interest, he added, sounding very much like Adam Smith, may be "strengthened by improved public sentiment" (1968, 78). Modern political oratory, consequently, should attempt to lead "considerate men to responsible action." It should wear a "serious and business character" (1968, 80). The modern political orator, he continued, "binds the truths and the wisdom of to-day to those of all past time, and to those that will be the fruit of a still larger experience in the ages to come. He is a *philosopher* in the best sense of the term, and yet as familiar with affairs and as safe in his deductions as a man whose whole life has been spent in calculations and details" (1968, 81). Echoing Ward's recommendations in his *System of Oratory,* Channing promoted the idea that the modern orator must be comprehensively well educated in all facets of knowledge. He must also be guided by what is right; he must seek the good; he must seek the truth (1968, 85).

Channing's objectives were weighty and of serious national consequence. He was a patriot. He believed that by adapting principles embodied in the study of the humanities, especially moral philosophy, to academic exercises in oratory, he could prepare his students for the economic marketplace and the American political arena. The tool he used to combine lessons in ethics, emotions, and public declamations was literary criticism.

Channing the Teacher

In his courses, Channing assigned poetry in English as well as prose readings because he believed that language courses generally should encompass all forms of discourse. They should be content-oriented and include in their purview poetry as well as oratory and expository writing as well as oral presentations. In the final analysis, what Channing was teaching after 1827, regardless of what the course was called, was oratory combined with literary criticism. He responded to the general temper of the age which, building on a new awareness of what the study of oratory could effect in the development of English studies, began to blur the distinction between oratory as simple speech making and other specialized forms of communication (1968, xxxiv). Owing to his predisposition toward the value of combining oral and written recitations on English literature, he decided, as Timothy Dwight had done earlier at Yale, to make the study of English literature available on a voluntary basis in the evenings, either to examine "some established Authors" or to read "some of the early English poets" (1968, xxxv). The titles of Channing's journal articles and reviews, all exercises in literary criticism, attest to his consuming interest in English and American literary study. Consider, for example, the breadth of his ongoing *North American Review* articles, written over a thirty-year period, on such topics as "On Models in Literature" (July 1816), "Cowper's Memoir of His Early Life" (May 1817), "Moore's Lalla Rookh" (November 1817), "Dunlap's Charles Brockden Brown" (June 1819), "Montgomery's Poems" (September 1819), "Periodical Literature of the Age of Anne" (April 1838), and "The Works of Lord Chesterfield" (April 1840), to cite but a few.

"The Orator and His Times" was the title of Channing's inauguration lecture, delivered on December 8, 1819. In it he observed that the task before Harvard's educators was "to determine the kind of eloquence" that suited the temper of the times. He added, "There never was a time when the disposition was stronger to make classical literature practically useful; to take it from the sophist, the disputant, the overloaded slumbering scholar, and place it in the hand of the philosopher, the soldier, the physician, the divine, the jurist, and the statesman." The pressing need, accordingly, he thought, was to "raise the moral character" of the state; public conduct should be the "result of settled principles, and not of vague, transient impulse" (1968, 20). To accomplish the task, he suggested, in an anticipation of Matthew Arnold's famous "touchstone" theory, taking "the best and most characteristic specimens of English eloquence in different ages" in order to "learn from them if the imagination had perished under the chilling restraints of an improved society" (1968, 21). The affections of the populace must be constantly addressed, he argued. "It is, indeed, true, that

the imagination and passions do not predominate in modern eloquence.
. . . Still we think it a false philosophy which tells us that it can ever be the
effect of general improvement to separate them from the judgment"
(1968, 21). In 1819, Channing was preoccupied with the question of
"judgment," i.e., "criticism," and how best to teach it. His response, it appears, was to teach it after a fashion that Arnold also would later advocate,
by encouraging the effect that "the best and most characteristic of English
eloquence" would have on the imagination. In essence, what he was advo-
cating was an early critical, all-encompassing program of study with literary
classics written in English as the foundation.

Channing's students wrote expository and persuasive themes on a wide
variety of subjects, many of them literary. In his oratory classes, his students
read aloud poetry and prose of their own choosing (Channing 1968, xli).
He assigned theme topics that demanded critical analysis, all done in the interest of improving the students' critical reading abilities. Among the literary topics for declamation listed by Anderson and Braden are the following:

- Evidences of the Moral and Literary influence of Shakespeare
- [The] Stability of Literary Fame
- Irving's Foreign Compared with his Domestic Titles
- The alleged want of variety in Scott's Chivalrous Characters
- What distinguishes a Play from any other composition?
- Gray's 'Elegy' and Bryant's 'Thanatopsis'—View of Death
- The English Poets as advocates of Liberty
- Describe the kind of character of Orations, which may be properly
called a part of Literature. Name some of the Eminent Orator-Authors.
- A Novel, designed to exhibit and enforce certain opinions in Theology,
Politics, or Education—distinct from what are called Historical Novels.

In support of one of the most basic principles of the oratorical tradition,
Channing believed that the teaching of rhetoric in its traditional form had
failed in his time to accomplish anything of real substance. In a lecture
called "The General View of Rhetoric," he argued that the term "rhetoric"
was at the time "one of reproach" or of "doubtful compliment" (1968,
27). That a course in rhetoric "should have been instituted among the ancient Greeks, in an age of civilization" was natural," he added, but it was
not the age Channing found himself living in. His age, he thought, was the
"age of books" (1968, 28–29). In fact, he added, poetry and drama in
many ways were then "nearly allied to what we specially denominate oratory." Rhetoricians, he thought, had already surrendered the study of

imagination and passion to the "writers on moral philosophy" (1968, 31).
As a result, he argued, much of the original strength of the discipline was
missing in contemporary efforts to teach rhetoric.

Echoing Hutcheson, he argued that to master the arts of declamation
and persuasion, students should understand more than grammatical rules
and simple techniques of argumentation. They should strive to appeal to
audience emotions in order to persuade and give pleasure. "Persuasion," in
that case, "would arouse, impel, deter, invite." Hence, lessons in persuasion as an art were best taught by appealing broadly to imagination and
taste, "to the sense of beauty and grandeur and moral excellence,—to [the]
sense of wit and humor and irony and satire." Students, therefore, were encouraged to turn to "the written book, the novel, the history, the fable and
the acted play" because the literary selections "make their approaches to
the heart in the same direction and by use of the same methods." The
course of rhetoric teaching, in Channing's time, was limited; therefore,
what was needed, he thought, was a new, more philosophically critical concentration on literature designed expressly to appeal to imagination and
taste. "A man's power of affecting others will be less," he added, "if he has
not acquainted himself with the modes in which other artists exercise that
power" (1968, 34).

Based on these ideas, Channing set out to teach courses in literature to
his Harvard students that combined criticism with oratory and that appealed to imagination and taste. In a lecture to the seniors on elocution, he
explained how studying Shakespeare, for instance, could assist speakers in
the practice of emotional self-control. Think how exactly Shakespeare has
discerned, Channing observed, "what the refined ear and taste demand."
"Use all gently," he quotes Shakespeare's Hamlet (Act 3, Scene 2) as saying
to the actors preparing to play before the king, "for in the very torrent,
tempest, and . . . whirlwind of your passion, you must acquire and beget a
temperance, that may give it smoothness" (1968, 58–59). The intent of
the lesson was to teach prospective orators how, like actors, to win over an
audience without losing control or resorting to sophistry. The methodology involved studying texts, not just to learn form and style, but to learn to
speak knowledgeably and with authority in order to appeal to the feelings—the "heart." The technique was at the center of Ward's *System of Oratory.* At one point in the lecture, Channing cited Adam Smith's *The Theory
of Moral Sentiments* on the value of acquiring the ability to speak with conviction, emotion, and wisdom in a manner that commanded respect.

What noble propriety and grace do we feel in the conduct of those who, in their own case, exert that recollection and self-command which constitutes the dignity of every passion, and which bring it down to what others can enter into. We are disgusted with that clamorous grief, which, without any delicacy, calls upon our compassion with sighs and tears and importunate lamentations. We . . . watch with anxious concern over our whole behavior, lest by any impropriety we should disturb that concerted tranquillity, which it requires so great an effort to support. (Smith [1759] 1976, 24)

It comes as no surprise that Channing's successor at Harvard, Francis J. Child, upon assuming the Boylston Chair in 1851 changed the title of the lectures delivered to the seniors from "Rhetoric and Criticism" to something more closely in line with what was being taught. He called the course "English Language and Literature."

Eventually, President Charles William Eliot would expand the Harvard curriculum to include philology and linguistics as well as literature. The old courses in rhetoric became "composition and rhetoric" and, taking on a more familiar modern look, were limited largely to freshmen and sophomores.

E. T. Channing was a transitional figure at Harvard. In his years there he succeeded in transforming the study of oratory from a traditional concentration on classical grammar and prescriptive exercises in style into a humanities course that was primarily content-oriented and geared to the critical examination of learned texts, most of them written in English. In essence, he was teaching English literature. His students regularly presented both oral and written recitations based on topics drawn from specifically assigned critical readings in English literature. He was a remarkable and highly influential teacher who placed great emphasis on the "interaction" between society and the individual and who grounded his revolutionary teaching, as Anderson and Braden remind us, "firmly in Scottish philosophy" (1968, li). He was a genuine pioneer in the history of vernacular literary study in American universities.

3

Scottish Education and Literary Study
on the American Frontier

In the 1820s, when E. T. Channing combined an experimental course of study in oratory with literary criticism at Harvard, the concept was new and revolutionary. By the time he retired in 1851, however, English literary study, promoted directly or indirectly by critical exercises in one or another form of oral or written literary analysis, was being taught in an impressive number of North American colleges, including a number of small experimental colleges located in villages along the western frontier.

1783: A College in the Wilderness—Dickinson College

Between 1763 and 1775, more than ten thousand Scots had left the Highlands and emigrated to North America. Many went to Canada and to what are now North Carolina, Tennessee, and Virginia. A lion's share, however, ended up in Pennsylvania, many in the western portion of Pennsylvania, which was still frontier (Bell 1954, 276). Scottish Presbyterians disseminated Scottish education along with lessons in Christian morality wherever they went. The village of Carlisle, in central Pennsylvania, was no exception. Charles Coleman Sellers, in his bicentennial history of Carlisle's Dickinson College, observes that even before Cumberland was a county with Carlisle as the county seat "classical learning was there with the Presbyterian congregations" (1973, 3).

The pattern for the advancement of education was predictable in frontier villages settled by the Scots-Irish: First an educated pastor tutored interested pupils; then a grammar school of sorts was organized and funded for a time by a church synod; then, if the grammar school was successful, an

75

effort was made to add an academy or, in the case of the village of Carlisle, to establish an actual college. The grammar school was preparation for college in those days. In many instances, grammar schools survived for years as adjuncts of colleges. Because educational opportunities were few and far between on the frontier, boys with some degree of formal education filled in what they needed by attending the local and relatively inexpensive grammar school.

Scottish and Scots-Irish grammar schools, academies, and colleges in North America that were established during the colonial period shared one major pedagogical characteristic connecting them directly with their Scottish roots—that was a concentration, as argued in the preceding chapters, on the study of moral philosophy and a desire to use education to improve moral conduct and promote civic responsibility. In most of the schools that were either founded by or came under the influence of Scottish Presbyterians, the study of moral philosophy was at the center of the curriculum, regardless of the level of learning.

The history of Carlisle and Dickinson College is part of the larger history of the development of Cumberland County in Pennsylvania, one that was directly indebted to Scottish immigrants. The area that would become Cumberland County—Carlisle would eventually be the county seat—was first settled around 1730 after Maryland's Lord Baltimore claimed for the British crown a large section of land along the western bank of the Susquehanna River. With a studied cynicism bred from earlier experiences with ragged pioneer settlements, the Proprietaries of Pennsylvania, i.e., the Penn family, decided in 1730 to establish two separate ethnic communities west of the Susquehanna in the new territory. One was to be Scots-Irish; the other, German. The object was to keep them separate. The rationale for the decision was based on the hypothesis that a shared common heritage enhanced a pioneer community's promise for the future. The Germans were settled in an area on the northern border of Maryland that eventually became York County. The Scots-Irish were directed farther west into an area north of the Yellow Breeches Creek and the Blue Ridge Mountains foothills. By 1732, migration into the area had increased considerably. In 1750, the land on which the Scots-Irish had originally settled was incorporated into Cumberland County, which at the time included all of the western frontier land that did not infringe on Native American titles. By 1751, Cumberland County was ready for a county seat, and the Proprietaries decided to build one. The town was Carlisle. Its early inhabitants, as late as the mid–1750s, still remained noticeably Scots-Irish.[1]

Carlisle in the 1750s was an outpost. Wagon roads literally ended there, and people moving west from Carlisle were forced to travel on pack trails. Life on the frontier in the 1750s was dangerous. Native American raids increased following the colonists' defeat of General Edward Braddock in the summer of 1755 and, as a planned act of revenge, the deadly assault on the Indian village of Kitanning to the west by Colonel John Armstrong's army of British regulars and colonial frontiersmen. The threat of native uprisings lasted well into the late 1760s; yet, as early in the town's history as the late 1750s, irrespective of the outlook for the immediate future, Carlisle's Scots-Irish Presbyterians were debating the prospects of adding a grammar or Latin school to the town. The date on which the school was established is not totally clear, but it was early. Sellers, in his history of the college, cites a January 11, 1770, entry in the *Pennsylvania Gazette* that referred to a grammar school that had existed in Carlisle "for several years" (1973, 27).

The desire to locate an institution of higher learning in the West was stimulated by developments stemming from the conflict at the College of New Jersey in the 1760s between Old Side and New Side Presbyterians. In 1766, Dr. Samuel Finley, president of the college, died. Francis Alison, a Scot and an Old Side Presbyterian conservative, saw Finley's death as an opportunity to change the course of study at the college. Although Alison wanted the presidency, John Witherspoon was elected. Witherspoon, also a Scot, was a liberal supporter of New Side principles. The New Side, consequently, won the battle. Old Siders were dismayed but not defeated. But there was still no institution of higher learning in the American colonies that was directly under their control. Consequently, they decided to look west for a prospect. The village of Carlisle with its predominant Scots-Irish population was their choice.

By 1770, a grammar school was in operation in Carlisle, run by the Reverend Henry Makinly, a Scots-Irish minister from County Donegal in Ireland. The school had three units: a Latin school, a mathematical school, and an English school. Handwriting, English composition, and declama-

---

1. In 1753, a group of Moravians traveling to North Carolina passed through Carlisle. They recorded seeing about sixty houses and remarked that they were "chiefly inhabited by Irishmen" (Flower 1944, 4).

tion were taught (Sellers 1973, 37). By 1780, James Ross, the son of Scots-Irish immigrants and later author of a series of popular Latin grammars,[2] was in charge of the school. The school was successful, and in 1781 Carlisle's Presbyterian congregation petitioned the Donegal Presbytery to change the school to an academy (Flower 1944, 27). At this point in the history of the college in the wilderness, Benjamin Rush, the famous American physician whose Scottish connections ran deep, entered the picture.

Rush had studied medicine at Edinburgh University, graduating in 1768. He was also a graduate, in 1760, of the College of New Jersey. Eight years in Scotland had left him with a strong admiration for Scottish educational principles and models, which shaped Rush's vision of what higher education could achieve in North America. Rush was particularly supportive of the egalitarian hope that basic courses in reading, writing, and arithmetic could be made available to all people, regardless of race, creed, or class. One of the key studies in his ideal curriculum, consequently, was English. He was admittedly antagonistic toward the old classical curriculum and thought, in fact, that English should be emphasized over all other languages, including other modern languages. Writing in English, he believed, was essential to a solid education, and he insisted that for models of good writing and good thinking, students be assigned to read and study the works of contemporary masters of English prose such as Swift and Hume (Sloan 1971, 204).

In 1781, when Rush learned of efforts to establish a Presbyterian academy in Carlisle, he saw an opportunity to go one better and get an actual college started in the village. He and John Montgomery, a Carlisle businessman who also was a Scot, undertook a vigorous effort to promote interest in establishing a college. Although they had limited support, their efforts succeeded, with financial help coming from wealthy Scottish Presbyterians of the Old Side persuasion and from Rush's wealthy Philadelphia connections. On September 9, 1783, the Pennsylvania General Assembly passed an act establishing Dickinson College in Carlisle as an institution charged with the responsibility of educating youth, "in the learned and foreign languages, the useful arts, science and literature" *(Dickinson College,*

2. In 1798, Ross published *A Plain, Short, Comprehensive Practical Latin Grammar.* It was in print until 1892. His *Latin Grammar, Comprising All the Rules and Observations Necessary to an Accurate Knowledge of the Latin Classics,* published in 1844, was in print until 1864.

Benjamin Rush. Unknown artist. Courtesy of the Blocker History of Medicine Collections, Moody Medical Library, University of Texas Medical Branch at Galveston.

Chartered 1926). The college was named after John Dickinson, the governor of Pennsylvania, who drafted the college's Articles of Confederation.

Rush's reputation as a physician and a dedicated American patriot devoted to social and educational progress ultimately influenced the results of the limited campaign for the college (Morgan 1933, 2–10). The fact remains, however, that, in spite of Rush's admirable motives and his commitment to higher education, a college at the time, especially on the unsettled western frontier, was premature. Even Samuel Miller, the contemporary biographer of Charles Nisbet, a Scot who was the first principal of Dickinson College, was convinced that the college was unnecessary, actually redundant, because the colleges of New Jersey and Philadelphia offered far more means of instruction and they had more money. Furthermore, enrollment was low at the colleges of New Jersey and Philadelphia, with no apparent promise of an increase in the immediate future (Biddle 1920, 8–10). The question thus arises: Why was another college established, especially on the frontier?

Part of the answer is to be found in Rush's desire to establish an institution west of Philadelphia that could develop with a minimum of pressure from influential easterners and that would remain Presbyterian with a definite leaning toward the Old Side, even though the Presbyterian congregation in Carlisle was essentially divided in allegiance. Rush was critical at the time of developments at the College of Philadelphia, which in 1779 had been reconstituted as a state college by the Pennsylvania legislature. He also disliked John Witherspoon and the dominating Presbyterian New Siders at the College of New Jersey. Placing a college in Carlisle, he surmised, would provide an opportunity to create an institution of higher learning that would remain Presbyterian and, if he had his way, sympathetic to Old Side ideals. On September 3, 1782, he composed "Hints for Establishing a College at Carlisle," in which he outlined his plans for the institution. Dickinson College, unlike the new state-funded and, hence, state-controlled college in Philadelphia, would adhere primarily to the old Presbyterian ideal for education by remaining independent, though sectarian, but nevertheless free of state control. The faculty would be exclusively Presbyterian and the school would be funded mainly by in-state Presbyterians. Given that he wanted to keep the college Presbyterian, one can assume that Rush also took into consideration the desire to preserve the homogeneity of the Presbyterian Scots-Irish community in Carlisle.

Scottish educational models were always uppermost in Rush's mind. In an essay titled "A Plan for Establishing Public Schools in Pennsylvania" that was published in 1789 in *Essays, Literary, Moral, and Philosophical*, he referred to Oxford and Cambridge as "seats of dissipation," while praising highly "the more numerous, and less crowded universities and colleges in Scotland," which, he argued, were "remarkable for the order, diligence, and decent behaviour of their students." Following Scotland's lead, he wanted free schools established in every township in the United States, where students would be taught the basics. To accommodate Pennsylvania's growing immigrant German population, he argued that both English and German should be taught. Students showing promise, he added, would also be encouraged to attend college regardless of their class status or background. He concluded the essay by acknowledging that his advice to the legislature and to the citizens of Pennsylvania was based on a conception of education "taken chiefly from the plans which have long been used with success in Scotland, and in the eastern states of America, where the influence of learning, in promoting religion, morals, manners, and good government, has never been exceeded" (1789, 3, 5–6).

For Dickinson College, in particular, Rush had a specific design in mind. In the first place, like Witherspoon at the College of New Jersey, Rush believed that a liberal education should "prepare youth for usefulness here, and for happiness hereafter" (Rush 1789, 21). Hence, he determined that studying classical languages for their own sake was relatively useless, particularly when compared with the study of English, which he thought practically more beneficial. Overall, the mode of education he preferred was intended to complement the independent enterprising character of the new nation. Because the new form of government, he wrote, "has created a new class of duties" for every American, it behooved American educators to adapt their teaching "to the peculiar form of our government" (1789, 6–7). An education based on pragmatic national objectives, then, would be "one general, and uniform system of education" that would "render the mass of the people more homogenous, and thereby fit them more easily for uniform and peacable government." The most "useful" educational training in a republic, Rush thought, would be "laid in Religion"; without religion, "there can be no virtue, and without virtue there can be no liberty, and liberty is the object and life of all republican governments" (1789, 8).

Students must be taught respect for their infant republic, he suggested. Consequently, they must be taught to understand that they do not belong to themselves, but that they are, in fact, part of a commonality, a *sensus communis*. They must be taught to "watch for the state, as if its liberties depended on [their] vigilance alone." Echoing Francis Hutcheson on civic virtue and Adam Smith's conception of the moral responsibilities of "economic man," Rush added that students must also be taught to protect the nation's interests "in such a manner as not to defraud . . . creditors, or neglect . . . family." Students must be ready to "decline no station, however public or responsible it may be, when called to it by the suffrages of [their] fellow citizens" (1789, 10–11). They also should be taught the value of money, but only to increase the power "of contributing to the wants and demands of the state." Study and business should "be . . . principal pursuits in life." A distinct concern for the art of life would also be emphasized so that students would desire to acquire as many of life's "conveniences as possible." The lesson followed with the admonition that life's "conveniences" were to be acquired mainly through "industry and economy" (1789, 12).

Moral philosophy, religion, and the teaching of conduct, therefore, were central to Rush's curriculum. The role of religion in education, in particular, he argued, must be comparable to the role traditionally played by the arts and sciences. "Do we leave our youth to acquire systems of geography, philosophy, or politics, till they have arrived at an age in which they are capable of judging for themselves?" he asked. Because the answer was no, he added, as much should be claimed for religion as "for the other sciences" (1789, 10). He even envisioned the inclusion of physical exercise and controlled diets in his plan as ways to enhance moral instruction. In his school, students would "subject their bodies to physical discipline," and to offset their studious and sedentary way of life, they would be fed a temperate diet consisting mainly of broths, milk, and vegetables. He recommended particularly the "black broth of Sparta," a soup made from pork stock or pig's blood and flavored with vinegar and salt, and, more to the point of this study, the "barley broth of Scotland"; both, he noted, were celebrated for their "beneficial effects upon the minds of young people" (1789, 13).

Language study was of singular importance in Rush's plan. He urged specifically the need to teach Americans how "to read and write [the] American language with propriety and elegance" (1789, 15). Also, he argued for the academic recognition of the link between vernacular language study and the demands of the commercial world. Reminiscent of Adam Smith on the responsibilities of "economic man," he wrote: "The advantages of a perfect knowledge of our language to young men intended for the professions of law, physic, or divinity are too obvious to be mentioned, but in a state which boasts of the first commercial city in America, I wish to see it cultivated by young men, who are intended for the compting house, for many such, I hope, will be educated in our colleges" (1789, 16).

Rush thought that young men desiring careers in merchandising would benefit particularly from his curriculum. He envisioned eventually offering them courses in the origin and present state of commerce and in the "nature and principles of money." Echoing Adam Smith again, he added that the wealth of nations, in and of themselves, merited close study. Understanding the workings of commerce, he argued, was "the best security" against hereditary monopolies and, thus, the "surest protection against aristocracy." He ranked knowledge of the effects of commerce next to religion as a potential humanizing force (1789, 17). In essence, Rush's plan of study recommended specifically by name, probably for the first time in the history of higher education in North America, a range of courses, including English, designed specifically to prepare young men for the commercial world.

Learning the principles of legislation was also high on Rush's list. Students, he suggested, should be urged to attend courts of justice where they would hear laws explained and observe how truth is discovered. In language reminiscent of Lord Kames, Rush noted that the need to attend to the deliberations of the courts was so essential to a young man's education that he wished to see more colleges established in urban centers or, as they were designated at the time, "county towns" (1789, 18). Rush even envisioned a place for women in his ideal college. "They must concur in all our plans of education for young men," he suggested, "or no laws will ever render them effectual." Women, he thought, should also be taught principles of government, and the obligations of good citizenship should be incumbent upon them as well (1789, 19).

The man Rush chose to implement his progressive curriculum at Dickinson College was, not surprisingly, a Scot. The Reverend Charles Nisbet of Montrose in Scotland was offered the job of principal of the college in 1784 and arrived in Philadelphia on June 9, 1785, after initially turning the position down owing mainly to the hardships he thought it would pose to his family. On June 30, Nisbet and his family left for Carlisle. The heat of the summer of 1785, illness, and the harsh living conditions at Carlisle produced grave doubts about the family's staying on. Nevertheless, they managed to overcome the initial difficulties, including Nisbet's own very serious illness and the tendering of his resignation in 1786, which was eventually recalled. In time, Nisbet and his family adjusted as well as they could to the rugged frontier life in western Pennsylvania; he remained in the position as principal until his death in 1804.

Belles Lettres at Dickinson

When Dickinson College first opened in 1785, the course in belles lettres, taught by the Reverend Robert Davidson, a close friend of Rush and the pastor of the Presbyterian Church in Carlisle, included the study of grammar, rhetoric, and criticism (Morgan 1933, 107, 166). Davidson was a 1771 graduate of the College of Philadelphia. For eleven years, from 1772 until 1783, he had held the professorship of history and belles lettres at Philadelphia. He appears to have been a vain but solemn person who never really captured the imagination or enthusiasm of his students. In August 1785, the *Carlisle Gazette* carried a notice on the plan for the college which claimed that the course outline was "extensive" and included "several branches of literature not hitherto taught in any of the American colleges." Davidson was listed in the notice as having been elected as "Professor of HISTORY, and the BELLES LETTRES, to teach also CHRONOLOGY and GEOGRAPHY" (Sellers 1973, 84). The notice also called attention to the establishment of a new "English school" attached to the grammar school, which was intended to give a full range to students' preparation for the college. Robert Tait, a Scot who had made the transatlantic journey with Nisbet, was in charge. The notice referred to Tait's plans "to teach the English and French Languages Grammatically" along with "Writing, Cyphering, and Bookkeeping" (Sellers 1973, 85). Tait was replaced in 1786 by Daniel Jones, who taught English and oratory (Morgan 1933, 106). It is worth pointing out that during Nisbet's tenure as principal, from 1786 to 1804, English was taught separately from belles lettres. After Tait left in 1786, Jones and Davidson, until 1804, taught the English course in combination with the study of "elements of oratory" as their schedules would permit (Morgan 1933, 117). The link between oratory and the study of belles lettres, by the turn of the century, was becoming increasingly evident not only at Dickinson College but also at other prominent colleges across the nation.

It was Nisbet himself who did the most to promote literary study at Dickinson, however. By 1786, he had instituted a course in "moral philosophy and belles lettres," which he personally taught until his death in 1804. Not much is known about Nisbet's course, but some of his lectures have survived in student transcripts. Sellers writes of his "confronting the boys with ideas [and] with authors from ancient to modern times," including Pliny, Pascal, Jean de la Bruyere, Sir Thomas Browne, Robert Boyle, Voltaire, Jean-Jacques Rousseau, Locke, and Hume, among many others.

One lecture that has survived, dated January 24, 1788, is on the topic of Scottish commonsense thinking and the logic of John Locke. The lecture, which attempts to illuminate Scottish "moral sense" thinking, reveals the influence of both Hutcheson and Thomas Reid. In it, Nisbet observed that Locke "has detailed to the world as a capital discovery . . . that secondary qualities of Matter do not exist in bodies themselves, but solely in the mind which perceives them, and is at great pains to prove that nobody ever questioned, viz. that inanimate bodies are not percipient beings, nor in the least conscious of the impressions which they make on beings endowed with the power of Perception" (Sellers 1973, 104). The Cartesians, Nisbet added, attribute "all the effects in nature to the immediate agency of the Deity, and allow external objects to be only the occasions of the ideas excited and the effects produced by them." Both sides of the question, Nisbet concluded, advanced "sundry things not easily conceivable. Mr. Locke and his followers, by affirming rashly that the mind perceives nothing except its own ideas, have laid a foundation of general scepticism. . . . And it is truly a scandal to the philosophic reputation of the present age that the ingenious Dr. Reid was obliged to write [an] octavo volume . . . merely to prove the existence of external objects." It is to be hoped, he continued, that the light of reason and common sense will "destroy the credit of these fanciful and mischievous theories, which tend to subvert the foundation of human knowledge, and to destroy all distinctions between truth and falsehood, virtue and vice." At this point, in support of his argument for questioning Locke's deference to the superiority of mind in all things and to the Cartesian surrender to authority, Nisbet deftly introduced a series of carefully chosen literary selections. For his support, he cited passages from Horace, James Thomson, and Pope. He concentrated then on the value of right thinking and the proper choice of words as he moved his argument forward to an affirmation of the value of learning to employ plain, commonsense language and good sense in the pursuit of truth. For his classroom examples, he turned again to literature, primarily English literature. He related a series of anecdotes on how Swift, Pope, and Moliere read selections from their works to common readers as a check on clarity and precision in their thinking and writing (Sellers 1973, 104–6).

What Nisbet promoted in his January 24, 1788, lecture was criticism; one might reasonably call it literary criticism. His objective was to teach his students that writing with clarity and precision required the ability to think and form judgments clearly, in the context of good common sense. Technically, Nisbet was teaching moral philosophy to that class, but he was also teaching literature. Roger Brooke Taney, a 1795 Dickinson graduate who became a chief justice of the United States Supreme Court, recalled how

Charles Nisbet. Unknown artist. Courtesy of Archives and Special
Collections, Waidner-Spahr Library, Dickinson College.

Nisbet's object was always to encourage the students to think for themselves and to think critically. He observed of Nisbet's lectures, that "his object was to teach the pupil to think, to reason, to form an opinion, and not
to depend merely upon memory. . . . He undoubtedly succeeded in fasten-
ing our attention upon the subject on which he was lecturing, and induced
us to think upon it and discuss it, and form opinions for ourselves" (Sellers
1973, 106–7).

    One might safely assume that, given his academic preparation, Nisbet's
course on moral philosophy and belles lettres regularly included the study
of Scottish moral philosophers and other prominent Scottish Enlightenment thinkers and authors who wrote exclusively in English. It is certain,
however, that whatever English literary study was being promoted at Dick-

inson College before 1804 was being advanced by Nisbet, mainly in combination with lectures on moral philosophy. He also taught logic, philosophy of the mind, and economics and sociology. Morgan notes that, in his economics lectures, Nisbet drew extensively on Adam Smith's work. Nisbet also lectured on subjects that these days would fall under the heading of sociology. Morgan suggests that Nisbet's economics and sociology lectures may well have been "the first on these subjects delivered in America" (1933, 110).

Dickinson College fell upon hard times after Nisbet's death in 1804. Lack of funds and bitter internal conflicts between trustees and faculty appear to have been the primary cause (Morgan 1933, 144). In 1834, after Dickinson had actually closed, the Methodist Episcopal Church accepted an invitation to assume control of the college. Anticipating an early reopening, the new administrators affirmed a plan for seven professorships and proceeded to elect first a professor of belles lettres who would teach rhetoric, elocution, and English literature. Merrit Caldwell of Maine was the unanimous choice. The Reverend Ebenezer Erskine, pastor of a Presbyterian church in Newville, Pennsylvania, in a sketch of the short career at Dickinson of William Neill, principal of the college from 1824 to 1828, observed that had Dickinson College been efficiently organized and effectively managed while in Presbyterian hands, "it would, in all human probability, have become one of the foremost institutions in our country." There was not a more "favorable location or larger constituency for a successful college under Presbyterian control in all this broad land," he added. "The Alumni of Dickinson College, while under Presbyterian patronage and management, took rank with those of the oldest and strongest colleges in the country" (Morgan 1933, 238). The Reverend William A. West, clerk of the Presbytery of Carlisle at the time of the transfer of authority to the Methodists, wrote, "There was in Carlisle, belonging to us, a literary institution which was the rival of Nassau Hall at Princeton. . . . Dickinson College was virtually ours then, and might and should have continued to be ours. . . . But there was division, and with it weakness, if nothing more, when it was permitted to pass out of our hands. Perhaps in no other period in the history of the Church could the transfer have been made. Proverbially," he added, "are Presbyterians 'God's silly people' " (Morgan 1933, 238).

Carlisle's Scots-Irish Presbyterians and Philadelphia's Benjamin Rush, at the time of the founding of Dickinson College in 1783, were hardly

"God's silly people." Nevertheless, the progress of the college after Nisbet was impeded by a lack of harmony among the supporters and, as the new century turned, an increasing lack of interest in its future.

Rush's deep sense of community had been an important factor in the original plans for Dickinson College. Rush and the members of the Carlisle community who drafted plans for the college believed basically that any enterprise that promised to provide increased opportunities for education in the new republic deserved support. Owing to their resolve, the resulting college was arguably, needed or not, the first college founded in the newly created republic after the War of Independence. Supporters also may have been inspired by what James Henry Morgan, college historian, called the "home feeling," which grew out of a sense of unity and purpose that characterized Carlisle's Scots-Irish citizens. Edward W. Biddle, in his brief history of the founding of the college, argued that, although the college's founding may have been premature, "its influence on the borough has been marked" by benefits gained from "the constant association" of faculty and students with the Carlisle community; this, he added, had served to increase the community's "intellectual tone" (1920, 10). The point, of course, was that Dickinson College ultimately benefitted from the belief, obviously popular among Carlisle's Presbyterians at the time, that a certain amount of parochialism in a college was not a bad thing. To unite a community, religiously and patriotically, around a popular, well-supported college would improve the community spirit and, therefore, was well worth the effort.

Dickinson College, consequently, was the first institution of higher education on the American frontier founded principally to promote an educational vision grounded in both ethnic and sectarian frames of reference. To that extent, it was the forerunner of the many ethnic and religiously centered colleges west of the Susquehanna River that have served other ethnic communities during the past two hundred years of American history. These institutions have vastly increased educational opportunities through an impressive proliferation of colleges designed with first-generation Americans in mind, that is to say, the sons and daughters of European immigrants who otherwise might never have had the opportunity to attend college. In this context, William Sweet, in his seminal study of the role of the Presbyterians in the United States, *Religion on the American Frontier,* notes that of forty American colleges and universities established between 1780 and 1829, thirteen were founded by Scots or Scots-Irish Presbyterians (1936, 2: 75).

1783: English and Teacher Education at
Kentucky's Transylvania College

In 1780, the year that Thomas Jefferson was elected governor of Virginia, the Virginia Assembly, in spite of an impending invasion by British troops under General Charles Cornwallis, entered into a series of spirited discussions on a proposed charter designed to establish a college or "seminary of learning," on the west side of the Allegheny Mountains in the Kentucky territory. The territory was controlled at the time by the Commonwealth of Virginia (Wright 1975, 1).

The Kentucky territory was first chartered in 1750. Thirty years later, most of the territory still remained wilderness. In 1763, after the Treaty of Paris had ended the French and Indian War, Britain had temporarily prohibited settlers from moving into the western portions of the Appalachian Mountains. Consequently, the area was left to hunters and fur traders to explore. In 1773, Daniel Boone persuaded six families to join him and his family in a move to Kentucky. A year later, a North Carolina land company negotiated a treaty with the Cherokees for rights to this vaguely defined tract of western land. A new colony was planned, which was to be called Transylvania. Boone was chosen to establish an outpost for the company on the Kentucky River, which he did in 1775; it later was named Boonesboro (Wright 1975, 2–4).

Eventually, after the Declaration of Independence was signed in 1776, the state of Virginia enacted a law vesting about eight thousand acres of escheated lands that previously had been deeded to British subjects in the name of several chosen trustees for the purpose of establishing the proposed "seminary of learning." In 1783, twelve thousand more acres of escheated land were added, bringing the total to twenty thousand acres. The new college was empowered from the outset to grant bachelor and master of arts degrees (Jennings 1955, 4–8).

Between 1775 and 1800, more than 150,000 settlers, mostly from Pennsylvania, Virginia, and the Carolinas, passed through the Cumberland Gap on their way to the new Kentucky territory. Many of them were Scottish; a majority were Scots-Irish Presbyterians. The matter of the seminary in Kentucky that came before the Virginia Assembly in 1780 had been introduced initially by Presbyterians who had already established similar schools in Virginia, including Liberty Hall (later Washington and Lee University) and Hampden-Sydney College. Now they wanted a college in Kentucky. The Reverend John Todd of Hanover Presbytery in Virginia; his nephew, Colonel John Todd; and Caleb Wallace were principal figures in the effort to persuade the Virginia Assembly to approve the charter (Wright 1975, 4–6). The Reverend Todd in 1784 presented the school with a library and some scientific equipment. The trustees were grateful but it took five years to get the books and equipment over the mountains, and the library was not functional until 1792 (Wright 1975, 11, 23). Walter Wilson Jennings, in his study of the pioneering status of Transylvania College, writes of an amendment to the original 1780 charter, which was drafted in 1783 by a committee of six trustees, chaired by Caleb Wallace, a Presbyterian minister and graduate of the College of New Jersey, and guaranteed that the new school was to be public, hence free from sectarian influences (1955, 6). Wallace would later be appointed to the Kentucky Supreme Court.

Of the trustees of the new western seminary of learning, none was more dedicated to the college than the Reverend David Rice, known affectionately to the early settlers as Father Rice. He was one of the earliest Presbyterian ministers to settle along the Kentucky River. He was likely a New Sider, having undergone a conversion experience while listening to the preaching of a local Presbyterian minister. Rice also graduated from the College of New Jersey, studied under the Reverend John Todd, and was ordained in 1763. In 1783, Rice responded to a request from three hundred Kentucky Presbyterians to establish a church in the wilderness. Accompanied by his wife and eleven children, he moved to the frontier and, as Wright observes, "laid the foundation for Presbyterianism in Kentucky" (1975, 9–10).

In February 1785, the college opened. Attendance was small. Classes were held in Father Rice's cabin, located between the towns of Danville and Fort Harrod, Kentucky. The school, little more than an elementary school, was at least a beginning. Not surprisingly, the first teacher employed was another Presbyterian minister, the Reverend James Mitchell. Born a Pennsylvanian, Mitchell had moved in his youth to Virginia, where he became acquainted with Rice and Caleb Wallace. Eventually, he moved to Kentucky, where he taught in Rice's cabin for slightly more than a year, returning to Virginia in 1786 to serve as a pastor. In 1789, the school was moved to Lexington (Wright 1975, 12–13).

From the outset, the question of how to teach morality without teaching any particular brand of Christian theology, Presbyterian or otherwise, was a key issue for the school. Wallace, for one, advocated the necessity of teaching theology. Others urged the removal of religion completely from the curriculum, often citing the new country's constitutional principle separating church and state. Lexington, with a population of 835 in 1790, was about as urban as any frontier town could be at the time. Consequently, the issue received considerable public attention. Town leaders wanted to make Lexington the Philadelphia of the West, a cultural oasis of libraries, schools, and churches, supporting education and the arts. The town leaders, therefore, welcomed Transylvania College when the decision was made in 1789 to relocate it.

Within ten years, amateur theatrical productions were being presented by Transylvania students on the courthouse stage. On November 12, 1817, a group of local musicians performed Beethoven's first symphony; the concert may have presented the first Beethoven symphony ever performed in the United States (Wright 1975, 19). Books, pamphlets, and literary magazines were available to the populace. In Lexington in 1812, Joseph Buchanan, who had graduated with a bachelor of arts degree from Transylvania College in 1809, published *The Philosophy of Human Nature*. The book was a series of lectures on medical theory that Buchanan had prepared for courses he taught at Transylvania.

In 1792, Kentucky had been admitted to the union as the fifteenth state. In 1794, Harry Toulmin arrived in Lexington from England to assume the presidency of the struggling college. Toulmin was not supported by the Presbyterians, and he resigned in 1796 when the Presbyterians once again regained control of the college. In 1804, the Reverend James Blythe assumed the college presidency. Blythe was a staunch, orthodox Presbyterian of the Old Side (Wright 1975, 47). That same year, Robert Hamilton Bishop was hired as professor of moral philosophy, logic, criticism, and belles lettres. Bishop, recently emigrated from Scotland, was also an Old Side Presbyterian and the author of *An Apology for Calvinism*, a strong defense of orthodoxy. Bishop had studied Latin, Hebrew, and moral philosophy at the University of Edinburgh (Jennings 1955, 58).

Bishop was a true pioneer of reform among early nineteenth-century American educators. A native Scot, he was born the son of Presbyterian tenant farmers in 1777 in Scotland's West Lothian. In 1794, at age seventeen, he entered Edinburgh University, and taught night classes to factory workers to earn his tuition. Although he was a conservative Presbyterian, his political sympathies were liberal and democratic (Rodabaugh 1935,

3–10). Bishop studied moral philosophy with Dugald Stewart, whose liberal influence permanently marked Bishop's political character. It was Stewart who first exposed Bishop to, among other intellectual wonders, the "glories of Milton, and Cicero, and Shakespeare" (Rodabaugh 1935, 13).

In 1798, Bishop entered the Theological Seminary at Selkirk. At this point in his life, he decided to become a missionary. He wrote in his *Recollections* that the success of missionary work depended almost solely on the need for "enlarged views of ecclesiastical action," adding that "in almost every case, the success has been in proportion to the enlarged and liberal views of those who entered heartily into the work, whether in Christian or heathen lands" (Rodabaugh 1935, 20). It is not surprising that Bishop, who had learned moral philosophy from Stewart, himself a student of Adam Ferguson, a pioneer in the study of sociology, was on the way to becoming a preacher with a distinct social mission. He wanted to be a Christian reformer. In 1802, he was licensed as a minister in the Scottish Presbyterian Church. A year earlier, he had made up his mind to emigrate to the United States. In late August 1802, with his new bride, Ann, he set sail. He was twenty-five years old (Rodabaugh 1935, 20–22).

Of Bishop's preparation for life in the United States, James H. Rodabaugh observes that Bishop's study of the contributions made to history, political science, economics, sociology, and the study of human relations by David Hume, Adam Ferguson, Adam Smith, Thomas Reid, and William Robertson, along with his personal exposure to the teachings of Dugald Stewart, provided him with the foundation from which his desire to humanize and secularize the educational curriculum emanated (1935, 170). Once in the United States, he was assigned to Kentucky. In early November 1802, he left New York for the western frontier. After a three-month stay in Chillicothe, Ohio, he arrived in Kentucky in March 1803. Initially, he worked as a circuit-riding missionary, charged with the establishment of new churches. In the summer of 1803, he was given a congregation in Jessamine County, directly south of Fayette County in which Lexington was the county seat. Almost simultaneously, he was offered a professorship at Transylvania University. He accepted the position of professor of moral philosophy, logic, criticism, and belles lettres in the fall of 1804, a position he would hold for the next twenty years. Shortly thereafter Bishop and his wife moved to Lexington (Rodabaugh 1935, 22–24).

Lexington in 1804 was the metropolis of the West, by far the wealthiest town in Kentucky. By 1810, its population numbered 4,326 citizens.

Robert Hamilton Bishop. Portrait by Horace Harding. Commissioned by the Miami Union Literary Society, Miami University; unveiled September 1830. Courtesy of Miami University Art Museum.

Bishop was very keen on the link he envisioned between education and civic responsibility. In the tradition of Scottish enlightenment thinkers, he believed, for instance, that Transylvania University had an obligation to its citizenry to provide education principally geared to the common good. Consequently, from the outset, he opposed what he interpreted as the "non-progressive spirit" of the university's administration (Rodabaugh 1935, 39). He lectured on history, logic, and moral philosophy. Because his primary interest was social history, his history courses ranged widely, incorporating the study of the political, social, and economic development of nations and cultures. He believed that history "in some form or other," supported "all the other arts and sciences" and was, therefore, "inseparably connected with all liberal pursuits" (Rodabaugh 1935, 171), including, one might surmise, the study of literary history.

He designed a course in history during the early years at Transylvania that Rodabaugh suggests was, for the years immediately following 1804, "the most extensive course of instruction in history" ever offered in an American college. Rodabaugh also notes that the term *history,* as Bishop understood it, was "all-inclusive," that is, it encompassed other disciplines, including one of the first, if not actually the earliest, programs of study ever offered in the United States in "sociology" (1935, 172). In "An Introduction to a Course of Lectures on History," which Bishop first delivered to his students and then published in 1823 at the request of the students, he observed that "history brings into one view all those plans, and experiments, and enjoyments, and makes the aggregate in a great measure the property of every individual." It also supports "all the other arts and sciences." For "every science and every art," he contended, "is just so far useful and worthy of cultivation as it is founded upon matter of fact, and as it can be applied to some practical purpose in the ordinary business of life" (1935, 3, 5–6). Even fictional literary works, he added, "whether in prose or verse, derive their value and their interest from their assuming the form and having something of the reality of history" (1935, 11).

Bishop's experimental history course covered four years, was centered on texts, and utilized literary works. In the first year, students studied the published biographies of distinguished historical figures. In the second year, they studied both ancient and modern historical texts. The third year, surprisingly, concentrated solely on the study of the history of the United States and of other nations whose history was directly connected with that of the United States. The fourth year involved an extensive review of previous readings with a concentration on applying what had been learned about the history of the world and the United States to the "the varied business of actual life" (Rodabaugh 1935, 14). The reading list for the course covered influential thinkers from the Renaissance or earlier through the period of the American Revolution. They were largely authors that

Bishop himself had studied at Edinburgh while a student of Dugald Stewart. They included Erasmus, Juan Luis Vives, Thomas More, Martin Luther, John Calvin, Niccolo Machiavelli, Francis Bacon, Thomas Hobbes, Michel de Montaigne, Rene Descartes, John Locke, Gottfried Leibniz, and Benedict de Spinoza (Rodabaugh 1935, 185). Although the course was not labeled "literary study," nevertheless, the list of representative authors would constitute the core reading for any respectable course in literary masterpieces in nonfictional prose from the Renaissance through the eighteenth century. The likely list of readings for Bishop's history course would have included Hume, Immanuel Kant, Francis Hutcheson, Adam Smith, George Berkeley, Adam Ferguson, Dugald Stewart, and Bishop himself. His essays and published lectures on social relations and the political economy, especially his observations on industrialism and the division of labor and on government responsibility for promoting the greatest amount of good for its citizens, clearly mirrored his reading of history. Ferguson's 1767 *Essay on the History of Civil Society,* in particular, was the direct source for much of Bishop's thinking on government, politics, evolutionary history, and social philosophy (Rodabaugh 1935, 176–87).

In 1816, the Reverend James Blythe, who had hired Bishop at Transylvania, resigned as president under pressure from the Kentucky legislature. The legislators were responding to what they considered the stagnant and divisively sectarian character of the college. As a result of Blythe's departure, the trustees could no longer expect to maintain Presbyterian control of the college (Rodabaugh 1935, 59). In 1817, they elected to the presidency Horace Holley, a Boston Unitarian minister and a Yale graduate who had studied with Timothy Dwight. In 1818, the Kentucky legislature dissolved the old Transylvania Board of Trustees and appointed a new one.

The new board, honoring the wishes of the old board, endorsed Holley's presidency. Bishop, of course, was still on the Transylvania faculty and actually had served as interim president after Blythe's departure. Bishop was dissatisfied and anxious to leave, particularly when he discovered that Holley's salary was three times larger than his own (Jennings 1955, 298). He wrote to the board insisting on a similar salary, and the board refused to comply. Once in place, Holley also took over Bishop's classes in moral philosophy. Bishop was not pleased. In 1824, he left Transylvania, convinced that his efforts had not been appreciated. Shortly thereafter he assumed the presidency of Miami University in Oxford, Ohio.

In spite of Bishop's departure, by the mid–1820s Transylvania was considered "the educational center of the west" (Rodabaugh 1935, 98). In 1825, Holley became embroiled in state and interdenominational church politics. In 1826, he was forced to resign as a result of ongoing accusations from the legislature that the college was catering to aristocratic students to the exclusion of poor students, particularly those from Kentucky. The college was in the process of losing its state support.

Holley's successor was Alva Woods. He was elected to the Transylvania presidency on February 7, 1828 (Jennings 1955, 156). Woods was an 1817 Harvard graduate and had attended Andover Theological Seminary. He spent two years abroad, traveling mostly in England and Scotland, and in 1824 he assumed the position of professor of mathematics and natural philosophy at Brown University. Under Woods, conditions at Transylvania University improved considerably and enrollment increased. More than one hundred students were enrolled in the Academic Department by late 1828.

Woods's main task was the total rebuilding of the Academic Department. To placate detractors, such as members of the Kentucky legislature who were critical of Holley's assumed "elitism," Woods made a show of effort that demonstrated his serious concern with the education of the masses. He believed that an educated electorate was essential to the survival of a democratic government. In his inaugural address of October 13, 1828, he contended that "freedom" ultimately depended on the measure of a people's intelligence and, in proportion, on their educated ability to "detect the sophistries of the artful demagogue" (Wright 1975, 121). He believed, consequently, in the necessity of formal schooling from the nursery through college. He also believed that a special effort should be made to educate people from the lower classes. Criminals, he asserted, were primarily products of illiteracy. His plans for the college involved a revolutionary departure from the traditional classical curriculum. In order to modify the course of study to meet the needs of the average student, he proposed that "for the purpose of political safety and of practical morality, a thorough education in the exact sciences and in English literature is all that is necessary" (Wright 1975, 121).

The trustees, in an effort to give the university a more democratic image, followed Woods's urging and created two separate tracks of study in 1828. One centered on the Department of Ancient Classics, the other on a newly formed Department of English Literature. The English literature concentration was designed for students who did not have an extensive grounding in the classical languages. Students planning careers in public school teaching, for instance, were especially encouraged to enroll in the English literature option. Wright observes that the effort to encourage teacher education was a first at Transylvania, and it reflected the hope that as the university's contribution to teacher education increased so would the generosity of the legislature. The minutes of the Board of Trustees for November 22, 1828, record a request of twenty thousand dollars from the legislature to establish a chair in English literature at Transylvania designed primarily to train teachers. Wright notes that many of the courses taught in the new Department of English Literature were similar to the courses required of all students. The only courses not offered were courses in the classical languages. Students studied English grammar, moral philosophy, natural and experimental philosophy, and, significantly, a course that was now called "Elements of Criticism" (1975, 122).

1824–1841: Bishop's Career at Miami University

During his years at Miami University in Ohio, following his departure from Transylvania in 1824, Bishop, who was Miami's president from 1824 to 1841, continued to expand his history course, delving ever deeper into the study of social philosophy. In an 1837 Miami publication, Bishop's course was described as offering instruction "in Political Philosophy, or what is otherwise called the Philosophy of Social Relations." The description also noted that the course was designed particularly for "young men who have . . . any taste for reading and investigation" (Rodabaugh 1935, 173 n. 22). The course appears to have included a critical assessment of readings in the vernacular, in all respects a course that one might designate "literary study," given particularly the broad latitude with which vernacular literary study of any kind was conceived by educators in the early years of the nineteenth century. It should also be noted in this context that, as pointed out, Bishop was originally hired at Transylvania to teach, along with logic and moral philosophy, criticism and belles lettres. With no evidence to the contrary, the wide-ranging nature of his history course suggests that he incorporated in the course all of the subjects he was initially hired to teach, including criticism and belles lettres. Rodabaugh suggests that there was a popular demand for instruction in English and other "practical" subjects that dated from Miami University's opening in 1824 and that Bishop promoted courses in rhetoric, composition and moral philosophy, and modern history (1935, 63–64).

Noteworthy also, in connection with Bishop's Miami years, was his close connection with William Holmes McGuffey. McGuffey, who was ordained into the Presbyterian ministry while at Miami, was the son of a colorful Scots-Irish farmer who, after settling in New Connecticut (northeastern Ohio), literally "chopped out his own road to the village of Youngstown" so that his children could be formally educated (Havighurst 1969, 63). William McGuffey had taught school in a number of frontier settlements. Bishop found him teaching in a smokehouse in Kentucky and subsequently hired him in 1826 as professor of languages, philosophy, and philology. McGuffey remained at Miami until 1836 when he became president of Cincinnati College. While McGuffey was at Miami, during Bishop's presidency, he responded to a request from Winthrop B. Smith, partner in the Cincinnati book publishing firm of Truman and Smith. Smith had an idea for a series of eclectic readers that would satisfy the growing market for texts in public schools and that would be particularly useful for the reading needs of pioneer children. He asked McGuffey to compile them, and McGuffey accepted, launching the now famous series of McGuffey *Readers* (Sullivan 1994, 57–58).

The *Readers,* though designed for public school use, were also available in libraries and widely distributed among families. Consequently, they were read and studied both in and outside of school by many generations of Americans. They contained carefully selected extracts from a wide variety of prominent American and English authors extending from Shakespeare to Dickens to Washington Irving. The extracts with their accompanying literary lessons, in the tradition of Adam Smith and other early Scottish, commonsense educators, were intended to teach patriotism and morality. The concern among Scottish teachers with using literary selections to educate good and useful citizens on the American frontier, as discussed in Chapter 1, can be traced back at least to 1753 and the publication of William Smith's *A General Idea of the College of Mirania.* McGuffey's objective, like Smith's, was primarily the promotion of Ciceronian or civic humanism in the students, colored always, however, by McGuffey's strict conservative approach to life. Any improvement, consequently, in his readers' rhetorical or oratorical skills, though welcomed, was subordinate to the object lessons communicated daily in the textbooks. The constant use of McGuffey's *Eclectic Readers* in nineteenth-century public and private schools, and their wide appeal among a general reading populace that was sold on the need for personal improvement, profoundly affected the shaping of the nineteenth-century American character and, subsequently, the direction of American history from about mid-century.

McGuffey's authoritarian nature and his obsession at Miami with what he considered a failed disciplinary program eventually set him at logger-heads with Bishop. Although they kept their distance from each other, they still shared a mutual respect and a firm commitment to the goal of educating good and useful citizens. But they were very different as people. McGuffey was a strict conservative in both religion and education and appears to have had Southern sympathies that made him suspect on the issue of slavery and human rights. Bishop, on the other hand, was an abolitionist, a liberal, and a progressive in his thinking on both educational and religious issues.

Although McGuffey and Bishop did not agree on much, they did collaborate for a brief time between 1828 and 1829 on a literary magazine. A third professor involved in the publication of the magazine was John E. Annan, a graduate of Dickinson College, who taught mathematics (Rodabaugh 1935, 56). The magazine, the *Literary Register,* first appeared in June 1828. It was published biweekly and included four separate sections: one on current news, a second on poetry and essays, the third on materials of literary and scientific interest, and the last on miscellaneous matters, which included market reports, letters, and other items (Rodabaugh 1935, 72).

Bishop also encouraged the formation of a number of literary societies while at Miami. These societies, most established during the 1820s and 1830s, were formed to promote literary study and printing, and were highly instrumental in the perpetuation of the oratorical tradition in western schools. Rodabaugh notes that books that were purchased by these societies, more than 6,200 volumes before 1840, formed the nucleus of Miami's young library. Initially only seniors could use the library, but in 1826, library privileges were granted to any student who had a faculty endorsement. Reading, even as a pastime, had become a respected and recognized means of moral and intellectual improvement, and it was encouraged by all levels of the faculty. In their desire to promote reading and oratorical training, the societies initiated a lecture series that drew famous American orators to the Oxford campus. During the early years of the societies noted western author-orators such as James H. Perkins, Charles Caldwell, and Lyman Beecher visited the campus (Rodabaugh 1935, 69, 78). The literary societies were also responsible in later years for the production of an impressive catalog of famous authors as honorary members, including Daniel Webster and Washington Irving, as well as Salmon P. Chase, the early American historian; Edward Everett, a noted orator who also edited the *North American Review* from 1820 to 1823 and was president of Harvard from 1846 to 1849; Elizabeth Palmer Peabody, social reformer and Boston transcendentalist, who opened the first kindergarten in the United States in 1860; and Robert Dale Owen, noted abolitionist and popular nineteenth-century author (Rodabaugh 1935, 69–70). Bishop appears to have been well pleased with the accomplishments of Miami's literary societies. Approvingly, he described them as "pure democracies . . . and miniature representations of the Two Houses of Congress and of the different State Legislatures" (Rodabaugh 1935, 77).

Miami grew steadily during Bishop's tenure, and its commitment to literary study as a vehicle for moral and civic improvement continued. Bishop was replaced by George Junkin in 1841. Junkin's ancestry also was Scottish, and he was a staunch Old Side Presbyterian. His years at Miami were filled with conflict and, hence, were generally unproductive. He was vehemently opposed to an antislavery movement that was gaining considerable momentum in Oxford at the time. Under pressure, he resigned the presidency in 1844. His career before he assumed the Miami presidency and, in particular, his influence on the promotion of literary study in emerging teacher education programs are discussed in more detail below in the section on Lafayette College.

1795: English Studies at the University of North Carolina

On January 15, 1795, the doors of the University of North Carolina opened for students. The new "presiding professor" was David Ker, a thirty-six-year-old Scots-Irish Presbyterian minister, a native of Ulster, and a graduate of Dublin's Trinity College who had emigrated in 1791 (Snider 1992, 3). Owing to a lack of money, the trustees had decided not to name a president. Ker, the presiding professor, would function in the meantime as the chief executive of the new institution, in Chapel Hill.

The dream of a college in North Carolina began with the hopes of Scottish and Scots-Irish immigrants who settled in North Carolina's western frontier in the waning years of the eighteenth century. William Richardson Davie, a graduate of the College of New Jersey, was credited with founding the university. He was elected governor of the state in 1789, the same year the university was established. Davie emigrated from England as a child and was raised in the home of his uncle, the Reverend William Richardson, a Presbyterian minister who had settled in the Waxham Mountains on the North Carolina-South Carolina border near Mecklenburg County and the frontier village of Salisbury. William Snider, in his history of the University of North Carolina, observes that most of the people who populated the region were pioneers, "largely Ulster Scot Presbyterians, Lutherans, and other Protestant sects" who had originally made their way south from Philadelphia. They were, in the main, Presbyterians and thus their ministers and preachers were also schoolmasters, among them the Reverend Samuel E. McCorkle, a College of New Jersey graduate who would be influential as a member of the University of North Carolina's Board of Trustees and also by 1795 as the professor of moral philosophy and history (1992, 5–8).

On October 12, 1793, a ceremony was conducted in which a cornerstone for the first campus was laid. McCorkle was chosen to deliver an address on the occasion, which concluded with the following salutation: "The seat of the University was . . . sought for, and the public eye selected Chapel Hill. . . . May this hill be for religion as the ancient hill of Zion; and for literature and the muses, may it surpass the ancient Parnassus!" (Snider 1992, 23). As Snider notes, "McCorkle's references to Zion and Parnassus as the university's antecedents vividly described the two major forces shepherding it toward birth" (23). Scots-Irish Presbyterians constituted one force, promoting mainly a balance of traditional learning with some experimental new subjects; the second force, the political influence came from Federalists and Republicans who promoted, under Davie's leadership, more practical support for the expansion of public education in the state and a concentration on useful subjects. McCorkle, particularly, thought that religious learning and moral training, though useful and important, were only part of a first-class education, and that the future of public education in North Carolina would necessitate allocating at least equal time for the more traditional fruits of Parnassus (Snider 1992, 23).

Davie and McCorkle agreed on the benefits to be gained by establishing a working public university in the state, but they disagreed on the curriculum. McCorkle's preliminary plan, drawn up in 1792 by a trustee committee, was literary and classical, but realistic. The committee recommended that "instruction in literature and science be confined to the study of the languages, particularly the English, the acquirement of historical knowledge, ancient and modern; Belles Lettres, Mathematics and Natural Philosophy; Botany and the theory and practice of Agriculture, best suited to the climate and soil of the State; the principles of Architecture" (Battle 1907, 1: 49). The curriculum was experimental. According to Kemp P. Battle, president of the university from 1876 to 1891, there is good reason to believe that the 1792 curriculum was also heavily influenced by Dr. Hugh Williamson, a trustee, a Presbyterian minister, and a medical doctor who was a graduate of the College of Philadelphia and who, like Benjamin Rush, had studied medicine at Edinburgh (1907, 1: 48).

When the University of North Carolina finally opened in 1795, the curriculum offered two tracks or "classes" of study. One was the Scientific Class, which involved the study of English, belles lettres, botany, agriculture, architecture, mathematics, natural philosophy, and ancient and modern history. The other was called the Literary Class. Students enrolling in the Literary Class for the first year, or the "first class," studied "English grammar, Roman antiquities, and such part of the Roman historians, orators and poets as the professors might designate, and also the Greek Testament." The "second class" studied arithmetic, bookkeeping, geography, Grecian antiquity and the Greek classics. The "third class" studied mathematics, natural philosophy and astronomy. The "fourth class" studied logic, moral philosophy, principles of civil government, ancient and modern history, and belles lettres (Battle 1907, 1: 55).

By December 1795, however, it was clear that some of the students were not properly prepared for college-level courses, so a new plan was devised. The university was divided into two branches, one called the Preparatory School with a practical program of study devised by Davie. The plan favored the sciences; the study of Latin and Greek were excluded. Under Davie's plan, with support from educators who favored usefulness over the traditional classical curriculum, Latin and Greek were reduced to electives. Science, English, and history were at the core of his course of study (Snider 1992, 25–26). The other program operated under the designation "Professorships of the University" (Battle 1907, 1: 93). Students in the professorships program studied rhetoric based on Thomas Sheridan's *Rhetorical Grammar of the English Language* and belles lettres based on Hugh Blair and Charles Rollin. The course was taught by the university's first president, the Reverend Joseph Caldwell. For the course of study in the English language taught by the professor of languages, Vicesimus Knox's *Elegant Extracts* and "Scott's Collections" were required. The professor of languages also taught Latin and Greek. Students in this program were designated to work under various professors. For instance, the students taught by the professor of languages were required to deliver twice a week translations into English of some Latin or Greek literary classic (Battle 1907, 1: 95–96).

Caldwell was a Scots-Irish Presbyterian minister, the son of an Ulster physician. He was also a 1791 graduate of the College of New Jersey where he had been a student of John Witherspoon. He served as president at North Carolina from 1804 to 1835. Caldwell was a staunch believer in the academic value of the classics. Subsequently, he restored the classical curriculum that Davie had largely scrapped. In 1800, the trustees had repealed the earlier ordinance that conferred the bachelor of arts degree on students "having passed an approved examination on the English Language and the Sciences." In its place they instituted a stiff Latin requirement that made proficiency in Latin mandatory for both admission to and graduation from the university. In 1804, under Caldwell's influence, Greek was also made a mandatory requirement for admission and graduation (Caldwell 1945, 6).

Following President Caldwell, advocates of the classical curriculum dominated the history of the university for the next fourteen years. In 1818, however, the curriculum was expanded to accommodate a growing faculty. The program approved by the university trustees in 1818 provided for studies in English, Greek, Latin, and mathematics during the first two years, and for English literature, rhetoric, moral philosophy, natural philosophy, natural science, advanced mathematics, and metaphysics during the junior and senior years (Caldwell 1945, 8). Noteworthy here is the separation, as early as 1818, of English literary study from rhetoric.

The fate of the English literature course, however, remains a mystery. According to Wallace E. Caldwell in a survey of the history of the humanities at North Carolina from 1795 to 1945, by 1824, Latin and Greek were being taught in the junior and senior years along with a new course in political economy. English literature appears to have been dropped. The university catalogue for 1825 included English grammar in the freshman year and rhetoric in both sessions of the sophomore year and in the first session of the junior year. In the senior year, moral philosophy was required for the first session—apparently the only moral philosophy course included in the entire four-year curriculum. Rhetoric and practical elocution (i.e., oratory) were also available—for the first and only time—during the first session of the senior year (1945, 15–16). The four-year course of study in 1825 heavily favored the classics, mathematics, and the natural sciences, with some noticeable concentration on ancient and modern history.

In 1835, David L. Swain was appointed president. Swain openly favored expanding the history offering, but failed to do anything substantial about the study of English literature. It obviously was still a consideration at North Carolina as late as 1849, when A. M. Shipp was hired as the professor of English literature and history. It appears, however, that courses in English literature were never taught. In 1850, barely a year after his initial appointment, Shipp was given a new title—professor of French and history. By 1854, he was identified solely as the professor of history. When he resigned in 1859, his ancient history courses were taken over by the professors of Latin and Greek. Swain continued to teach the modern history courses (Caldwell 1945, 13–14).

As late as 1856, North Carolina, under the leadership of President Swain, still had made no apparent provision for courses either in English or American literary study. A course in English composition was taught during both sessions of the sophomore year in 1856. The freshman year was given over almost totally to the classics and ancient history, with algebra and geometry offered respectively in the first and second terms. Juniors also studied English composition and classical Greek tragedy, along with ancient, medieval, and modern history. Juniors also studied chemistry, mineralogy, and astronomy, along with calculus, natural philosophy, and a course labeled "analytical mechanics." Seniors took political economy, logic, chemistry, geology, and a course that Swain instituted on international and constitutional law. Seniors also—for the first time—studied moral philosophy. They also had the option of either studying Plato and Cicero or taking a course called "studies in the scientific school" (Caldwell 1945, 16–17).

Courses in the classics, the natural sciences, and history dominated the curriculum at North Carolina right up to the time of the Civil War when most of the faculty and students left the campus to embrace the Confederate cause. The development of courses in English and American literary study was among the many reforms destined to be instituted during Reconstruction, but they would come much later. Plans for a complete reorganization of the curriculum on an elective basis were proposed in 1867, but they were never carried out. Instead, as Caldwell notes, the program that went into effect directly after the war was mainly a continuation of the program offered during Swain's years as president, only with the added provision that students could pick their courses more freely. By 1870, however, owing to low enrollment and lack of funds, the university closed (1945, 19–20).

When it opened again in 1875, the winds of change were more favorable. In 1876, Kemp P. Battle was named president. He would remain president until 1891, guiding the university through a major reconstruction. Battle promoted a new curriculum that included, among traditional courses in the classics, mathematics, and the sciences, courses in agriculture, history, moral philosophy, and, finally, English literature. The continuing link between moral philosophy and English literary study was attested to at North Carolina by the official appointment of Adolphus W. Mangum as the new professor of moral philosophy and English literature. Mangum was followed in 1885 by Thomas Hume, who was hired strictly to teach English language and literature (Caldwell 1945, 21). Although late in coming, from the time of Mangum in the late 1870s, North Carolina's commitment to English and American literary study gradually expanded this area of study into one of the foremost undergraduate and graduate programs in the nation. Eventually North Carolina would become home to some of the preeminent scholars of American literature, including Howard Mumford Jones, Norman Foerster, and C. Hugh Holman. But, as the early history of the university shows, literary study came to North Carolina initially as a dream of its Scots-Irish founders who recognized at the outset the practical value of offering courses that combined the study of the classics with studies in English.

Literary Study and Teacher Education

1802: Jefferson College

Jefferson College was founded in 1802 as another frontier experiment in higher education promoted by Scots-Irish Presbyterians. Located in Canonsburg, Pennsylvania, Jefferson College traced its history back to 1791 and the establishment of an academy at Canonsburg by the Scots-Irish. Joseph Smith, author of the *History of Jefferson College; Including an Account of the Early "Log-Cabin" Schools and the Canonsburg Academy,* a work published in 1857, notes that the Canonsburg Academy, although not the first academy chartered on the west side of the Allegheny Mountains, actually was the first frontier academy to open for students (1857,

26). Canonsburg is approximately twenty miles southwest of present-day Pittsburgh and approximately the same distance from the Ohio-Pennsylvania border.

The Washington Academy, also a Presbyterian school, had been originally chartered in 1787 but it did not open. Its three organizers were Presbyterian ministers and graduates of the College of New Jersey. The Reverend John McMillan, whose parents were Scots-Irish immigrants, arrived in Pennsylvania's western frontier in 1775; the Reverend Thaddeus Dod, whose parents were New England Puritans, came in 1777; the Reverend Joseph Smith arrived in Pennsylvania in 1780. All three were graduates of the College of New Jersey and, like most New Jersey graduates, they were steeped in moral philosophy. McMillan and Dod had been students at New Jersey during the time of John Witherspoon. Smith, who was older, had graduated in 1764. The three founders of the Washington Academy were joined by the Reverend James Power and in 1781, they formed the pioneer Redstone Presbytery. They taught out of their homes in typical Presbyterian clerical fashion, eventually erecting log cabin schools on their property. Finally, in 1791, the Presbyterian Synod of Virginia gave approval for the formation of an actual educational facility in Washington County, Pennsylvania, and the Washington Academy began to take shape (Coleman 1956, 2–14). In 1806, the Washington Academy became Washington College.

By 1792, Canonsburg Academy was already open and welcoming students. David Johnson from the Washington Academy came to Canonsburg to teach the classics to the older students. Samuel Millar taught geometry, trigonometry, astronomy, navigation, algebra, bookkeeping, and English to the younger students (Coleman 1956, 46–47). Helen Coleman notes that, in spite of the presbytery's endorsement, which implicitly expected divinity studies, the Canonsburg Academy emphasized the teaching of the liberal arts (1956, 50).

When the Canonsburg Academy became Jefferson College in 1802, the curriculum included three departments or divisions of study: the first, called the school of the languages, was traditionally classical; the second was the mathematical school; the third, unnamed, emphasized rhetoric, logic, and moral philosophy and was taught by the language instructors (Coleman 1956, 57). Modern languages were firmly embedded in the curriculum by 1834. By 1840, English literature was being taught along with rhetoric and English composition. In 1865, Jefferson College and Washington College were finally united in Washington, Pennsylvania, as Washington and Jefferson College. The Jefferson College campus in Canonsburg subsequently closed in 1869.

In a grateful acknowledgment of the courage and tenacity of the Scots-Irish pioneers who settled in southwestern Pennsylvania and of the dedication of their Presbyterian ministers, Smith offers the following tribute:

> The Scotch-Irish emigrants, who began to pour out on the Western frontier, a little before the last quarter of the 18th century, and to form settlements through Western Pennsylvania, were a remarkable race. They brought with them a deeply cherished love for the *House of God* and the *School House*. The ministers of the gospel of the Presbyterian Church . . . were well-educated men, most of them graduates of the college of New Jersey [who] devoted their untiring efforts to organize and build up churches in the new settlements. They also co-operated with their people in organizing schools; and in most cases took them under their care, becoming teachers themselves, or providing adequate instructors. (1857, 5–6)

Early contributions to the support of the Canonsburg Academy came mainly from congregations of Presbyterians and seceders located in the western Pennsylvania and eastern Ohio area. By 1796, a literary society had been formed which Smith designates as the "first literary association of the West" (1857, 35). By 1797, there were two literary societies in Canonsburg, the Philo Society and the Franklin Society, both founded by College of New Jersey graduates and formed on the model of College of New Jersey literary societies (1857, 40). Historically, the societies were useful in the promotion of discipline and "in training the minds of the students to habits of attention, accurate discrimination, and argumentation," which improved their performance particularly in courses in composition and oratory. Smith adds that the Canonsburg literary societies had also introduced something that in 1797 was not yet practiced at the College of New Jersey or at any other eastern college—i.e., a literary contest between the two societies in composition, in oratory, and in debate (1857, 41–43).

The list of faculty charges at the time of the opening of Jefferson College in 1802 designated moral philosophy as the core of the curriculum. The list called for the professor of moral philosophy to teach logic, geography, and rhetoric. The course of study for the first year included readings from Horace, Cicero's *Orations,* Xenophon, Homer, and Longinus; courses in Greek, Roman antiquities, geography, and algebra were also required. The second year was given over mainly to mathematics, with additional courses required in natural philosophy and rhetoric and history. In the third year (designated the "philosophical year"), logic, moral philosophy, and metaphysics were required, along with "a careful review of the Languages, and of the . . . arts and sciences." Strict attention, the catalog noted, would be paid to student compositions and to speaking orations (Smith 1857, 59–60).

In 1805, the Philo and Franklin societies petitioned the trustees for the location of society libraries on the college grounds. As a result, two college libraries were established that made titles in a variety of literary subjects available to Jefferson's students. In 1832, the library of the Franklin Society numbered 676 volumes. By 1857, it numbered nearly three thousand volumes and included some of the "most valuable standard works in the English language, in History, Poetry, Philosophy, Theology and the Natural Sciences" (Smith 1857, 166). In 1841, the college appointed the Reverend Alexander B. Brown professor of belles lettres. In 1845, his title was changed to professor of belles lettres, logic, rhetoric, and general history. In 1852, the Reverend William Ewing was named "professor extraordinary" of history and modern languages.

The English studies program at Jefferson College directly influenced the development of English literary studies at Lafayette College to the east, in Easton, Pennsylvania. The faculty that staffed Lafayette College when it opened, including the Reverend George Junkin, its first president, were all Jefferson College graduates.

1832: Lafayette College

Lafayette College, although not on the extreme western frontier, nevertheless was another academic pioneer in the history of English literary study. The college had a direct tie to Jefferson College and owed most of its early support to the Scottish Presbyterians who lived in Easton. By the 1820s, Easton, located on the Delaware River, was a key link in the riverboat transport of coal and lumber to Philadelphia from upcountry Pennsylvania forests and anthracite coal mines. It was also directly on the route to the West for settlers coming from New York and New England. In 1824, in a single month, 511 covered wagons carrying more than three thousand immigrants passed through the town on the way to the frontier (Skillman 1932, 1: 5–7).

The desire for a college in Easton dated from 1824, when a memorial requesting a charter and legislative support for a college was drafted by Joel Jones, an Easton lawyer, and forwarded to the Pennsylvania legislature. The memorial testifies to a surprisingly progressive attitude toward education among the trustees, especially James Madison Porter who would head the college's Board of Trustees. Porter and Colonel Thomas McKeen, who was Scots-Irish, were the two most instrumental trustees in the promotion of the plan. They were also members of Easton's First Presbyterian Church, originally established in 1819 by the Reverend Stephen Boyer, who would later return to Easton to teach in the college (Skillman 1932, 1: 27).

The memorial cited the need for a college that would combine "a course of practical Military Science with the course of Literature and General Science" (Skillman 1932, 1: 32). The document also addressed the need for a course in civil engineering and argued strongly for the importance of the study of modern languages, particularly German and English. W. B. Owen, in an essay on the college's history published in 1902, quotes the founders as addressing what he refers to as "the germ of the present course in English studies" (1902, 16).

An addition will be made to the language course usually adopted. In this branch students commonly limit their attention to the dead languages. This is to be regretted. The living languages certainly have some claim to attention which the dead have not. Particularly is it to be regretted that after acquiring the Latin, the Romantic dialects of modern Europe should not receive that small portion of time which is necessary to acquire them.

But the language most neglected in our seminaries of learning is the English. It is, we think, one of the follies of the learned to expend time and toil and money in the minute investigation of the languages of other times and other people, at the expense of omitting the equally curious and more useful investigation of their own. (Owen 1902, 16–17)

In 1824, Easton's population was made up predominantly of German immigrants who, unfortunately, showed no discernible interest in supporting the fledgling college. Yet the board realized that the college, if it was to survive, needed the support of the Germans. Hence, when a notice of a meeting of Easton citizens was posted to enable townsfolk to discuss the idea of a college in their town, the notice made it clear that of the modern languages, German would be taught in the new college (Skillman 1932, 1: 27). The move was well timed and successful. The promise to teach German increased community interest somewhat, but it also increased the possibility of formal courses in other vernacular European languages, including, of course, English. As the memorial that was forwarded to the legislature noted, the "richness" of the German language "and its intimate connection with the nobler part of the English, entitle it to the attention of every American, and particularly of every Pennsylvanian." A fair portion of the students' time, the document added, therefore would be committed to the study of "the modern languages," particularly German (Skillman 1932, 1: 33). As will be discussed in Chapter 4, the modern language curriculum at Lafayette College, with its emphasis on the German-English connection, formed a natural setting from which the first courses in Anglo-Saxon, taught by the renowned philologist Francis A. March, eventually would emerge.

In 1825, however, the Pennsylvania legislature was by no means unanimous in its support of the college plan. One member of the House, Jacob F. Heston of Philadelphia, tried rigorously to defeat the bill. He objected to the course in military science, which he said would foster militarism in the country; he also objected to the inclusion of courses in the classical languages. He called them "dead languages" and argued that they were a "useless waste of time" and would keep students from studying "really useful" subjects. In an unintended but still forceful endorsement of English language study, he noted that knowledge of all the classical languages "would not furnish a single idea, that could not be communicated in English." The study of classical languages, he concluded, "added no more to scientific knowledge than the croaking of frogs" (Skillman 1932, 1: 35). The debate was as heated in the Senate as it was in the House. Finally, on January 6, 1826, the Pennsylvania House of Representatives approved the establishment of a college in Easton. On March 7, the bill passed the Senate and was approved by the governor on March 9. Although, technically, Lafayette College existed, nothing much happened to get it up and running until six years later in 1832.

The Board of Trustees, which intended the college to incorporate the underfunded, almost defunct Easton Union Academy, thought that finally having a real college in the town would encourage support from the citizens. But their efforts to encourage the town citizenry, especially the Germans, to help fund the college, in spite of the German community's early enthusiasm for courses in German, met with little success. On October 15, 1827, in a desperate effort to find a way to open the college, the board posted a letter to officials at Mount Airy College, a small private school in Germantown, outside of Philadelphia, that prepared young aristocrats for military careers. The letter was essentially an invitation for Mount Airy to consider an affiliation with Lafayette. The hope was that the financially solvent Mount Airy College would provide the financial base that would enable Lafayette College to open. In the letter the board outlined the ambitious course of study the trustees envisioned for Lafayette.

> The Trustees propose to establish a Seminary, which, in a literary and scientific point of view, shall ultimately be inferior to none in our Country. The course of instruction . . . shall embrace the learned and the more useful of the Modern European Languages—an extensive course of English Literature—of the Mathematics—of Natural Philosophy—Ethics and Military Science and Tactics will be pursued to a considerable extent, and perhaps far enough for every useful purpose, though it will be much subordinate to the literary and civil purposes of the Institution.

The description continued with an acknowledgment of the need for financial support and a comment on the proposed special concentration of the new college on military science, a move designed to accommodate the Mount Airy commitment to officer training.

> We are, at present, entirely out of funds, and for that reason only, have delayed so long the opening of the college. . . . No College at the West of us [is] nearer than Dickinson College. . . . The military part of our system, we anticipate will give it some attracting and many advantages, and the subordination of it to literature and general science, will remove objections from the minds of parents, who wish to have their sons to be prepared for the civil purposes of life. (Skillman 1932, 1: 39–40)

Mount Airy appears not to have taken the bait, and as late as 1831, Lafayette College still was not open. Finally, however, in 1831, interested Scottish Presbyterians took up the cause. The Reverend John Gray, pastor of Easton's First Presbyterian Church, of which James Madison Porter and Colonel Thomas McKeen, college trustees, were members, wrote to the Reverend Robert Steel, pastor of the Abington Presbyterian Church near Philadelphia. Steel was a trustee of the Manual Labor Academy of Pennsylvania. The manual labor academies that had sprung up around the nation were similar to Britain's Mechanics' Institutes. They were modeled essentially after Emanuel von Fellenburg's experimental Swiss academies devoted to the study of the mechanical arts. The impetus for the experiment derived from Johann Heinrich Pestalozzi's well-heeded theories about the need to direct educational training at the whole person and not just at the mind.

Schools of science and industry were becoming increasingly popular in the United States even as early as the 1820s. There was a distinct economic advantage to the system. The products of student labor could be sold, subsequently reducing the cost of educating the student in the first place. In Germantown in 1829, a group of Philadelphians established just such a school. Not surprisingly, they were Presbyterians, and the school was called the Manual Labor Academy of Pennsylvania. It was founded upon the commonsense principle that enabling young men to earn while they learned would make it easier for them to pay for their education. Even though most of the young men in the academy were in programs aimed at the ministry, they worked as manual laborers. The school opened on May 1, 1829, with four students; by the end of the year the enrollment had increased to twenty-five (Skillman 1932, 1: 50). At this point, the Reverend George Junkin entered the picture. In July 1830, Junkin was elected president of the academy; he was forty. His lineage was also Scottish. His grandparents had emigrated from Scotland around 1737 and had settled in Cumberland County.

Junkin, as an 1813 graduate of Jefferson College at Canonsburg, well knew the value of and need for a practical language study program, especially in the preparation of teachers. He was an Old Side Presbyterian. As it turned out, most of the trustees of the Manual Labor Academy were New Siders. Eventually, Junkin alienated them when he attacked a New Side pastoral appointment in Philadelphia. Junkin, in 1831, however, was anxious to move. The Manual Labor Academy was in financial trouble, owing mainly to the high cost of transporting needed manufacturing materials from Philadelphia. The Reverend Steel, in the meantime, had received the Reverend Gray's letter and informed Junkin of the vacancy at Lafayette College and of the opportunity to start fresh in Easton with a brand new college.

In January 1832, Junkin was invited to Easton to meet with the trustees. He was offered and accepted the college presidency with the proviso that the trustees institute the manual labor system of education in lieu of the unit on military science (Skillman 1932, 1: 53–54). As a result, the founders had to abandon their dream of a grand military college with drills, uniforms, and students from affluent backgrounds, and accept instead a scenario involving boys from poor backgrounds laboring and studying for the ministry under the tutelage of an Old Side Presbyterian divine. Students from Germantown's Manual Labor Academy who followed Junkin to Easton built an addition to a rented farmhouse chosen to house the students. On the morning of May 9, 1832, Lafayette College finally opened for classes.

In the beginning, the college had only two teachers sharing one recitation room. One taught mathematics, the other the classics. The classics teacher was James I. Coon, a graduate, like Junkin, of Jefferson College. Charles Francis McCay, another Jefferson College graduate, was the professor of mathematics and natural philosophy. He would later become president of the University of South Carolina. When the school opened, the standard course of study included Latin and Greek for all four years; mathematics for the first three years; evidences of Christianity for the second, third, and fourth years; and mental philosophy in the third year. Seniors were offered natural philosophy, mineralogy, botany, political economy, history, moral philosophy, rhetoric, and history (Skillman 1932, 1: 63).

There was an increasingly recognizable need for trained teachers on the American frontier at the time. Transylvania College, as noted above, had responded to the need earlier, in 1828, with the establishment of a chair in English literature designed primarily for the training of teachers. Now Junkin, seizing an opportunity for Lafayette to train teachers, instituted a preparatory program of study for prospective teachers which consisted, along with a variety of mathematics courses, of courses in reading, writing, English grammar, geography, vocal music, bookkeeping, and moral philosophy (Skillman 1932, 1: 64). Two popular literary societies were also formed at the college, the Washington Literary Society and the Franklin Literary Society. The societies encouraged reading and, to that end, provided books, many of which were literary selections. Through the societies' efforts, students consequently gained a firsthand knowledge of English literature, but, even more importantly, one that was acquired in conjunction with debating and declamation. In the efforts of the societies to combine literary study with critical disputation, we mark another important example of the effect of the combination of criticism and the oratorical tradition on the history of English and American literary studies in the United States in the early years of the century.

By 1834, Lafayette was offering instruction in German, as had been promised. In 1837, the college hired an actual professor of belles lettres. He was the Reverend David X. Junkin, the youngest brother of the Reverend George Junkin, the college president. At the time of his appointment, the Reverend David Junkin was pastor of the Presbyterian Church in Greenwich, New Jersey. By 1838, as a result of hiring the new belles lettres professor, the college was able to offer a complete course in belles lettres for the junior year. By 1841, regular lectures on rhetoric and belles lettres were offered to sophomores and seniors during both the first and second sessions *(Catalogue 1841–42* 1842, 15).

George Junkin resigned his presidency in 1840 to assume the presidency of Miami University in Oxford, Ohio. Junkin later returned to Lafayette College to resume the duties of president. By 1855, Lafayette College could boast what Francis A. March, the renowned philologist, referred to as "a higher plane" of English study than any he had previously experienced (1895, 26). March's enthusiasm for the developing experimental program in philology at Lafayette, discussed in more detail in Chapter 4, helps to explain why, in 1857, he readily accepted the Chair of English Language and Comparative Philology at the college. It was the first chair designated exclusively for English language study in the United States, and it foreshadowed a new direction for English studies that eventually would eclipse both the oratorical tradition and the critical study of belles lettres.

4

Marketing Literary Study, 1820 to 1870

"This Literature of England Must Be Forever Ours"

> The Academic bowers, the lyceums, and the universities of the mother country have all poured their treasures into our land most readily. This literature of England must be forever ours.
> —Samuel Lorenzo Knapp, *Advice in the Pursuits of Literature*, 1832

By the late 1820s, emerging trends in the study of oratory, rhetoric, and criticism in many American universities supported the classroom use of English and American literature. The progress was aided by an impressive selection of essays and books, many of which were anthologies and textbooks, published between 1800 and 1870 that directly addressed the need for the study of vernacular literature, both British and American, in American schools. Kermit Vanderbilt, writing in *American Literature and the Academy*, notes that in 1820 school texts accounted for one-third of the $2.5 million publishing market in the United States. By 1830, income from textbooks had increased by a third, up to $1.1 million in a $3.5 million book market; by 1850, the market for school books had grown by 500 percent (1986, 31). Public literacy was also on the rise as was the availability of printed books and journals designated for the trade market. In 1819, Washington Irving had observed, in an essay titled "English Writers on America," that "every one knows the all pervading influence of literature at the present day, and how much the opinions and passions of mankind are under its control" (1978, 46). If Irving was correct, the "all pervading influence of literature" in the early years of the nineteenth century was also a force shaping public opinion.

By the mid–1840s most American towns with a measurable population had some kind of public library or town reading room. American college and university libraries by mid-century held a combined total of more than six hundred thousand monographs; the books in public libraries around the nation at the same time numbered nearly nine hundred thousand. By 1825, the Napier steam-driven press was in use, increasing the rate of printing time for many publishers. By 1832, books were coming off the presses regularly in single runs of at least one thousand copies (Spiller 1963, 234–35). The improvements in printing increased production, keeping costs down while increasing availability among the populace, many of whom could now afford to buy books. The improvements also eventually encouraged the production of pioneering literary anthologies, most of which were intended for the increasingly profitable American textbook market.

British authors and British publications retained their dominant popularity during the first half of the century. English literature enjoyed favored status as the cultural standard by which other vernacular literatures, including American literature, were measured. Washington Irving's *Sketch Book,* heralding the adolescence of American literature, did not even appear until 1819. In the very early years of the nineteenth century, the British critic Sydney Smith could still wonder whether anyone read an American book and whether there was such a commodity as American literature. Robert Spiller also describes an attitude that prevailed throughout New England in the early decades of the century that was critical of designs on developing a national literature in spite of the efforts toward nationalism of professors and critics such as Edward Tyrell Channing at Harvard and his more famous brother, William Ellery Channing. As Spiller puts it, in their criticism of Jefferson's Embargo on British shipping and their general lack of enthusiasm for the War of 1812, many New Englanders, particularly those from the "more prosperous classes" and those living "in the vicinity of Boston," displayed a discernible "Anglophile tendency." At their Hartford convention in 1815, for instance, members of New England's Federalist Party pondered whether New England, if the action were necessitated by unfavorable circumstances, might actually choose to secede from the federal Union and become an independent state (1963, 233).

Neither an Anglophile nor a separatist, George Tucker from Virginia as early as 1814 began the publication of a series of essays in which, among other concerns, he questioned why the United States lacked a recognizable national literature. In his essay "On American Literature," he examined the problem, citing the absence of a literary center as a possible reason for the neglect. He also accused American educators of failing to promote literary study adequately. To strengthen his argument that the United States, regardless of its youth, should cultivate a literary heritage independent of English literature, Tucker invoked the example of the Scots as successful latecomers in the creation of a vital national literature. He observed that, "until within little more than the last fifty years, Scotland had scarcely a poet or a dramatic writer to balance [against the English literary tradition]. . . . Yet since that time, Scotland has produced its full quota of literary genius" (1822, 65). In 1816, Tucker would be named professor of moral philosophy and political economy at Central College, Jefferson's infant college in Charlottesville, Virginia, which, in 1825, became the University of Virginia. Tucker remained at Virginia until 1845. Like the Scottish moral sense theorists, Tucker also promoted the use of literary study as a way to teach morality and conduct. "If we consult . . . history," he wrote, "we shall find abundant evidence to show that the state of literature in every country depends upon moral causes . . ." (1822, 63). He also recognized the implicit importance of the theories of Adam Smith in the future development of the American national economy.[1] In particular, he lauded the theory of the division of labor as a basis upon which to advance "industry" and the subsequent manufacture of "all those various commodities . . . produced by human ingenuity and skill" (1822, 70). An educated work force of managers and laborers capable of promoting a national economy that would foster a cultural identity which supported American literature was a foregone conclusion in Tucker's prescript for national prosperity, a prescript that, as Vanderbilt also acknowledges, was greatly inspired by intellectual developments in eighteenth-century Scotland (1986, 40).

The promotion of English and American literary study in the early years of the nineteenth century benefited considerably from the increased availability of primary and secondary texts intended particularly for classroom use. Professional authors and schoolmen alike realized the growing potential for classroom literary study, and they supplied the market with a wide choice of texts, many of which were still in print and being used in the early years of the twentieth century. Among the most influential (because they were the most successful) textbook authors of the nineteenth century were John Seely Hart, Samuel Lorenzo Knapp, William Ellery Channing, Rufus

---

1. All of Tucker's publications on political economy are directly indebted to his reading of Adam Smith.

Wilmot Griswold, James Robert Boyd, Thomas B. Shaw, and William Spalding.

John Seely Hart

In 1819, John Seely Hart, a prominent American educator and editor, published the *Class Book of Poetry: Consisting of Selections from English and American Poets, from Chaucer to the Present Day, with Biographical and Critical Remarks*. The book, along with a companion study on English and American prose published in 1845, was widely used in American colleges and academies. Hart, who graduated with honors from the College of New Jersey, eventually held the professorship of rhetoric and English language at the college. He is now best remembered for having taught there, in 1872, what is believed to have been the first course in American literature ever offered for college credit. The *Class Book of Poetry* and the *Class Book of Prose* were among the first anthologies used in the United States for the study of English literature. Hart's interest in English literary study was also the motive for his publication of an American school edition of *Spenser and the Fairy Queen* in 1854 and a summary outline of the life of Shakespeare in 1888.[2] Hart also published a number of popular and profitable English grammars for the growing American textbook market, including *An English Grammar; or, An Exposition of the Principles and Usages of the English Language,* which was originally published in 1845 and remained in print in various editions until 1877; and *A Manual of Composition and Rhetoric,* first published in 1871, and still in print and being used in 1903. His *Grammar of the English Language, with an Analysis of the Sentence,* published in 1874, was in print until 1937.

It is also much to Hart's credit that, in his ongoing desire to popularize and, hence, promote the formal study of literature, he published an anthology of American women prosaists in 1852, titled *The Female Prose Writers of America. With Portraits, Biographical Notices and Specimens of Their Writings.* He noted in the preface that he was inspired to produce the book

2. The Spenser school edition was originally a trade book published in 1847 under the title *An Essay on the Life and Writings of Edmund Spenser, with a Special Exposition of the Fairy Queen.* Hart's summary biography of Shakespeare was included in a volume edited by W. G. Clark and W. A. Wright, titled *The Complete Dramatic and Poetical Works of William Shakespeare* (1888).

on the prose writers because of "the unwonted favour" extended to Thomas Buchanan Read's *Female Poets of America: with Portraits, Biographical Notices, and Specimens of Their Writings,* which appeared in 1848 (Hart 1852, 7). Hart claimed to have produced *Female Prose Writers* particularly for the American trade market in an effort to promote interest in American literature among women readers. A selling point, a testament to the popularity of biography at the time, was the inclusion of biographical sketches of all of the women represented because, as he surmised, "it seems to be an instinctive desire of the human heart, on becoming acquainted with any work of genius, to know something of its author" (1852, 7). Hart's anthology, which sold well in the United States, went to five editions, the last edition being published in 1930. The anthology included prose samples from the works of forty-eight American women from the late eighteenth century and early nineteenth century, including S. Margaret Fuller, Harriet Beecher Stowe, Susan Fenimore Cooper, Catherine Sedgwick, Lydia H. Sigourney, Caroline Gilman, and a host of others, some known, some now long forgotten.

Hart also published in 1872 survey histories titled *A Manual of English Literature* and *A Manual of American Literature.* Both were intended primarily as texts for college and university classes. The two books were abridged and combined in 1873 in a survey history titled *A Short Course in Literature, English and American,* which also had considerable trade market appeal as a self-teaching resource for learners denied access to formal courses in literary study. Hart's *Short Course,* which was arranged by chapters intended to be studied as individual units, provided a glimpse at how the formal study of English and American literature was being perceived in the United States by mid-century. The book was done in two uneven parts. Part 1 included fourteen chapter-units on English literature. Part 2 devoted five chapter-units to American literature.

The chapter breakdown for American literature was chronological and gives some sense of how Hart and others may have considered organizing a course in the subject in 1870. Chapter 1 treated "The Early Colonial Period"; Chapter 2, "The Revolutionary Period." Chapters 3, 4, and 5 were arranged arbitrarily by years: 1800 to 1830, 1830 to 1850, and 1850 to Hart's "present," or approximately 1870. The last two chapters were divided generically into sections: eight sections in Chapter 4, eleven in Chapter 5. The section headings covered a wide variety of literary types, including "Poets," "Novelists," "History and Biography," "Literature and

Criticism," "Political Writers," "Scientific Writers," "Theological Writers," "Magazinists," "Journalists," "Humorists," and "Politics and Political Economy," all of which Hart subsumed under the title "American Literature." He included authors without specific generic distinctions under "Miscellaneous." Obviously, *literature* for Hart meant any written work of cultural or political significance that was, in his estimation, worth preserving, for his conception of what formal literary study should entail included much more than what would have been classified even at the time as "belles lettres."

The long list of names that constituted the American literary canon to Hart in 1870 is informative. Almost all of the major figures whose reputations have survived into the twentieth century are represented: e.g., Cotton and Increase Mather, William Byrd, Anne Bradstreet, Jonathan Edwards, Benjamin Franklin, Thomas Jefferson, Edgar Allan Poe, James Fenimore Cooper, Washington Irving, Ralph Waldo Emerson, Henry Wadsworth Longfellow, Nathaniel Hawthorne, Herman Melville, Louisa May Alcott, Henry David Thoreau, and Mark Twain. Most of the minor figures covered in the text, however, have not fared as well. For example, almost all of the writers contemporary with Hart who were included in Chapter 3 as representative of the period from 1800 to 1830, with the exception of Charles Brockden Brown and Noah Webster, are all but forgotten. Among them are Robert Treat Paine Jr., the Federalist poet; Thomas Green Fessenden, the satirist who attacked Jefferson and the Democrats; Joseph Rodman Drake, the poet-patriot; and Samuel Woodworth, the author of "The Old Oaken Bucket." Hart also included in his list of notable American "authors" for the period 1800 to 1830 the unlikely names of Francis Scott Key, John James Audubon, and Chief Justice John Marshall—unlikely, because, in spite of Audubon's *Journal* and Key's poems, they are not generally remembered as "literary" figures (1873, 233–36). But to Hart, they were literary enough to earn a place in the history of early nineteenth-century American literature, which again speaks directly to what, at the time, was a much broader understanding of exactly what at mid-century constituted American literature.

The arrangement of the fourteen-chapter section on English literature was different from that of the section on American literature. Like so many of the classroom manuals and literary histories that preceded it, Hart's short course in English literature was arranged primarily biographically, that is, by prominent authors presented as representatives of various period divisions in English literary history. The course breakdown, as it did for the American section, indicates how Hart conceived the study of English literary history in the 1870s. Chapters 1 through 4 are brief, covering the period from Layamon's *Brut* to the later fifteenth and early sixteenth centuries and the works of Thomas More, John Skelton, Bishop Hugh Latimer, and Sir Thomas Wyatt and Henry Howard Surrey. The chapters include brief biographical sketches with some occasional criticism on "the plan of a work," its "influence," or its form. Chapters 1, 2, and 4, in particular, include discussions of a rather conventional list of medieval authors, e.g., Geoffrey Chaucer, John Gower, Sir John Mandeville, et al. All of Chapter 3, however, addresses the Scottish influence on Hart's conception of early English literary history, for it is given over totally to a discussion of "Early Scotch Poets" who lived and wrote in the fifteenth century. The chapter includes sketches with some critical commentary on the writings of John Barbour, Andrew Wyntoun, James I, Robert Henryson, William Dunbar, Gawin Douglas, and Sir David Lindsay. Hart observed that "from the time of Chaucer . . . the succession of minstrels and poets seems to have been limited to the northern part of the island, nearly all the poetical writers of any note in this period being Scotchmen" (1873, 28). Significantly, Hart addressed the intrinsically Scottish character of the works produced by these authors, including the works of Robert Henryson, the Scottish poet remembered mainly as Chaucer's imitator.

With the sole exception of Chapter 6, which was an accounting of the various English versions of the Bible, all of the chapters from 5 to 14 were given titles that cited the representative figure or figures who, for Hart, epitomized the essential literary contribution of the age and against which other writers from the time were measured. Always, the rationale for literary greatness in Hart's eyes was the degree of public attention and popular appeal the author had originally generated and continued to generate, even in the United States, as late as the 1870s. For Chapter 5 (1550–1625), the representative figures are Edmund Spenser, William Shakespeare, and Sir Francis Bacon; for Chapter 7 (1625–1675), the figure is John Milton; for Chapter 8 (1675–1700), John Dryden; for Chapter 9 (1700–1740), Alexander Pope; for Chapter 10 (1740–1780), Dr. Samuel Johnson; for Chapter 11 (1780–1800), William Cowper; for Chapter 12 (1800–1830), Sir Walter Scott; for Chapter 13 (1830–1850), William Wordsworth; and for Chapter 14 (1850–1873), Alfred, Lord Tennyson. Hart's choices, in most cases, were conventional and, for the 1870s, very much in line with how English literary history from a major authors' perspective is still conceived.

The exceptions are Cowper, Scott, and Wordsworth. They represented the time from 1780 to 1850 for Hart, suggesting the not too surprising conclusion that he based his choice of the three on his perception of their continuing popularity into the nineteenth century rather than on their influence as accountable shaping forces on a still developing literary canon which was probably too close to Hart in time for an accurate assessment. His overestimation of the representative role of Cowper at the end of the eighteenth century is particularly telling. He claimed that no English writer appeared during the 1780-to-1800 period who was his "equal in originality and power." Cowper, Hart added, "created a new era in English poetry," attributable mainly to a popular following that was "far more firmly established, far more deeply set, than Pope had ever attained." Pope was "the poet of the wits." Cowper's fame, however, rested on his role as "the poet of the race" (1873, 120).

For the period from 1800 to 1830, Hart deemed Scott more representative than Lord Byron because the poet's negative popularity had convinced Hart that Byron's reputation in England and the United States by the 1870s was suffering "the neglect" toward which he was "surely gravitating" (1873, 140). Percy Bysshe Shelley was passed over because he was too much like Byron. Hart gave John Keats two sentences; one acknowledged his promise and his premature death and the other listed his principal poems as "Endymion," "Hyperion," and the "Eve of St. Agnes" (1873, 141). The now forgotten Henry Kirke White, favorite of Robert Southey, also a poet who died prematurely, earned a full paragraph. Samuel Taylor Coleridge, Hart noted, was "endowed by nature with genius" but "the fitful and irregular character of his mental action prevented his accomplishing any great and completed work commensurate with his acknowledged genius" (1873, 144). Again, the argument from popularity at mid-century carried the day for Hart. In 1870, according to Hart, Scott best represented the years from 1800 to 1830 because no other author "filled so large a space in the public mind" (1873, 138). "Scotland's greatest poet," Hart could claim as late as 1870, was also the age's "greatest novelist" (1873, 149).

Wordsworth was Hart's representative author for the period from 1830 to 1850, the years immediately preceding Wordsworth's death. Although he acknowledged that Wordsworth was actually contemporary with Coleridge and Southey, nevertheless, he chose him for the 1830-to-1850 period because Hart believed that Wordsworth's star rose at mid-century. Coleridge's and Southey's did not. The argument, as in the case of Scott, was again to public popularity as a measure of greatness. "From 1840 to 1850," he wrote, Wordsworth "was by general consent the first of living poets in England" (1873, 161). Hart attributed Wordsworth's popularity to a poetic style that had awakened "a love for the lowly both in nature and in man" and had, consequently, "given a healthier tone to popular sentiment." He linked Wordsworth with Charles Dickens. Through Wordsworth's exaltation of the lowly, Hart contended, he "prepared the public for the folk-sketches of the great novelist" (1873, 163). The observation is fascinating, especially when one considers that for most contemporary critics and literary historians Wordsworth's later poetic efforts pale by comparison with his earlier work. Obviously, critical consensus on Wordsworth's major contribution to English literature was based on a considerably different measure of greatness in the later years of the nineteenth century.

Hart's *Short Course* also accorded ample space and attention to Scotland's Enlightenment philosophers and rhetoricians, suggesting that he had no difficulty including both Scottish moral philosophy and rhetoric in his scheme for the teaching of English. He adjudged Dugald Stewart "the leading metaphysical writer" in early nineteenth-century Britain (1873, 154). Hart recognized the role of Thomas Reid as Stewart's teacher and as the founder of "a new school of metaphysics" that had combatted the "errors of Hume and Berkeley and other advocates of the Ideal Theory." In the United States, Hart added, Reid's philosophical principles constituted a large share "of the commonly received doctrines" of the time (1873, 130). He recommended Adam Smith as "the ablest writer of the age on political economy" (1873, 128–29). He also cited Dugald Stewart's observation that Lord Kames's *Elements of Criticism* was a "literary wonder" and recommended it to his students as the standard work for the study of the link between metaphysics and the fine arts (1873, 107). Hart also included a section on Francis Hutcheson, calling him the "founder of the modern Scottish school of philosophy" and the original promoter of the doctrine of the "existence of an innate moral sense" (1873, 98). Hugh Blair's *Lectures on Rhetoric and Belles Lettres* was also cited for its continuing popularity as a basic school text, both in England and in the United States (1873, 131).

Keep in mind that Hart's recognition of the value of the Scottish moral sense philosophers to the age was included in the book he designated as *A*

Short Course in Literature. Vanderbilt notes that Hart's "manuals" provide a fairly accurate idea of how he thought American literature should be taught (1986, 86). The same insight applies as well to his publications on the teaching of English literature. Vanderbilt also notes that, from 1873 to 1874, Hart's course in American literature was required of the seniors at the College of New Jersey for all three terms. It was one of seven required literature classes at the time (1986, 86).

Samuel Lorenzo Knapp

Samuel Lorenzo Knapp was another nineteenth-century American textbook author and critic who played a notable role in the early promotion of English literary study in the United States. Knapp, from Massachusetts, was a well-published self-styled historian whose specialty was biography. He published a biography of Lafayette in 1824, *A Memoir of the Life of Daniel Webster* in 1831, and a *Life of Aaron Burr* in 1835. The year before, in 1834, he had published a truly pioneering work titled *Female Biography; Containing Notices of Distinguished Women in Different Nations and Ages,* about which I will have more to say below. In 1821, he had published a similar book on men titled *Biographical Sketches of Eminent Lawyers, Statesmen, and Men of Letters,* which included brief biographies with some commentary mainly on prominent New England lawyers, most of whom have long since been forgotten. Among the few "men of letters" he included, Cotton Mather was dismissed as an affected "pedantic" who was "an incorrigible lover of conceits and puns," yet whose style had been greatly imitated for more than half a century (1821, 139). Writing about Mather later in his *Lectures on American Literature,* Knapp again took him to task for his rhetorical flourishes but acknowledged the eclectic nature of Mather's "mighty mind" and the persuasive power of his writing style (1829, 60–62). Knapp's object in publishing *Biographical Sketches,* it seems, was to provide some insight into the "manners, habits and institutions of New England" by highlighting the lives of prominent authors and lawyers (1821, 5). He argued that U.S. history in particular lacked informative sectional histories, and his sketches of New England lawyers and men of letters provided a step toward remedying the problem (1821, 8). A promised second volume appears never to have been published. The book did have some reference value. Moses Coit Tyler, in his *History of American Literature, 1607–1765,* first published in 1878, cited it twice, once while assessing the career of Francis Knapp, the New England imitator of Pope, and again in a section on Joseph Green, the popular eighteenth-century Bostonian wit (1949, 296, 302).

Knapp's 1834 anthology of *Female Biography* was very much ahead of its time both in acknowledging the value of famous women in history and in satisfying an obvious market demand among American women in particular for books about women. The anthology provided sketches of the lives of 172 prominent women in world history, beginning with Hannah Adams, "a name identified with American literature" (1834, 2), and ending with Mary Washington, George Washington's mother. Of the 172 women included, thirty-one were English. Most of them had literary connections. He included a section on Jane Austen, which attests to her American popularity as early as 1834. Austen "composed . . . novels," he noted, "which for ease, nature, and a complete knowledge of the features which distinguish the domesticity of the English country gentry, are very highly estimated" (1834, 44). He also included biographical sketches of Anna Letitia Barbauld, the eighteenth-century poet who, according to Knapp, taught William Taylor how to write in English. She was an abolitionist who also, in 1810, edited one of the earliest collections of British novelists. Knapp claimed that "she was acquainted with almost all the female writers of her time" (1834, 93). Knapp also included a sketch of Fanny Burney, who was herself, he noted, "almost an Evilina" (1834, 202). There were sections on Queen Elizabeth and Lady Jane Grey. Sarah Fielding, the little known sister of Henry Fielding, who wrote romances, was also included. Knapp dubbed her a woman of literary taste. He also included a sketch of Cicilia Fleron, Thomas More's daughter, whose claim to fame, according to Knapp, depended primarily on her friendship and correspondence with Erasmus.

Among Scottish women, he included St. Hilda, princess of Scotland; Esther Inglis, the Scottish calligrapher; and Margaret Lambrun, a Scot in the service of Mary, Queen of Scots, who, to avenge Mary's death, attempted to murder Queen Elizabeth. Of Mary herself, Knapp concluded that if her circumstances had been different she likely would "have taken the veil" (Knapp 1834, 314). Of Lady Mary Wortley Montague, Knapp observed that both England and the United States were indebted to her "for the weeping willows, which hang their pensive boughs over the hallowed graves of the dead." A basket which she sent Alexander Pope from Constantinople contained a sprig of the Asiatic willow. Pope planted it in his garden at Twickenham, and from it, Knapp whimsically conjectured, "came all the weeping willows in England and America" (1834, 310). He also included fourteen pages on Hannah More, a sketch, he contended, that contained "more facts than any other" existing at the time (1834, 351). He included sketches of Katherine Phillips "Orinda," a seventeenth-century English poet and translator, and of Mary Sidney, Countess of Pembroke, sister of Sir Philip Sidney. Mrs. Ann Radcliffe earned twenty-five pages with lengthy critical commentary on her novels. Of Radcliffe, he mused poetically, "how many nights have we been under the influence of this enchantress, the dagger stained with blood, the dying groan, the pale light, the hoarse voice of the raven, croaking upon the battlement, have all come up to us as the bell tolled one, and the stars shot wildly from their spheres by the potent magic of her pages" (1834, 406). Among other notable Englishwomen represented in Knapp's anthology were Elizabeth Rowe, a poet, and Margaret Roper, eldest daughter of Sir Thomas More.

Knapp intended *Female Biography,* as he noted in the introduction, as a corrective for the "many wrong opinions" entertained at the time "in regard to the treatment and influence of women" throughout history. Knapp also made a plea for women's rights and the improvement of education for women in his introduction (1834, iii). Knapp's was not the only early anthology intended for women. John Seely Hart's anthology of *Female Prose Writers of America,* as noted, was published in 1852; and Rufus Wilmot Griswold, another early American anthologist who played an important role in the promotion of literary study in the United States, and about whom I will say more below, published a work titled *Gems from American Female Poets* in 1844 and in 1848, a 487-page anthology of *The Female Poets of America.* There was also, as noted, Thomas Buchanan Read's popular book on *Female Poets of America* that also appeared in 1848.

Writing about the expanding American market for books on women, Knapp observed in his introduction that he had intended *Female Biography* "to be attractive to young ladies in . . . schools and at home." Because much of the "general reading of the present time among females, as well as others," he added, "has been novels," which, properly chosen, may "do much good," nevertheless, he suggested, "they should be mixed with history and other studies" (1834, x).

Knapp's conception of the literary canon, both British and American, was broad-ranging for the time. He found a place in his canon not only for women but also, like John Seely Hart, for authors who were producing works that were not generally considered belles lettres. His *Lectures on American Literature with Remarks on Some Passage of American History,* published initially in 1827, with later editions appearing regularly throughout the century, was a testament to the value he attached to good writing of all kinds—"moral, literary, or scientific." As he noted at the end of his introduction to *Female Biography,* "being well versed in geography, biography, and history, all things seem to come into one vast panorama." Education, he noted, "whether moral, literary, or scientific," had the ability to throw "a charm over every hour of life" and entered into all phases of our lives with considerations of life's "duties, pleasures, and hopes, from the cradle to the grave" (1834, xii).

Knapp's *Lectures on American Literature* was one of the earliest attempts to deal critically and historically with the subject of an indigenous American literature. Vanderbilt devotes an incisive lengthy section to the *Lectures* and concludes that Knapp did, indeed, [as the *Cambridge History of American Literature* editors claimed in 1917] "throw a floodlight on America's colonial writing" (1986, 29). The *Lectures* included fifteen "lectures" set off as chapters. Lecture 1 surveyed the history of English as a language. Lectures 2 through 7 advanced Knapp's pioneering concept of a generic American literature that closely paralleled the progress of American history from the time of the pilgrims to the Revolutionary War. Lectures 6 and 7 in particular were thoughtful accounts of the importance of the oratorical tradition in the history of American letters before and during the war. They included descriptions of prominent orators along with observations on the role that political pronouncements such as Washington's speeches and the various congressional debates and publications, considered as American literature, played on the outcome of the war. Lecture 8 surveyed the writings and careers of prominent early American physicians and clergymen who were also prominent and successful authors. Knapp wrote: "Among the literati of our country . . . may be numbered many eminent physicians, who were not only useful in their profession, but distinguished for a spirit of inquiry and a knowledge of letters" (1829, 118).

He had in mind works such as the treatises on smallpox and measles by Thomas Thatcher of Massachusetts and a later treatise on smallpox by Dr. William Douglass, the Scottish-born Boston physician who wrote in opposition to inoculation for smallpox and in 1736 published a major work describing scarlet fever (1829, 119). The fact that Knapp included medical treatises in his account of American literature seems odd, but, like John Seely Hart, who also included scientific, theological, and political tracts in his assessment of American literature, Knapp's interest in medical writing spoke directly to the broadly inclusive nature of what he thought American literature was all about as early as the 1820s. Near the end of Lecture 8, he cited Thomas Thatcher's *Biography of American Physicians,* calling it an important and "valuable addition" to the study of American biography, which again seems idiosyncratic, but does makes some sense in the context of an historical or archival study of the early eighteenth-century popularity of biography as a legitimate literary genre (1829, 133).

Lecture 9 was headed "A General Description of Poetry and Its Uses" and included a "succinct view" of English poetry from the twelfth century to Shakespeare, followed by an account of exclusively American poets who wrote after the time of Shakespeare. Knapp's point was that "a fair view of American poetry" required some knowledge of the British "springs from whence it flowed" (1829, 139). Lecture 10 was on the state of American poetry at the outbreak of the American revolution and included the full text of an anonymous "addition" to Thomas Gray's famous "Elegy in a Country Churchyard." As Knapp explained, the author of the "addition" thought "that Gray had not given the subjects of his muse enough of a religious character to make the charm complete" (1829, 184). Lecture 10 also acknowledged the importance of contemporary British models—especially Southey, Scott, Byron, Coleridge, George Crabbe, Thomas Moore, Thomas Campbell, and Robert Montgomery, the highly popular religious poet lionized by the press—on the progress of poetry in the United States during Knapp's lifetime (1829, 186).

In spite of Knapp's effort in Lecture 12 to provide another section on the importance of the oratorical tradition in the progress of American literature, including sketches of prominent American orators contemporary with him and of opportunities afforded in the United States for learning the art of disputation, Lectures 11 through 15 carried the book's focus far afield from any logical accounting of actual literary accomplishments. Lecture 11, for instance, was about American painters, engravers, and sculptors. Lecture 12 was mainly about language variety but with a concentration on "Indian history" and its "passion for eloquence" and what Knapp deemed the "maternal" as opposed to the "patriarchal" nature of language learning.[3] Lecture 13 was on the American military character ("which gave a hardihood to the people") and surveyed American military commitments from the French and Indian War to the Revolutionary War (1829, 227). Lecture 14 was an extended biographical sketch of George Washington. Lecture 15 examined the "naval character of our country."

Like his anthology on *Female Biography,* Knapp's *Lectures on American Literature* was intended to be used as a textbook. Knapp acknowledged in the preface that he published it as a handy single volume, in spite of the broad nature of the subject, specifically so it might "find its way into some of our schools, and be of service in giving our children a wish to pursue the subject of our literary history" (1829, 4). Aside from being the first organized history of American literature as well as, more specifically, the first history of colonial American writing, the *Lectures* was a testament to Knapp's unflagging patriotism, his commitment to Jacksonian democracy, and his faith in the promise of a dignified and respectable future for American letters.

In 1825, he began the publication of *The Boston Monthly Magazine,* a creditable but short-lived journal that was out of print by late 1826. The journal contained short reviews of recent publications, memoirs of eminent persons, brief articles on advancements in science and medicine, historical and travel articles, and notices of new publications. It also provided some foreign news, some poetry, and general notes on music.

In 1832, Knapp published *Advice in the Pursuits of Literature: Containing Historical, Biographical, and Critical Remarks,* which is geared more to the concerns of this study than any of his earlier publications. His objective in *Advice in the Pursuits of Literature,* as explained in the preface, was to provide an outline of English literature for interested Americans. It was, consequently, one of the earliest efforts—if not *the* earliest—by an American to promote the benefits of a formal historical and critical study in the

---

3. On the "maternal" nature of language learning, Knapp observed, "The seeds of eloquence are sown while on the maternal bosom, and are developed with the first powers of utterance. . . . All property that comes down to us from our ancestors receives the name of patrimony, as coming from our fathers. . . , except our language, the most noble of all things we inherit, and this is called our *mother tongue*—a just and beautiful compliment to maternal instruction. It goes to say, that the elements of our language are acquired before the father's care begins" (1829, 218).

United States of the many distinguishable periods, genres, and styles of English literature.

Knapp believed that English literature was a legacy that every American, by birth, had a right to study and use. He also envisioned English literature as an intellectual source, a bright light, pointing a direction that eventually could stimulate public interest, as a companion study, in the promotion of American literature.

> This literature of England must be forever ours. No non-intercourses or wars, can long keep the intellectual rays of that nation from us. This settled, we must respect our own literature to bring out the genius of the American people. This should not be done by a tariff on English literature, but by bounties on our own. There is mind enough and a good disposition every where seen among us for the high pursuits of learning, but our authors must shine only as scattered and flickering lights along our shores, unless these fires are cherished and new ones kindled up by the breath of public patronage. (1832, 167)

The time had come, he urged, "when no one can be ignorant, and still respectable" (1832, ix). Hence, his book was intended to "point out some of the most valuable authors" in the history of English literature, whose works, he thought, American readers "may safely peruse." He also intended *Pursuits* as an anthology of poems and extracts from poems and dramas that would introduce American readers in the 1830s to "some . . . passages in the progress of human knowledge with which it [was] necessary to be familiar, in order to give one a reputable standing" in the community (1832, ix). His arrangement was primarily historical, based on his interpretation of how specific eras in English literary history were best defined. He recommended that his readers use *Pursuits* to launch a circular study of the discipline. He advised, first, reading "the writers of Queen Anne's reign, . . .Young, Addison, Swift, Pope, Parnell, Akenside, Chesterfield, [et al.]" and from there to go back to "the earliest ages . . . and come down to the present day, enlarging the circle of reading until it embraces the best portions of English literature." But in order "to form the sweep and compass of knowledge," he reiterated, readers should begin with the reign of Queen Anne (1702–1714), the period he deemed the "age of taste and pure English" (1832, x).

Knapp's *Pursuits* was intended for study both in school and at home. As one of the earliest historical surveys of English literature published in

North America, it adds to our understanding of how the English literary canon was perceived in the United States in the late eighteenth and early nineteenth centuries. Some of Knapp's assessments of the timeless importance of English authors and works continue to ring true; this especially applies to authors who by the nineteenth century had achieved fame by historical consensus. Chaucer, Spenser, and Shakespeare, for instance, he placed at the center of the English literary tradition. Milton, surprisingly, was omitted, but the inclusion of other known major figures in his survey comes as no surprise. On some authors, however, particularly those who were his contemporaries, Knapp was predictably less accurate. His assessment of those late-eighteenth- and early-nineteenth-century authors who are now largely forgotten provides us with interesting insight into their solid, though fleeting, success.

Pursuits is divided into nine chapters. Chapters 1 through 6 were on English literature exclusively. Chapters 7 through 9 surveyed classical literature from ancient Greece (Chapter 7) to the Roman Empire (Chapter 8) to the fall of Rome and the emergence of European exploration up to the time of the earliest settlers in the American colonies (Chapter 9). All of the chapters included the full text or abstracts of selected representative works that Knapp wanted his readers to read. Chapters 7 and 8, along with examples of classical writing, also included excerpts from Milton used to help explain classical history. Chapter 9 included a brief section on the "spread of literature and philosophy" and a section on "reflections upon the settlement of America."

In Chapter 1, after briefly surveying the history of English as a language up to the Norman Conquest, he traced developments in the language from 1135, the time of Layamon, to 1300, the time of Robert de Brunne. Next he surveyed what he considered to be the "subjects" of romances of the fourteenth century: e.g., King Arthur, Richard Coeur de Lion, Amadis de Gaul (1832, 15). Lacking primary texts, he acknowledged the generic importance of "modern" treatments of the romance tradition in the hands of Samuel Johnson *(Rasselas)*, William Godwin *(St. Leon, Caleb Williams)*, and Sir Walter Scott. A lengthy section on Chaucer followed (1832, 17–20), after which he took up, in short order, John Gower, Thomas Occleve, John Lydgate, and John Kay (he referred to Kay, who lived during the reign of Edward IV, as "the first poet laureate," yet he acknowledged that, though he had read that Kay was the first laureate, "there is not a vestige left" of his poetry!). He cited, in passing, representative authors from the reign of Henry VIII: e.g., Alexander Barclay, John Skelton, and Henry Howard, Earl of Surrey (he acknowledged Surrey as the father of blank verse and the translator of Virgil but said nothing about his relationship with Sir Thomas Wyatt and his role in the generic history of the sonnet). He next went back in time and surveyed prominent prose writers beginning with travel writers: Sir John Mandeville (more of his tales "are believed at this day, than they were then!") and Ralph [Ranulf] Higden (in 1482 Caxton printed John Trevisa's translation of Higden's Latin *Polychronicon*, a history of the world to the fourteenth century). A brief account of the prose writings of John Wycliffe followed (Knapp dubbed him "the founder of the Protestant religion"). He also commented on the prose works of Bishop Reginald Pecock ("a learned writer of his age") and Sir John Fortescue (chief justice under Henry VI) (1832, 22–26).

A section on William Caxton, the invention of printing, and Caxton's *Chronicles of England* followed. He cited Thomas More as "the first literary character of his time, not only in England, but in Europe" (1832, 28). He also included a section on Thomas Wilson, the author of *The Art of Rhetoric* (1553). He called Wilson one of the sturdiest "advocates of English literature," and he suggested that the *Art of Rhetoric* had provided "the first system of criticism in our language." Wilson "read nature and the poets," Knapp added, with a "true spirit" of literary criticism" (1832, 29). Knapp also cited the work of the now forgotten William Fullward, the author of "Enemy of Idleness, teaching the manner and style how to endite and write all sorts of epistles and letters" (1832, 30). Of Mary, Queen of Scots, and her reign, Knapp had little to say, concluding only that "it may be said of her reign, that every sun rose and set in blood."

Chapter 2 surveyed the Elizabethan age. He listed the "characteristic traits" of Spenser's *Fairy Queen* as imagery, feeling, and melody of versification. He included extracts from Spenser's poetry. Richard Hooker's *Ecclesiastical Polity*, he observed, was being read by most students in divinity at the time; but, like Bishop Joseph Butler's *Analogy of Religion*, it was also "found in the hands of . . . young physicians and lawyers, as they [marked] out the great outlines of their professional course. In such works there is matter and forms of reasoning which every professional man should be master of" (1832, 43). On Shakespeare, he wrote, "he understood human nature, and he wisely wrote for two purposes, in some sort to please those of his own times, and to secure all those who should come after him" (1832, 47). He called Bacon "the greatest reformer the world ever knew"

(55). He noted that Robert Burton's *Anatomy of Melancholy* was currently available in an American edition, and, being "now much read," it amply repaid "the modern reader for his pains" (1832, 56). A lengthy section on Milton followed with an excerpt from *Comus* printed at the end of the chapter.

Chapter 3 surveyed the age of Milton, the seventeenth century. Knapp included a lengthy critical section on Dryden whom he acknowledged as a great but currently neglected writer in America:

> There are passages in the works of Dryden that will be quoted for ages, but as a whole it must be confessed that he is not now so much read, as he was by those who preceded us, and for good reasons. He wrought up events, political events, and party circumstances, into sarcastic wit and cutting irony, that sunk deeply then; but which circumstances and events are out of date now. So it must always happen to those who build their fame on local or transitory matters. (1832, 67)

He assessed Dryden's "Ode on St. Cecilia's Day" in some detail, citing excerpts from the poem to make the point that Dryden's ode was less religious than Pope's on the same subject. He deemed Pope's ode "superior in devotion, and more direct to the subject." He included a brief seventeen-line selection from Pope's ode (1832, 69). He added, in a telling statement on his estimate of the utility of secondary works in literary study, that some "ready" though "curious" criticism was to be found in Edmond Malone's life of Dryden (1832, 70). The chapter concluded with the printed text of Isaac Watts's ("a name dear to every pious mind in this country") "The Indian Philosopher" (1832, 80–83).

Chapter 4 surveyed the years from 1700 to 1760. "The tone of English literature at this period," he wrote, "can be traced in no small degree to a few fashionable writers," particularly Lord George Lyttelton and the Earl of Chesterfield (1832, 83). He observed that Laurence Sterne "was an author once much read" in the United States, but that because his moral tone was questionable, he never "awakened any true piety in the enamoured reader" (1832, 87). Knapp added that many contemporary critics and authors thought that Sterne pilfered material from Burton's *Anatomy of Melancholy*. Knapp disagreed, however, arguing that Sterne imitated Burton's style here and there but that imitation was not synonymous with plagiarism (1832, 88).

He included the text of an excerpt from Mark Akenside's *Pleasures of the*

Imagination. Although Akenside had failed to get Dr. Johnson's endorsement, his reputation, according to Knapp, unlike Dryden's, was solid in the United States in 1832. Knapp approvingly dubbed him "the great moralist" (1832, 88). Knapp also included the full text of William Shenstone's "Jemmy Dawson. A Ballad," after observing that Shenstone continued to be read by Americans who loved simplicity and nature (1832, 90). He also included the text of William Collins's "To Fear" and predicted that his odes on the passions would be "preserved as long as the language" existed. He cited them as the first recognizable odes "in the entire range of English poetry" (1832, 94). He also printed the full text of Thomas Gray's "To Adversity," noting that Gray's "Elegy in a Country Churchyard" remained a favorite of all classes of contemporary American readers (1832, 96). He included a section from Oliver Goldsmith's *Deserted Village.* Goldsmith, Knapp concluded, "sought the pulsations of the heart, as they beat in friendship and affection" (1832, 100). He called Edmund Burke a scholar whose "pen was superior to his eloquence." His works abound "with a great variety of matter, and are presently as familiar" to Americans "as to his own countrymen" (1832, 104). Knapp discussed the works of Thomas and Joseph Warton; he called them "scholars by profession." Thomas Warton's *History of English Poetry,* although uncompleted, Knapp labeled "a labor of great magnitude." He recognized Thomas's popularity as professor of poetry at Cambridge, saying, "his lectures were much attended and were considered both sound and brilliant." Joseph Warton, Knapp concluded, was also a genius but given more to theological pursuits. He ended the chapter with the full texts of Thomas Warton's "The Suicide" and Joseph Warton's "To Superstition" (1832, 113–19).

Chapter 5 surveyed the years from 1764, the date of Johnson's founding of the Literary Club, to 1800. "From the best days of the literary club," Knapp observed, to 1800, "there was thought to have been a great dearth of English poetry" (1832, 119). Knapp disagreed, and to set the record straight, he cited the works of William Cowper and, interestingly, the now forgotten Sir William Jones as literary giants of the time. Cowper was important, Knapp observed, because he preached morality in his verse (1832, 119). Jones he called "confessedly the most accomplished man of his age. He was a mathematician, poet, lawyer, linguist, and in all branches was superior to most men." Knapp called him "the first orientalist of his age." As a jurist, Jones administered justice to millions in India and to that purpose translated the laws of India. He made the Western world acquainted with the Veda and Indian mythology, and he translated oriental poetry into English. In tribute, Knapp included a lengthy selection from Jones's translation of *Solima: An Arabian Eclogue* (1832, 122–27).

Next, and with noticeably less enthusiasm, he turned to the Lake poets. Knapp identified them as the "new race of poets" who had emerged in England around the time of the French Revolution (1832, 127). These gifted writers, he concluded, "were dissatisfied with things as they were, and were determined to adhere to no ancient rules. They considered mankind as going on in error, and were engaged by bonds of sympathy to revive the world. . . . Southey . . . was at their head. . . . They contemplated migrating to the western world and there forming a literary society on the banks of the Ohio. Coleridge was of this society" (1832, 128). Knapp's opinion was that generally most of the authors, even the prosaists, associated with the Lake school were mentally deranged. Godwin, in particular, he thought, "was as wild in his *Political Justice* as any rhymer of them all, and his followers were numerous. Southey . . . moderated his feelings at first, and then changed them, and after a few years reformed them altogether. In this delirium, however, Southey wrote some of his best poems" (1832, 128).

The English poets of the period that Knapp lionized were Samuel Rogers, Oliver Goldsmith, and Thomas Campbell. Rogers, he cited as "well educated, and well disciplined." Goldsmith had been his model. Knapp judged Rogers's "Pleasures of Memory" one of the most "finished compositions" in English (1832, 129). He included no examples of the works of Southey or Coleridge, but he did include the full text of Rogers's "Verses Written to Be Spoken by Mrs. Siddons" (1832, 129). He praised Campbell highly, acknowledging his lectures on poetry which, he noted, were in print in the United States at the time and available to his readers. He called them "learned and smooth" with "striking passages" (1832, 132). Campbell's "Pleasures of Hope," he deemed "a splendid poem"; an example of poetry that was "philosophical and plain . . . full of imagination." Of Campbell's *Gertrude of Wyoming*, Knapp observed that it was "a sad tale told with tenderness as well as genius," and was preferred by some American readers to "Pleasures of Hope." Knapp was particularly taken with Campbell's patriotic war songs. "Ye Mariners of England," he thought, would live as long as there was "a timber left of the British navy" (1832, 132, 133). He printed all of Campbell's "Hohenlinden" at the end of the chapter.

Chapter 6 surveyed Knapp's "modern" period, his present, 1800–1832.

George Crabbe was "now an old man," he observed, but his works remained admirable and novel. "Crabbe probed deep," he added. "His works are yet to be more known and admired than they have yet been, for in time the poor will read them, which is not the case now" (1832, 137). Knapp included the full text of Crabbe's "Phoebe Dawson."

Poetry, Knapp concluded, was not the only genre that made up the best of "modern" literature. Histories have now entered "into the motives of men in power, and look . . . to the springs of human action." Instead of being mere describers of events, he added, modern historians were researchers, drawing on "philosophy and criticism to assist in their labors." They exhibited "a most interesting variety of matter for lessons of study and reflection." David Hume, he continued,

> had been the ne plus ultra of historical power, but the investigations of his successors have left him in the rear; and they have gone on to more accurate relations and sounder reasonings upon human actions. Lingard [John Lingard, author of an eight-volume *History of England* (1811)] with profound research and patient investigation has removed many of the stumbling blocks in English history. . . . The best history I have ever seen of England (and *her* history is the most important to us of any other except our own, though the history of the two countries be intimately connected) is that of Sharon Turner. . . . There is a spirit of research an elegance and an eloquence in it, not surpassed by any one who has ever attempted the great work of English history. (1832, 142–43)

Knapp also cited Sir James Mackintosh's *History of England* (1830–31), histories written by William Godwin and Charles James Fox, and George Croly's history of George IV (a "most interesting production of modern times") (1832, 143–44). Of Thomas Moore as a biographer, Knapp noted that "it is to be regretted that he should ever have written the lives of Sheridan and Byron." The two biographies, Knapp concluded, can do no good, for "the exposure of the follies of these extraordinary men neither deter the rising generation from vice nor enlighten the minds of those who are out of danger from such examples" (1832, 145). As a poet, however, Moore was in his prime, Knapp noted. Knapp included the full text of Moore's "Go Where Glory Waits Thee."

Next, Knapp took up the work of William L. Bowles, a minor sonneteer and editor, who influenced Coleridge and exchanged barbs with Byron and Campbell over the value of Pope's poetry. Bowles, Knapp judged, enjoyed "a respectable rank in the republic of letters, but is now probably more known for his controversy with Campbell and Byron" (1832, 147). Surprisingly, Knapp included the full text of Bowles's sonnet "To Time." He also singled out the poetry of Henry Hart Milman (professor of poetry at Oxford from 1821 to 1831. He was also a historian; in 1830, he published *History of the Jews*; in 1854 he published his most famous work, *The History of Latin Christianity*). Knapp approved of Milman and his work because he was "a sound believer, a good moralist." Knapp hoped that Milman would soon be as popular among American readers as Byron and Moore. He included Milman's heavily moralistic "Ode, to the Saviour." On Byron, Knapp wrote "it has not yet gone from our ears that the great poet is dead" (Byron died in 1824). He added, "It is well to know enough of his character as a poet to find the best portions of his works, and of history not to dwell on it. His course from the dawn of reason was wayward. His vices commenced early and lasted as long as he lived. He . . . offended every religious creed . . . and was selfish in his feelings" (148). Knapp predicted that when the excitement over Byron had ended, "the world . . . will select many parts of his works, and bind them up together for posterity." Byron's moral failing Knapp blamed on "want of parental example and domestic instruction" (1832, 151). In spite of his reservations, Knapp printed the full text of Byron's elegy from 1812, "And Thou Art Dead, as Young and Fair."

On Shelley, he concluded that his name "excites unpleasant feelings," and he "was a being to be pitied." He never accepted God—never acknowledged that "the Most High reigneth among men." He was a tortured man, but his poetry was powerful and revealed an obscurity that heightened its sublimity (1832, 155). Like the Lake poets generally, Knapp concluded, Shelley was mad. At the end of the Shelley section, he included only Shelley's dedication "To Mary" taken from "The Revolt of Islam."

Although Knapp had reservations about Shelley, he had high praise for the now obscure Thomas James Mathias, whose *Pursuits of Literature, or, What You Will: a Satirical Poem in Dialogue* (1794) satirized contemporary writers, specifically, much to Knapp's satisfaction, the Lake poets. Given the similarities in titles, Knapp obviously envisioned his *Advice in the Pursuits of Literature* as something of a sequel to Mathias's earlier work, minus the heavy satire. The bibliographical record indicates that Mathias's *Pursuits* remained popular right up to the 1830s. It was a best seller, going to sixteen editions before going out of print. Not surprisingly, Knapp devoted an entire section of his book to Mathias's work (considerably more than he gave Byron or Shelley); and he quoted lines from George Canning's poem, "New Morality," in which Canning, a British politician who became premier in 1827, praised Mathias as:

> the nameless bard,—whose honest zeal
> For law, for morals, for the public weal,
> Pours down impetuous on thy country's foes
> The stream of verse, and many languaged prose.
>   (1832, 161)

Knapp admired Mathias for his satires on "the wild and unprincipled writers of that period." Mathias also promoted the doctrine, which Knapp endorsed, "that on literature, well or ill conducted, depends the fate of a nation" (1832, 160). Knapp noted approvingly that the Lake poets "received a serious castigation" from Mathias. Yet Knapp conjectured that Mathias may have sacrificed energy attempting to crush every stinging gnat of literature and might have better concentrated his efforts solely on the real "monsters of mischief" (1832, 162).

Of fiction, Knapp noted that it was "now the rage in the republic of letters." He provided a short history of fiction. The first English novel, "as it is now understood," he surmised, was Sir Thomas More's *Utopia*. For Knapp, the novel was a work of fiction that provided "an exhibition of action or passion, and incident, such as belongs to nature, and is a dark, or bright or beautiful picture of human life." He added that, although the novel had no discernible prototype, "still all must be after nature." The value of the novel was compounded, he thought, addressing the eighteenth-century penchant for fictionally chronicling history, by blending into its narrative "public or private history, with . . . remarks put into the mouths of those who did, or did not exist; or by giving to ideal characters the air, manner, and words of real ones." The distinction helps to explain his rationale for calling More's *Utopia* the first English novel. Although he disapproved of Godwin's *Political Justice,* he found his novels admirable. Among the novelists contemporary with him, Knapp singled out Mrs. Radcliffe because "her imagination was of a high order" and she chronicled a feeling for Italian history, "always full of romance and taste," into her novels. He thought that Maria Edgeworth had no superior in terms of "just and powerful exhibitions of human life." Her work was full of "instruction," which he approved highly, and was "well calculated to teach all classes their duties." Sir Walter Scott, Knapp observed, had "the influence of genius." His readers also were "improved" by his works. Yet, Knapp thought, Scott had published too much, too fast: "His works have come too rapidly for the reader who had many avocations" and they have come with "less finish" than they should have (1832, 163–66).

Knapp concluded this final chapter on the history of English literature with a following prophetic observation:

> There is a great mass of English literature now extant, which contains immense stores of thought, and which, if read judiciously, would make a very learned man. It is every day increasing, and it will soon require large books of indexes and references for one to get fairly at it; in fact, they are numerous now. Much time is often wasted for want of proper guides in our studies. We not only should have finger-posts and mile-stones, but maps and directories constantly with us, whenever we go out to increase our knowledge, or for amusement. (166)

Outlining the major topics of Knapp's course of study produces what amounts to a hypothetical syllabus for a course in English literature as it might have been offered in 1832 (for an outline of Knapp's course see the appendix). At a glance, it also provides a sense of how English literary study and, subsequently, the English literary canon were conceived in the United States in 1832. The outline shows clearly that he recommended the study of more than just belles lettres. Of particular interest are his units, however brief, on the value of reading histories and works categorized as "oratory," attesting to his awareness of the significance of the oratorical tradition that was shaping, as I have argued in the preceding chapters, the study of English and American letters in the United States in the early years of the nineteenth century. Also of some historical importance is the space he allotted to obscure authors such as Sir William Jones, Thomas James Mathias, William L. Bowles, and Henry Milman. Mostly unknown or forgotten now, they received as much or more attention than Byron, Shelley, or Southey. Coleridge was only mentioned in passing, and the Lake poets generally were given short shrift, most of it critical.

As the course model also makes clear, Knapp was a moralist through and through. Like the Scottish moral sense philosophers, but with a heavy-handed catalog of specific authors and titles in mind, he argued the case that English literary study was a way to promote character and virtue. The majority of the poems he included in his text, as a glance at the titles will indicate, were heavily didactic or overtly moral in tone. Only the purest and best of models were offered for his readers to study and emulate. The fate of the heroine in Crabbe's "Phoebe Dawson" and the messages at the center of Thomas Moore's "Go Where Glory Waits Thee" and Milman's "Ode, to the Saviour" make the point.

William Ellery Channing

In 1830, two years before the publication of Knapp's *Advice in the Pursuits of Literature,* William Ellery Channing published an essay titled "Remarks on National Literature." The essay was written as a review of Charles J. Ingersoll's *A Discourse Concerning the Influence of America on the Mind,* a lecture which had been delivered before the American Philosophical Society at the University of Philadelphia in 1823 and was made available in print the same year. Ingersoll was a vocal utilitarian, who argued that Oxford and Cambridge, unresponsive to the "spirit of the times," were dated and unprogressive, and that American education, by contrast, was "better adapted to enlarge and strengthen the mind, and prepare it for practical usefulness" (1823, 8). In the field of imaginary literature written in English, however, Ingersoll thought the United States was deficient and unlikely to "contribute in any comparative proportion to the great British stock of literature," which, he added, almost "supercedes the necessity of American subscriptions," given that the American mind was generally linked more to "political, scientific, and mechanical" pursuits.

He concluded that, because the standard of American belletristic literature was "below that of England, France, Germany and perhaps Italy," if American writing were to have any national merit at all, it was in fields such as history, biography, science, research, philology, geography, oratory, and moral philosophy (1823, 14–16). On oratory, in particular, he argued that the United States demonstrated more talent than Britain. Finding "an eloquent professor or lecturer" of oratory in England was "very rare," he thought. In contrast, in the United States, it was generally understood that even the medical school of Philadelphia owed its success, "in part, to the . . . eloquence of its lecturers." He cited that specific example as but one small instance of the importance Americans attached to oratory (1823, 34). In addition, the American press had created a business climate by the 1820s that made the publication of books in the United States less expensive and more affordable than in Britain. For evidence, Ingersoll cited the popularity and sales among Americans in the 1820s of the Scottish authors Dugald Stewart and Sir Walter Scott. More than 7,500 copies of Stewart's *Philosophy of the Human Mind* had been published in the United States since its first appearance in print in 1792, he noted. And nearly two hundred thousand copies of Scott's Waverley novels, comprising five hundred thousand volumes, had issued from American presses within the previous nine years alone. Basing his assumptions on the records of more than two hundred itinerant wagons traversing the United States selling books, Ingersoll conjectured that, of all the many types of literature available to Americans, biographies, particularly biographies of prominent Americans, rather than belletristic works, were the books most often purchased.

His point was that belletristic American publications were less popular than belletristic British publications and, hence, much less marketable than American publications that dealt with more pragmatic American subjects. The argument, of course, logically questioned the value of promoting an indigenous American literature that had at its core mainly belletristic selections. If Americans wanted to read about their country, he was suggesting, they should turn to histories, biographies, and scientific writings and leave imaginary literature to European authors.

William Ellery Channing was incensed by Ingersoll's conclusions and responded to them in the essay, "Remarks on National Literature." Channing also was at the forefront of American writers and scholars in the early years of the nineteenth century who were actively promoting the need for an indigenous American literature. He believed that the subject was important to the future of the country, and, like the Scottish moralists, he promoted the argument that literary pursuits and literary study had "intimate connections with morals and religion, as well as with other public interests" (1899, 124). Unlike Ingersoll, Channing believed that a national literature should express "a nation's mind." Like Hart and Knapp, he interpreted the label *literature* broadly to include writing on all subjects directed at "the improvement of human nature" (1899, 125) rather than simply selected subjects that, as Ingersoll had argued, addressed "political, scientific, and mechanical" concerns.

Literature, Channing suggested, again echoing the Scots, was "plainly among the most powerful methods of exalting the character of a nation" in order to form "a better race of men" (1899, 126). Understanding that the influence of literature was increasing mainly through the efforts of the press and through "the spread of education" was an important consideration. Consequently, he argued, Americans must "attach special importance to those branches of literature which relate to human nature, and which give it a consciousness of its own powers." History was important, because it revealed human beings "in their strength and weakness, in their progress and relapses," but poetry was equally useful and important because it had the capacity to touch "deep springs in the human soul" and to create "beautiful forms of manifestations for great moral truths" (1899, 129). And it was on the subjects of morals and human nature, he continued, "that the mind especially strengthens itself by elaborate composition; and these . . . form the staple of the highest literature." "Moral truth," he concluded, "under which we include every thing relating to mind and character, is of a refined and subtile, as well as elevated nature" (1899, 132). And, he asked, to what impulse in particular should we look for a higher literature? The answer was to be found in what he referred to as "the religious principle" (1899, 136).

For Channing, a Unitarian, the "religious principle" was not what one might expect. He meant by it a code of belief that "higher literature" could address with more facility than literature devoted to current topical concerns or, as Ingersoll had argued, to the progressive "new spirit" that was abroad in the land (1899, 9). Channing thought that the study of "higher literature" had as its main objective moral development, spiritual enhancement, and the overall improvement of conduct. The problem with the American literary scene in the 1830s, Channing surmised, was that the reading of belles lettres was in fact "confined too much to English books." In this, we err, he conjectured, because he believed that England and, it would follow, English literature were both wanting in philosophy (1899, 137). Channing therefore urged American writers and educators to look beyond belletristic English literature for a philosophical direction that would benefit the United States, American readers, and American literature in general. His plea was for the value of cultivating a national literature that was in fact humanistically and philosophically centered.

His argument did not extend to any explicit endorsement of the Scottish moral philosophers as guides, but his acknowledgment of a lack of philosophical substance in the direction that American literature had taken up to the 1830s implicitly helps to explain why so many other American authors and educators at the time were embracing Scottish moral philosophy. For, if for no other reason, the Scottish Enlightenment philosophers provided the only descriptive contemporary philosophical basis readily available in

English for a nation that claimed English as its native tongue. I take John Seely Hart's and Samuel Lorenzo Knapp's anthologies as representative of a conviction, right or wrong, but peculiarly American, that English literature at the time had no visible or satisfying philosophy at its center. The conclusion one must draw from examining those texts, as suggested above, was that Kantian idealism, Coleridgean metaphysics, and British romantic philosophy in general had little impact on American criticism and American assessments of what constituted a British literary canon in the early decades of the nineteenth century. In fact, as both Hart and Knapp made clear in their anthologies, which were designed primarily for the American market, Coleridge, the Lake poets, and what we now understand as the romantic movement in general were seen by many influential American literati as little more than cultural aberrations.

Rufus Wilmot Griswold

In 1898, Rufus Wilmot Griswold, another early nineteenth-century American anthologist and editor, observed, in an edition of his correspondence and personal papers, that in 1831, at the ripe age of fifteen, he had commenced reading the works of the romantic poets and prosaists and, subsequently, was not greatly impressed. It was also in 1831, he noted, that he had met twenty-year-old George G. Foster, an upstate New York poet and journalist, known later in the East as "Gaslight" Foster owing to his book on *New-York by Gas-Light.* Foster also authored *New York in Slices* and *New-York Naked,* and he co-edited a variety of successful gossip journals before he was sent to jail for forgery in 1853. Together in 1831, according to Griswold's account, he and Foster pursued an organized course of reading "in romantic and poetical literature." This was Griswold's introduction to English and American literary giants. "All the masters of literary art who had written in the English language contributed to our entertainment and were subjected to our critical discussions," he noted. But he added that, though he and Foster "had warm controversies" about Pope and Goldsmith, he continued to prefer the more classical eighteenth-century authors to what he called in 1898 "the romantic and passionate school" of English authors (1898, 7–8). On Shelley, in particular, Griswold observed in his 1845 publication of *Poets and Poetry of England in the Nineteenth Century* that "the claims of Shelley" were only then beginning "to attract a share of the attention" that had been given mainly in the early years of the century to Byron and Wordsworth (1845a, 6).

Griswold was regarded during the first half of the nineteenth century as a foremost advocate of "Americanism" in literature. In 1842, he published an anthology of *Poets and Poetry of America*. In 1843, he published a school text titled *Readings in American Poetry*. In 1847, he published *Prose Writers of America* and in 1848, *The Female Poets of America*. He is best known today for his role as Poe's literary executor and for his malicious "memoir" of Poe that was included in the 1850 edition of Poe's *Works*. Griswold, by all accounts, was not trustworthy, but he adopted the posture of a strident Christian moralist. He claimed to have been a licensed Baptist minister and to have studied theology, although where he acquired the credentials remains uncertain. He was also a staunch and vocal advocate of the need for an infusion of "moral purity" in American letters (Vanderbilt 1986, 50). Significantly, for this study, along with his important anthologies of American authors, he published full-length editions of the poetry of Thomas Campbell and Sir Walter Scott. He also edited the *Poetical Works of James Montgomery. With a Memoir of the Author,* about whom he wrote in his edition of *Poets and Poetry of England in the Nineteenth Century* that the now forgotten Montgomery, born in Scotland in 1771, was "the most popular of the religious poets who have written in England since the time of Cowper" (1845a, 73). Griswold also included selections from the poetry of James Hogg, the "Ettrick Shepherd," in *Poets and Poetry of England,* citing Southey's adulatory observation that Hogg was "altogether an extraordinary being, a character such as will not appear twice in five centuries" (1845a, 81).

There is no concrete evidence that Scottish authors and, in particular, the Scottish moralists influenced Griswold's conception of what he thought literary study could accomplish in the United States, but he appears to have been at heart a "closet" Anglophile. Joy Bayless, Griswold's biographer, notes that "as the years passed [he] retained his belief that America could produce an original literature, but he lost his conviction that it should be distinctly American" (1943, 93). It comes as no surprise that his desire to connect literature and morality and his conviction that prose worth anthologizing was morally instructive and socially responsible had distinctly British roots (Miller 1955, 195). Perry Miller observes of *Prose Writers of America* that, given the moral of Griswold's "Survey of the History, Condition, and Prospects of American Literature," which served as a preface to the anthology, he was opposed to the idea (one promoted by his editorial rivals, Evert and George Duyckinck) that the American genius would "break through the barriers of propriety and decorum." Griswold, in contrast, promoted the idea that "genius must cease to strain after originality" and must instead seek its truth "under the inspiration of an enlightened love of country, and the *guidance of a high cultivation*" (emphasis mine, Miller 1955, 195–96). One wonders where the source of the concept of "high cultivation" originated; with Griswold, true to his erratic character, the location remains uncertain.

James Robert Boyd

Contemporary with Griswold in the 1840s was another colorful American educator named James Robert Boyd whose Scottish connections were obvious and deep. Boyd, a Presbyterian clergyman who graduated from Union College in 1822 and subsequently studied theology at the College of New Jersey, published numerous popular textbooks that were used in schools, academies, and colleges throughout North America from approximately 1844 to the 1880s.

Boyd was an upstate New Yorker who held the Chair of Moral Philosophy and Belles-Lettres at Hamilton College from 1849 to 1850 (*Appleton's* 1887, 1: 340). He published what were called "school editions," and, hence, they figured prominently in what young Americans were learning about literary history during the middle years of the nineteenth century. Boyd's Scottish connections began very early in his career when, after completing his theological studies at the College of New Jersey, he traveled to Edinburgh. While in Edinburgh in 1832, he attended the lectures of Dr. Thomas Chalmers, who held the Chair of Moral Philosophy at St. Andrews University for a time in the 1820s and was later, in 1828, appointed professor of divinity at the University of Edinburgh. Chalmers, like Adam Smith, sought to apply ethical principles to economic issues. Chalmers, as mentioned in Chapter 2, also was an acknowledged philosophical source for Francis Wayland, the president of Brown University from 1827 to 1855. Not surprisingly, Boyd cited Wayland as the primary source behind his own work on moral philosophy. Boyd, at some point, had been one of Wayland's students. Wayland, in 1864, would publish a *Memoir of the Christian Labors . . . of Thomas Chalmers.* The link between Wayland and Chalmers was significant, because Wayland was a source for Boyd's vision of the value of moral philosophy in the education of youth and, ultimately, in the role of literary study in that education.

Boyd's most important and direct contribution to the history of English studies in the United States was a textbook he published in 1844, his first major publication, the full title of which is, *Elements of Rhetoric and Literary Criticism, with Copious Practical Exercises and Examples for the Use of Common Schools and Academies, Including, also, a Succinct History of the English Language, and of British and American Literature from the Earliest to the Present Times. On the Basis of . . . Recent Works by Alexander Reid and Robert Connel.* The book, a significant contribution to the growing American textbook market, went through eighteen reprints and eight editions from 1844 to 1876. As Boyd acknowledged in the first edition, the text was based on his reading of critical works by Alexander Reid and Robert Connel, both of whom were Scots. Reid's *Rudiments of English Composition,* a school text, was published in 1839; his *Rudiments of English Grammar* was published in 1837. He also produced a *Dictionary of English Language, . . . Pronunciation, Etymology and Explanation of All Words Authorized by Eminent Writers* in 1844. Reid, who published numerous "school books" between 1833 and 1846, was educated at Edinburgh University and was for a time the headmaster of the Edinburgh Institution. Robert Connel remains a mystery. He is referred to as "Robert Connel of Edinburgh" in the *Catalogue of the British Library* and the *National Union Catalog.* Other than that, I have been unable to find any information on him. Connel did publish *A Catechism of English Composition with a Succinct History of the English Language and Its Literature* in 1831 in Edinburgh with a second edition appearing in 1839. In 1834, in Glasgow, he published a work titled *Improved System of English Grammar . . . Adapted to Use of Schools.* It was his *Catechism of English Composition* that Boyd used in drafting *Elements of Rhetoric and Literary Criticism.* He cited Connel on the value of studying English: "If to compose well be an object of importance, no less so is a knowledge of the history and the character of the English language and literature" (Boyd 1844, xii). Boyd's textbook was designed to be used to teach both composition and literature in the schools.

Boyd acknowledged his debts to other sources, particularly "Beattie's Rhetoric, Blair's Rhetoric, Dr. Spring's Lectures, Dr. George B. Cheever's [the trinitarian] Lectures, and . . . other similar productions." He also acknowledged the use of Robert Chambers's 1836 *History of English Lan-*

guage and Literature (Boyd 1844, xii). Chambers, of course, was a Scot. He and his brother William were prominent Edinburgh-based publishers who would publish, among other notable books, the famous 1843–44 two-volume edition of Chambers's *Cyclopaedia of English Literature; Consisting of a Series of Specimens of British Writers in Prose and Verse*. The text was published simultaneously by Lippincott in Philadelphia in 1843, appealing to a growing market for British literature that was developing in the United States at the time. Chambers's *Cyclopaedia* continued throughout the century as a supplemental classroom guide for students of English literature in American schools and universities.

Boyd's *Elements of Rhetoric and Literary Criticism* was well received when it first appeared in 1844. The *Jeffersonian* for November 26, 1844, recommended that the book "should be in the hands of every student and every man who writes for the press or for public speaking" (Boyd 1844, 6). In the preface, Boyd observed that his intention in producing the book in the first place was to present in a convenient method the best, meaning "the most useful," portions of the "works of Blair, Whately, Beattie, Campbell, and Watts," and also to supplement the selections with practical exercises, selections from representative British and American poets, and a history of the English language and literature (1844, iv).

Part 1 dealt with spelling, punctuation, diction, structure, and the arrangement of sentences; Part 2 with matters of style and the use of figurative language; Part 3, "Of the Different Kinds of Composition," included selections of letters and essays, but also selections excerpted from novels, blank verse, pastoral poetry, lyric poetry, epic poetry, dramatic poetry, and the sonnet. The term *novel*, Boyd argued, was understood at the time in its widest sense to include allegories, fables, as well as other "stories of all kinds" (1844, 142). He added that the form was believed to have originated in Asia. And on the critical difference between a *novel* and a *romance*, he borrowed terms used to explain the difference between the comic realistic tradition and sentimental or sensationalist fiction that emanated from the eighteenth century. He wrote: "A novel is a fictitious work, either founded upon the events of real life, or at least bearing some resemblance to them: while a romance was a work of a similar kind, having something wild and unnatural in it; and, if not purely imaginary, resting upon some extravagant tradition, and extending far beyond the limits of probability." Like Samuel Lorenzo Knapp, who made a claim for More's *Utopia* as the first novel in English, Boyd also traced novel writing back to the Elizabethan period, adding that its popularity had gradually increased until "now more novels issue from the press than works of almost any other description" (1844, 142–43).

Novels in the United States in the 1840s, however, were a subject of controversy, according to Boyd, with some critics extolling them as "the best teachers of morals," although others condemned them as "corrupters of principle, and . . . contaminators of the mind." He warned his readers that too great a love of novels tended to "distract the mind" and was an obstacle to "the pursuit of useful knowledge" (1844, 143). Among the greatest English novelists, he cited Daniel Defoe, Jonathan Swift, Oliver Goldsmith, Samuel Richardson, Henry Fielding, Tobias Smollett, Sir Walter Scott, and Maria Edgeworth. Curiously, he also included among the "greatest" an unknown novelist called Miss Porter (i.e., Jane Porter, 1776–1850), who authored a now forgotten historical novel titled *Thaddeus of Warsaw* in 1803 and, more to the purpose of this study, an historical novel, very popular at the time, called *The Scottish Chiefs*. Published in 1810, it was based on the historical events of the life of William Wallace, the legendary Scottish rebel. Boyd also included the name of a Mrs. Ellis in the "greatest" list, about whom I have found nothing except the titles of her novels. In his final judgment on novels, Boyd ranked some as "remarkable for the high moral tone that pervades them" and others as "infidel and licentious . . . ephemeral novels"; the latter, he added, were read "by that very class of persons who have no moral strength to resist their vicious influence" (1844, 144).

Part 4 of Boyd's *Elements of Rhetoric and Literary Criticism* covered types of essays—narrative, descriptive, etc.; Part 5 was a "History of the English Language"; Part 6, "Modern British Literature," was divided into sections on "English Literature under the Tudors and the First Stuarts," "English Literature from the Restoration to the Reign of George III," "English Literature of the Present Age," "English Novels and Romances," "The English Periodical Press," and "English Philosophers and Critics of the Present Century." There was also a section on "Criticisms and Specimens" of the works of British poets in Part 6, which included selections from Shakespeare, Milton, Samuel Butler, Edward Young, Pope, Gray, James Beattie, James Thomson, Cowper, Goldsmith, Crabbe, Samuel Rogers, Thomas Campbell, Mark Akenside, Coleridge, Southey, Byron, Wordsworth, Burns, Scott, and Thomas Moore. It also included Samuel Johnson's critical essay on

Milton and selections from such lost and forgotten writers as Mrs. F. D. Hemans, Henry Kirke White, and Robert Pollok.

In a particularly relevant section in Part 6, titled "Philosophers and Critics of the Present Century," Boyd included an excerpt from the *North American Review,* 1835, that cited Dugald Stewart as "by far the most distinguished of the English (British) philosophers who have lived since Adam Smith" (1844, 204). Stewart's popularity in North America as a moral philosopher was at its peak in the early years of the nineteenth century. Charles Ingersoll, as noted, had observed in 1823 in *A Discourse Concerning the Influence of America on the Mind* that more than 7,500 copies of Stewart's *Philosophy of the Human Mind* had been published in the United States since its original appearance in 1792 (1823, 18). The *NAR* article noted that though Stewart struck "out no new paths," he had pursued with patience "the track of the masters whom he venerated" (1844, 204). The idealistic Coleridge, in contrast, Boyd suggested, possessed very slender claims to philosophical distinction. He praised Coleridge's intelligence, his "great deal of reading," and his poetic talents. But he was critical of Coleridge's style, his "almost total want of clearness and precision of thought." Boyd suggested that a person curious about the distinctions between "reason" and "understanding" would learn more from the first ten pages of Kant's *Critique of Pure Reason* than from all of Coleridge's attempts to explain the concepts, "in which the English language breaks down with him at every step" (1844, 205). Then who in Boyd's estimation was the best living philosophical voice in Britain in the 1840s? Who else but Thomas Carlyle, the Scottish sage, who was, according to Boyd, "the most profound and original of the living English philosophical writers" (1844, 205–6).

Part 7 was devoted to American literature, beginning with a section titled "Poets of Our Revolutionary Period," followed by a lengthy series of sections on rather curiously paired American poets. For example, James K. Paulding was paired with John Pierpont; Richard H. Dana with James A. Hillhouse; Charles Sprague with Charles Wilcox; William Cullen Bryant with Fitz-Greene Halleck; Nathaniel Parker Willis with Mrs. L. H. Sigourney; Hannah F. Gould Lucretia with Margaret Davidson and James G. Percival; and J. G. C. Brainard with Henry Wadsworth Longfellow. Separate sections were included on John Greenleaf Whittier, A. B. Street, and the political orator E. W. B. Canning. There was also a sketch of American literature since 1815 and a section on "The Present State of American Literature and Its Relation to That of England," which was taken from the July 1844 *Democratic Review.* The article lauded American authors—Washington Irving, Richard Henry Dana, Nathaniel Parker Willis, and Nathaniel Hawthorne, in particular—who were said to be "without an equal in English contemporary literature." The article also claimed that "the best popular moralists of the day," the best contemporary examples of oratorical literature, and the most promising examples of "periodical literature" were American (1844, 303–4). Part 8 included a selection of critical essays on a variety of subjects, including a "Critical Examination of the Style of Addison," "Critical Notes upon a Portion of Paradise Lost," and "Defects of Dr. Johnson's Style of Writing."

In 1846, Boyd published a work titled *Eclectic Moral Philosophy, Prepared for Literary Institutions.* On the title page he cited Thomas Reid, the founder of the eighteenth-century Scottish school of metaphysics. The epigraph from Reid gracing the page observed that "moral conduct is the business of every man; and therefore the knowledge of it ought to be within the reach of all." Reid was not the only Scottish thinker represented in Boyd's *Moral Philosophy.* He also acknowledged his debt to Dugald Stewart's *Philosophy,* James Beattie's *Moral Science,* and Thomas Chalmers's *Natural Theology* and *Moral Philosophy.* Adam Smith's *Theory of Moral Sentiments* was also cited. Hugh Blair was represented, as well as Timothy Dwight, the Yale president whose lasting debt to Scotland was discussed in Chapter 2.

Because Boyd contended that William Paley's popular treatise on ethics, his *Moral Philosophy,* was "defective . . . pernicious," loaded with error, and generally "of little interest or practical utility" (1846, iii) and that Francis Wayland's book on ethics, his *Moral Science,* though excellent as a source, was not designed to attend to the needs of the "great mass" of American "instructors and students" in need of extended delineations of moral duties (1846, iv), he had decided to publish his own textbook on moral philosophy to meet the needs of that wider audience of American students. Because Boyd, essentially, functioned more as a compiler than an original author in all of his publications, this one being no different, he acknowledged that he intended to produce a text that combined, in a "connected form," what were *"the best thoughts of not a few of the most gifted moral writers of the present century"* (1846, v). His text, drawing handily on Adam Smith's *Lectures* and on other works by eighteenth-century Scottish rhetoricians, was designed to assist in the formation, "after the purest rules, [of] the character and conduct of the young" (1846, vi).

Boyd's concern for the formation of character led him to conclude, reminiscent of Scottish commonsense educators, that the study of character should be the preeminent objective of American education. In a section of *Eclectic Moral Philosophy* titled the "Moral Lesson of Biography," he observed, after a fashion that recalls, particularly, Adam Smith's *Lectures,* that the study of biography was an invaluable source in the classroom instruction of moral duties. "The biography of those who have carefully studied, and most exactly conformed to, the various delineations of duty furnished in the sacred scriptures, supplies a very pleasing and instructive means of learning how to feel and act under the varied circumstances, and in the various professions of human life" (1846, 407). He suggested that literary biography and the history of literature overlap in tracing the rise of Western civilization from the time of the Protestant Reformation.

> The Reformation in the time of Luther gave birth and prominence to many illustrious examples of the Christian and human virtues; and, from that period to this . . . providence has been greatly multiplying their number, so that in our own day biographical literature is sufficiently extensive to constitute, of itself, a respectable and a most valuable library—valuable, as furnishing one of the most agreeable, practical, and impressive modes by which a knowledge of human duty may be learned to advantage. (1846, 408)

He added that the prominent object of biographical literature, "when properly written," was to teach "men, women, and children, their duty in the various relations and circumstance of life, *by example*—most persuasive of all methods of instruction" (1846, 409).

Boyd's commitment to English studies reflected much more than just an interest in using literature to teach rhetoric. His Scottish connection was deeply rooted, including not only his admiration for Chalmers, Beattie, Stewart, and the use of Reid's and Connel's texts, but also an edition of Lord Kames's *Elements of Criticism* that he published in 1855 and a textbook in 1856 titled *Elements of Logic* based on William Barron's lectures at St. Andrews University. Both books were designed to be marketed as textbooks.

The impact of Kames's *Elements of Criticism* on education in the United States in the early years of the century was acknowledged by Boyd, who noted in the 1855 edition the volume's revered position, in particular, "in the colleges and academies of our own land." No other work, Boyd added, had appeared to date "to supply its place, nor, without great disadvantage to the cause of education, can it be laid aside" (Home 1855, 3). Boyd's typical (precopyright) publishing technique was to take an already published text and to add whatever he thought would improve it. Hence, using Kames's *Elements* as a base text, Boyd expanded it, as he put it, "for the improvement of the work" in order that "its usefulness may be increased" (Home 1855, 4). He freely added bits and pieces of literary selections from other authors and omitted some material that he deemed of "no utility, or objectionable on account of its indelicacy" (1855, 4). He also provided analytical notes at the bottoms of the pages, with paragraph designations, as a gloss on Kames's observations and recommendations.

The full title of Boyd's edition of Barron's *Elements of Logic,* published in 1856, the year after the appearance of his edition of Kames's *Elements of Criticism,* was *Elements of Logic: On the Basis of Lectures by William Barron . . . Professor of Belles-Lettres and Logic in the University of St. Andrews, with Large Supplementary Additions, Chiefly from Watts, Abercrombie, Brown, Whately, Mills, and Thomson.* As the long title indicates, Boyd used the same technique in publishing Barron's *Elements of Logic* as he did in publishing Kames's *Elements of Criticism.* Barron's text formed the foundation; Boyd added material from other sources in an effort to "improve" its usefulness. As he explained it, he supplemented Barron on logic principally "on points where, for practical utility, a more full discussion of the subject was needed; and also to introduce various important topics upon which Professor Barron had neglected to offer observations" (1856, 3). To his mind, he had produced a better, because more useful, text than the original.

On Barron's merits, Boyd observed that "the method of treating the general subject" which Barron had pursued "seems to be philosophical, and well adapted to secure all the most valuable ends of Logic, in a large and popular sense of that term." Barron concluded his lectures, Boyd added, with self-revealing statements of his own thoughts on the value of utility to the democratic or the "common life," "with an exposition of the nature of the Syllogistic Process, and of its great want of utility, for all the legitimate purposes of reasoning in common life" (1856, 7–8). At the end of his "Introductory Observations," Boyd continued his promotion of the value of utility in the "common life" by launching his text "on a mission of *usefulness* among the Academies, Female Seminaries, and Colleges of this Western Hemisphere, with the earnest desire that it may be found eminently serviceable in forwarding the cause of Truth, and in promoting a sound and useful education" (1856, 10). Again, on the subject of the value of a "useful education" to America, he quoted from Barron's "Introduction":

> Some people imagine that Logic is a frivolous, and ostentatious, at best an unnecessary art, which may serve to puzzle and perplex, but can be of little utility in business or philosophy . . . [yet] there is nothing in [the study of logic] either so uninteresting, so dry, or so difficult . . . which every person must surmount, who expects to acquire, either in philosophy, literature, or business as much use of his understanding as to attend to any train of thought. It is by the proper use of his understanding that man attains his eminent characteristic of being rational. It is by the proper use of his understanding that he can make any progress in knowledge. (1856, 14)

From Lecture 1, Boyd quoted Barron as saying, "The object of education is to increase knowledge, to refine imagination, to improve taste, and to prepare us for acting a part in life, respectable and useful in itself, as well as advantageous and honorable to the public" (1856, 15).

In 1860, Boyd published *Elements of English Composition, Grammatical, Rhetorical, Logical, and Practical,* which, as the subtitle indicated, was "Prepared for Academies and Schools." In 1860, he also published a *Memoir of the Life, Character, and Writings of Philip Doddridge, D.D., With a Selection from His Correspondence.* Boyd also provided colleges and academies in the early decades of the century with affordable classroom editions of Milton, Young, Thomson, and Cowper. His motives for promoting literary study were always heavily didactic and moralistic. A clergyman, he was essentially a student of moral philosophy. Eighteenth-century rationalism, which continued to dominate the study of the humanities in American schools and colleges during the 1830s and 1840s, formed the foundation of his thought. Adam Smith and the eighteenth-century Scottish Enlightenment philosophers were his primary influences, as he acknowledged in his edition of *Elements of Logic* based on Barron's lectures. He noted that, in contrast to the Anglican Archbishop Richard Whately and other predominantly English philosophers who endeavored to revive the logic of ancient scripture, the Scottish philosophers—Adam Smith, Thomas Reid, and Dugald Stewart, in particular—had succeeded in altering the course of philosophical thought in a direction away from orthodox metaphysical concerns and toward more progressive practical concerns. Drawing from Stewart's *Account of the Life and Writings of Adam Smith,*

Boyd cited in *Elements of Logic* one of Smith's pupils who said of Smith that while at Glasgow "he soon saw the necessity of departing widely from the plan that had been followed by his predecessors, and of directing the attention of his pupils to studies of a more interesting and useful nature than the logic and metaphysics of the schools." The student emphasized how Smith, after explaining enough ancient logic "to gratify curiosity with respect to an artificial method of reasoning," dedicated the remainder of his time to the study of rhetoric and belles lettres (Boyd 1856, 5–6). Boyd added the observation that a similar view of the artificiality of ancient logic was expressed by Lord Kames in "Progress of Reason" in his claim that Aristotle's "artificial mode of reasoning is no less superficial than intricate" (1856, 6).

For Boyd, the development of English literary study in the United States in the early years of the nineteenth century was at least as much indebted to Scottish moral philosophy as it was to Scottish works on rhetoric. The teaching objective was closely linked to a utilitarian ideal that promoted rationalism, civic humanism, and the moral improvement of the society in the name of economic and social progress. Progress in education was measured, consequently, in terms of the production of a literate and ethical populace capable of promoting ideals and objectives that were directly associated with the marketplace. The implicit influence of Adam Smith's arguments for the shift from a centrally directed government economy to a self-regulating, free enterprise economy was paramount. The debt to Chalmers, Barron *(Essay on the Mechanical Principles of the Plough,* 1774), Stewart, Reid, and other Scottish thinkers was greatest where American teachers in preparatory and secondary schools and professors in colleges, during those early years, went beyond teaching language, grammar, and composition in order to teach literary selections for their thematic, philosophical, and economic value. Boyd argued, for instance, that the study of authors such as Milton or Young "cannot fail to raise the mind above the danger of contaminating and degrading itself with . . . inferior and worthless productions so common at the present day" (1856, 2). Boyd never discounted the importance of grammar and composition. Nevertheless, it remained true, he added, that the great English poets were used extensively in school, and "in almost all instances, it was for no higher purpose than grammatical parsing."

Though he found the study of grammar beneficial, he suggested that "there are much higher purposes to be attained in the proper study of these authors." He suggested that they might be used to attain a full acquaintance with the English language, for one thing. They might also be used to gain an enlarged view of the principles and philosophy of rhetoric as a means for improving literary taste, "a more vigorous fancy, and a more chastened imagination." They might also be used to attain "clearer perceptions of truth and sounder judgments, besides a higher tone of moral and social character" (1856, 2–3). The objectives for English literary study were clearly outlined. His publications, particularly *Elements of Rhetoric and Literary Criticism* and his editions of the poets, were designed particularly to assist in the classroom realization of those objectives.

Thomas B. Shaw

In 1849, Thomas B. Shaw's popular *Outlines of English Literature* was published in London. In 1852, an American edition was published in Philadelphia and included a *Sketch of American Literature* by H. T. Tuckerman. Shaw's *Outlines* was used widely in the United States during the 1850s and 1860s; thirteen editions appeared before it went out in print in 1876. It accommodated, what Rufus Griswold had earlier reported: the growing American market for books of a historical and biographical nature. The book, similar to an encyclopedia, included mainly a list of names, dates, and places that students were supposed to memorize, but it was instrumental in promoting English literary study in the United States in the last half of the nineteenth century.

Shaw had been a professor of English literature in the Imperial Alexander Lyceum of St. Petersburg. While there, he realized that he needed a manual to supplement his lectures because the plan usually adopted in foreign countries of allowing students to copy the lecture notes of the professors was impracticable. He contended that at the time of his St. Petersburg tenure (circa 1847) no such manual that was affordable and that could function as the "framework or skeleton of the course" existed in English. Warton's volumes were too large and only treated poetry to the Elizabethan age. Chambers's two-volume *Cyclopaedia of English Literature* was also too large, and Shaw dismissed the shorter version of the *Cyclopaedia* as "dry and list-like" (1852, iii). His volume was intended to serve "as a useful outline Introduction to English Literature both to the English and the foreign student." The work was not intended as a substitute for a course in English literature. It was primarily an effort to describe the causes or the great revolutions in taste which produced what he called "Schools of Writing." Consequently, he concentrated on the "greater names" in English literature, first as representative "of the religious, social, and intellectual physiognomy of their times"; second, for their individual merits and messages (1852, iv).

Shaw's first chapter dealt, surprisingly, with the heretofore neglected influence of the Celts on the development of English. Chapter 1 also covered the role of Anglo-Saxon and other representative developments in the history of English up to the eighteenth century. The second chapter began the section on literature with "Chaucer and His Times." Chapter 3 concentrated on Sir Philip Sidney and Edmund Spenser as representative writers of the Elizabethan age. Chapter 4 was on Sir Francis Bacon, exclusively. Chapter 5 treated the "Origin of the English Drama." Chapter 6 concentrated on Christopher Marlowe and Shakespeare. Chapter 7 was on other Renaissance dramatists—Ben Jonson, Francis Beaumont, John Fletcher, et al. Chapter 8 surveyed the "Great Divines": Richard Hooker, Jeremy Taylor, and Isaac Barrow, particularly. Chapter 9 covered Milton; Chapter 10 was on Samuel Butler and John Dryden; 11 on Edward Hyde, Lord Clarendon, John Bunyan, and John Locke. Chapter 12 dealt with Alexander Pope and Edward Young; 13, with Jonathan Swift, Joseph Addison, Richard Steele, and Samuel Johnson; 14, with the novel from the romance tradition of Spain, Italy, and France to Daniel Defoe's "air of reality" and the works of Samuel Richardson, Sir Charles Grandison, Henry Fielding, Tobias Smollett, Laurence Sterne, and Oliver Goldsmith. Chapter 15 shifted the focus to the "Great Historians"—David Hume, Edward Gibbon, and William Robertson, author of *History of Scotland during the Reigns of Queen Mary and of James VI* (1759) and a *History of America* (1777); in Chapter 16, titled "The Transition School," Shaw discussed James Thomson, George Crabbe, and Robert Burns. Chapter 17 covered Scott and Southey; 18, Moore, Byron, and Shelley; 19, "The Modern Novelists," included discussions of Horace Walpole, Mrs. Ann Radcliffe, Monk Lewis, Charles Maturin, Mary Shelley, William Harrison Ainsworth, Edward Bulwer-Lytton, Fanny Burney, Maria Edgeworth, William Godwin, Jane Austen, Charles Dickens, Anthony Hope, and Frederick Marryat, among others. Chapter 20 surveyed the tradition of comedy from William Congreve and Richard Sheridan and also the tradition of "Oratory in England," including the works of William Paley, Bishop Joseph Butler,

Sir William Blackstone, and Adam Smith. Chapter 21 was on the "New Poetry" of Wordsworth, Coleridge, Leigh Hunt, Keats, and others, who revealed, he concluded approvingly, in marked contrast to Hart, Knapp, and Griswold, a more "passionate and lyric tone" in their poetry.

On the subject of the value of English oratory, which from the early years of the nineteenth century was a bone of contention among U.S. textbook editors and publishers, in Chapter 20, Shaw observed that "English public speaking, at the bar or in parliament" was "eminently and essentially practical." A British audience, he added, although it listened "with patience to a cogent and practical reasoning, however inelegantly expressed," had no interest in "mere flowery rhetoric or vain general declamation." Nothing was more contradictory to eloquence, "in its highest sense, than the *air* of being eloquent." He suggested that the Greeks understood that principle, "as the English had done"; and there was, consequently, "in the oratory of both nations, a singular resemblance in point of directness, *muscularity* of expression, and practical application" (1852, 407). He cited William Pitt, Charles James Fox, and Sir William Wyndham as particular examples of the best of British parliamentary oratory. He thought Edmund Burke singular as a political theorist but not as an orator (1852, 408). Among theological proponents of British practicality and reason, he cited Paley and Butler. Adam Smith was singled out for his work on political economy; Dugald Stewart was cited as "the most distinguished of modern British metaphysicians" (1852, 410). Metaphysics, he added, had been "more cultivated in Scotland than in England." In fact, he concluded, "the Scottish intellect appears to possess a peculiar tendency and aptitude to this kind of disquisition. In the present age . . . it is Edinburgh which has produced the most distinguished of the metaphysicians of Great Britain" (1852, 411).

Shaw's extended defense of the British oratorical tradition inadvertently may help to explain why American editors in the early nineteenth century found British oratory both less inspirational and less marketable than American oratory. If Shaw was correct in his estimation of the strength of British oratory, it emphasized a concentration on practicalities and, as he put it, a *"muscularity* of expression." American oratory, quite to the contrary, was characterized by a rhetorical effusiveness that was particularly evident in the delivery of political orations and orations that were designated "pulpit eloquence." By 1864, Shaw's section on British oratory in the newly titled *Complete Manual of English Literature*,[4] revised expressly for the American textbook market, was deleted and replaced by a Chapter 18 that contained a survey of "Historical, Moral, Political, and Theological Writers of the Eighteenth Century." Although the revised edition included nothing on British oratory, it continued to provide a *Sketch of American Literature*, written by Henry T. Tuckerman, that included a lengthy section on American oratory. American oratory was praised as a special and original literary genre because it was characterized by a "mental life . . . identical with religious discussion" that traced its history from the time of the colonists. The struggle between the advocates of the various religious sects prominent at the time in the colonies, Tuckerman suggested, "gave birth to a multitude of tracts, sermons, and oral debates which elicited no little acumen, rhetoric, and learning." As a result, every sect had what Tuckerman called "its illustrious interpreters" who first bequeathed and continued to contribute "written memorial of their ability." American clergy, in particular, he added, had always been among the most "prominent laborers" in this "field of useful literature" (Shaw 1867, 480). Hence, a genre that Tuckerman now labeled "ethical literature" was cited as peculiar to American literature, giving "a literary value and interest to pulpit eloquence which soon exercised a marked influence on the literary taste of the community." At the head of the class, he thought, was, not surprisingly, William Ellery Channing (1867, 480).

On the place of oratory in American literary study, he added that, because oratory was "eminently the literature of republics," the fame of American oratory was in part traditionary. The expression of thoughts on

---

4. Shaw's 1849 *Outlines of English Literature* was the prototype for four other, later textbooks that were widely used in American schools throughout the nineteenth century. The first, Shaw's *History of English Literature*, was published in London in 1864. It went to seven editions, the last appearing in 1897. The second, an anthology, was published in 1864 under the title, *The Students' Specimens of English Literature. Choice Specimens of English Literature. Selected from the Chief English Writers, and Arranged Chronologically, with Additions by William Smith*. An 1869 edition "Adapted to the Use of American Students" by Benjamin N. Martin, went to four editions, the last appearing in 1889. The third textbook, Shaw's *Complete Manual of English Literature*, was initially published in London in 1865; it went to twelve editions, the last being published in 1879. The fourth, *Shaw's New History of English Literature. Prepared on the Basis of "Shaw's Manual,"* was published in the United States in 1874 under the authorship of Truman J. Backus; it was in print in the United States as late as 1891.

public interest was a "requisite accomplishment" for every "intelligent and patriotic citizen" and helped to explain why oratory was "a decided feature of American literature" and why so many large and "remarkably creditable" editions of discourses had been published in collected editions in the United States by the 1860s (1867, 486).

In Chapter 2 of his *Sketch of American Literature,* Tuckerman cited the importance of a tradition of criticism in the development of American literature, which he associated directly with the increase in American education in the nineteenth century. He quoted Joseph Buckminster, a prominent Boston Unitarian minister, from an August 1809 Phi Beta Kappa address at Harvard called the "Dangers and Duties of Men of Letters" which was subsequently printed in the *Monthly Magazine.* Buckminster said that "the genius of our literature begins to show symptoms of vigor, and to meditate a bolder flight. . . . The spirit of criticism begins to plume itself, and education, as it assumes a more learned form, will take a higher aim. If we are not misled by our hopes, the dream of ignorance is at least disturbed, and there are signs that the period is approaching, in which it will be said of our own country, *tuus jam* regnat Apollo [Apollo now reigns with you]" (1867, 148).

William Spalding

Another widely used English literary history in nineteenth-century North America was William Spalding's *History of English Literature.* Spalding, a prominent Scot who contributed considerably to the early development of academic literary study in the United States, held the Chair of Rhetoric and Belles Lettres at Edinburgh from 1840 to 1845. He left Edinburgh in 1845 to assume the Chair of Logic, Rhetoric, and Metaphysics at St. Andrews University, a position he held until his death in 1859. His popular and influential *History of English Literature: With an Outline of the Origin and Growth of the English Language* was originally published in Edinburgh in 1853. Strictly a literary history, it was still being used as late as the end of the 1880s in American and Canadian universities (Tilson 1991, 469).

Spalding acknowledged the influence of Chambers's earlier two-volume *Cyclopaedia of English Literature* and George Craik's six-volume *Sketches of the History of Literature and Learning in England* (1844–45) as larger companion histories that had attempted to survey the field in depth (1853,

28). His book, by contrast a single volume and much less detailed, was intended specifically, like Shaw's *Outlines,* for classroom use in schools and academies. Consequently, like Shaw's *Outlines,* it had a more immediate effect on the development of academic literary study in the United States than its more cumbersome predecessors. In the preface, Spalding acknowledged that the book was "offered, as an Elementary Text-Book, to those . . . interested in the instruction of young persons" (1853, 1). He also expressed his desire eventually to see the systematic study of English literature universally in place in programs of study in the liberal arts throughout the English-speaking world. Like the Scottish moral philosophers, he also believed that literary study could assist the promotion of the doctrine of sympathy and the improvement of conduct. He noted that he wanted students "to reflect, how closely the world of letters" was "related . . . to [the] world of reality and action"; how literature originated from "thought . . . emotions, and wishes"; and how, in its effects, it was "one of the highest and most powerful of those influences, that have been appointed to rule and change the social and moral life of man" (1853, 1–2). In Part 1, Chapter 1, he reiterated the idea by observing that literature "in itself" tended "towards moral improvement." And in another observation, reminiscent of Adam Smith's earlier claims for literary study as a complement to character building, he noted that literature was in fact, a "moral power . . . modifying the character of mankind, and aiding in the determination of their position now and hereafter." Knowledge of the importance of literature in the formation of character underscored, he added, the importance of choosing books wisely (1853, 26–28).

In Chapter 12 of Part 3, titled "The Eighteenth Century . . . Literature of the Third Generation, 1760–1800," Spalding identified a generally inclusive category he labeled simply as "Philosophy." Under the category, he identified four classes of writing. He linked the first class of works, "disquisitions on the Theory of Literature or any of its applications," with a theory of literature that he claimed "now began to be known among us by the name of Philosophical Criticism, and which is really a branch of philosophy properly so called" which he labeled "the philosophy of the human mind" (1853, 351). The association between "philosophical criticism" and human development recalls earlier nineteenth-century claims made by Jonathan Maxcy of Rhode Island College and Edward T. Channing of Harvard, which I have discussed in Chapter 2, for philosophical criticism as a combination of moral philosophy, rhetoric, oratory, and literary criticism.

As his representative philosophical critics, Spalding named two Englishmen and four Scots. The Englishmen were Edmund Burke and Sir Joshua Reynolds. Not surprisingly, the Scots were Adam Smith, Lord Kames, Hugh Blair, and George Campbell. Of the Scottish philosopher-critics, he observed that their works were "confined to literature; and, all the writers being Scotsmen, it was perhaps natural that they should occupy themselves much with the laws of style" (1853, 351).

The specific Scottish works cited were Campbell's *Philosophy of Rhetoric,* Lord Kames's *Elements of Criticism,* Blair's *Lectures on Rhetoric and Belles Lettres,* and what he called Adam Smith's very original "contributions" to this field of inquiry (1853, 351). The middle of the eighteenth century, he added, was a particularly important epoch in the development of "Philosophical Writings." During that period, Scottish thinkers appeared "whose opinions . . . were . . . in most departments of philosophical study, entitled to be regarded as new." Many of their works, he added, continued in the mid-nineteenth century to influence contemporary thinking (1853, 350–51).

The second class of works considered under the "philosophical" category, included works on "political economy." Spalding listed Adam Smith's *Wealth of Nations* as the standard work on the study of political economy. Smith was cited again in the third category, which Spalding labeled "ethics or moral philosophy." Here he referred to Smith's *Theory of Moral Sentiments* with special attention to its "leading doctrine," an "ingeniously defended paradox" on "the resolution of all moral feelings into Sympathy" (1853, 352). He also cited Abraham Tucker[5] and William Paley.

The fourth class of works listed under the heading "philosophy" dealt with "metaphysics and psychology." Here, Spalding discussed Thomas Reid, in particular, as the founder of the Scottish school of metaphysics. Spalding concluded that Reid's major contribution to philosophical literature was his antagonism to dominant philosophical theories of the time. Specifically, Reid opposed Locke's sensualistic vision, which, Spalding observed, held "all our ideas to be primarily derived from sensation." Reid

---

5. Abraham Tucker (1705–74) was a follower of David Hartley who believed that ethical convictions were better understood by employing the principle of association. He called it "translation." His major work, *The Light of Nature Pursued,* was published in seven volumes in 1805.

also opposed the idealistic vision of Berkeley, which, according to Spalding, allowed for the existence of mind but denied the existence of matter. Reid also opposed the skeptical vision of Hume, which denied that we can know anything at all. Reid successfully disputed all three, Spalding maintained. Spalding's conclusion was that Reid's original, positive perspective on knowledge and consciousness paralleled the fundamental metaphysical philosophical position of his more famous German contemporary, Kant, leading one to speculate that, in Spalding's eyes, Reid was a force in the development of basic aesthetic theories that contributed directly to the promotion of vernacular literary study in the nineteenth century (1853, 352–53).

Textbooks and the Literary Canon

The theoretical basis upon which nineteenth-century textbooks in English literary study were founded was essentially philosophical. The prosaic and often drill-oriented nature of the texts, as well as the tendency toward the simple cataloging of authors and dates, do not obscure the fact that the authors recognized the primary aesthetic value of the study: the promise of influencing students in terms of levels of appreciation as well as levels of cognitive thinking. Nor do they diminish the importance of the profit to be gained from a ready market for literary texts that was expanding commensurate with the increase in student enrollments throughout the nation.

Spalding, Hart, Knapp, Griswold, Boyd, Shaw, and the many other authors and editors of textbooks on English literature designed for schools and colleges in nineteenth-century North America provided affordable books for use by students who read them, learned from them, and then often abandoned them. As Alistair Tilson points out in an essay on the impact of Spalding's texts in Canada, despite the fact that tens of thousands of his books were printed and studied over the years, very few now survive except in libraries with specialized archival collections (1991, 469–70). The same observation applies to the many other authors and editors of school texts who helped shape the history of literary study in North America into the nineteenth century.

The wide availability of school texts in literary study, however, promoted the idea, one obviously taken to heart by generations of students who studied from those books or, at least, had sections dictated to them that they in turn copied into notes, that English literary study was an organized discipline that had at its basis a canonical body of fundamental works. If the new subject was to be taken seriously, especially in North America, it had to be presented scientifically as a body of knowledge capable of being read, examined, and dissected in order to create the kind of academic challenge that would benefit students. In some respects, the textbooks aided the argument that the close study of vernacular literatures could indeed provide students with the same kind of mental discipline that was traditionally associated with the study of Latin and Greek classics. As the market for textbooks in the study of English and, later, American literature accelerated, so did the popularity of the subject. The ready market perpetuated the demand because most Americans, in particular, found that textbooks on English and American literary study required no particular linguistic expertise to both read and appreciate.

The subject was readily accessible and could satisfy both a natural curiosity about the cultural history of the English-speaking peoples and an aesthetic yearning for the inspirational experience that comes simply from reading quality literature. Although teachers and professors may have found the teaching of aesthetic appreciation less conducive to the everyday drills and assignments designed to challenge the students intellectually, they always could—and regularly did—turn the study of literature, English and American, into object lessons on civic conduct, proper behavior, and moral prescription. Often, the tried-and-true questions, "So what does the work mean to you?" and "What do you get out of it?," resulted in moral lessons ultimately designed to turn out better citizens and, consequently, better people.

The essential pattern upon which the object lessons were built, however, had, as this study has argued, a long history extending well back in time to the days when professors and teachers first decided to combine the study of moral philosophy, most of which emanated from eighteenth-century Scotland, with literary selections written in English. From the late eighteenth century to the middle years of the nineteenth century in North America, the link between moral philosophy and literary study remained solid. By the 1870s, however, the emphasis changed.

The Rise of Philology

At Columbia University, in the 1860s and 1870s, the professor of philosophy and the professor of English literature were one in the same. The professor was Charles Murray Nairne, a Presbyterian minister educated, not surprisingly, in Edinburgh. In 1867, Moses Coit Tyler, an ordained Congregational minister, was named professor of rhetoric and English literature at the University of Michigan. Of his responsibilities as an English professor at Michigan, Tyler observed as late as 1869, "above all other considerations," he wished to carry "into this sphere . . . the whole force of my moral nature. . . . I never could, I never can," he added, "do my best, unless backed up and energized by my moral activities" (Austen 1911, 43). In 1878, Tyler's classic two-volume *History of American Literature, 1607–1765* was published. In 1881, Tyler, by now a specialist in American colonial history, moved to Cornell where he assumed the first professorship of American history in the United States.[6]

In spite of Tyler's claims in 1869 for the moral value of literary study, by the 1870s, the impetus behind English teaching had begun to shift. In the 1870s, graduate education in the United States was instituted, and a new study—comparative philology—imported mainly from Germany, began to make inroads into courses that had previously concentrated on belles lettres. By the 1870s, the Scottish influence on literary study had waned considerably. The shift of emphasis from the study of belles lettres to philology and to the scientific study of English as a language had been anticipated as early as the mid–1850s. Francis James Child, who succeeded Edward Tyrell Channing as Harvard's Boylston Professor of Oratory and Rhetoric in 1851, offered courses on language and literature, including a new course designated simply as "History of the English Language." By the mid–1870s, Child, as Harvard's first official professor of English, was offering regular courses in philology.

Francis March, another noted philologist, installed an experimental program in English at Lafayette College in 1855 that drew heavily on comparative grammar. Lafayette College, as discussed in Chapter 3, was originally founded in 1826 by Scottish Presbyterians. March's Lafayette College professorship in English language and comparative philology was the first of its

6. For additional information on late nineteenth-century appointments in English literature at American colleges, see Graff and Vanderbilt. See also John W. Burgess, *Reminiscences of an American Scholar,* 1934; William Riley Parker, "Where Do English Departments Come From?" *College English* 28, no. 5 (Feb. 1967); Morris Bishop, *A History of Cornell,* 1962; Harold Williamson and Payson S. Wild, *Northwestern University: A History, 1850–1975,* 1976; and Ernest Earnest, *Academic Procession: An Informal History of the American College, 1636–1953,* 1953.

kind in North America. By the 1880s, owing to the efforts of philologists like Child and March and to the development of a program of study at the newly established Johns Hopkins University that favored the scientific study of modern languages, philology reigned in the United States, ironically accelerating interest in the study of selected literary works that raised serious philological issues. Shakespeare's plays, for instance, eminently satisfied the linguistic preoccupations of word-oriented philologists obsessed with the complexities of morphological history. As Applebee observes, "with the sanction of philology," though it seems contradictory, nevertheless, "the teaching of literature spread quickly through the American college and university system" (1974, 27). In fact, as late as 1895, the emphasis at Lafayette College was still on philology.

In 1895, March published an essay titled "English at Lafayette College" in a volume edited by William Morton Payne on the subject of *English in American Universities,* one of the earliest extant publications solely devoted to the history of English studies in the United States. In the essay, March noted that English studies at Lafayette College from mid-century had focused on developing in students a facility with English primarily as a means of communication. The goal was the teaching of word usage rather than morality, conduct, or "literary appreciation" (1895, 75). A number of influential English professors at the time—i.e., William Lyons Phelps at Yale, Bliss Perry at Williams, and Hiram Corson at Cornell—resisted the spread of philology in the universities. They offered as an alternative the benefits of "literary appreciation," but, as Applebee notes, "they lacked an adequate methodology to offer in place of the new-found rigor of philology" (1974, 28). The study of philology appeared to have at its basis a scientific methodology; the study of literary appreciation was reduced to exercises in subjective emotional responses. Literary criticism, as such, was limited mainly to impressionistic ramblings, some colorful, some merely solipsistic, but none that actually dealt in any depth with the literary content itself.

Lafayette's English literature courses, as the century waned, March noted, were increasingly shaped by the belief that "English should be studied like Greek." Hence, a special professorship was eventually instituted that coordinated Greek and Latin courses with ancillary studies in classic English authors such as Chaucer and Shakespeare and were taught "after the same methods as Homer and Demosthenes" (1895, 75–76). The objective was to teach the English classics, in the words of Rugby's Dr.

Thomas Arnold, by dwelling upon Shakespeare and others "line by line and word by word" (1895, 76). Even in 1895, March noted, the English courses were "still constant to this central idea." Three recitation hours a week were conducted in the fashion of Dr. Arnold—worthy literary passages were read line by line and word by word. Given that approach, a full term could be dedicated to a single play of Shakespeare. The lesson plans involved memorizing lines and interpreting the meaning of the words.

Lafayette's English literature program under March concentrated mainly on linguistic interpretation—etymology, vocabulary, definition, metrics, grammar, and sentence parsing—allowing little consideration for any moral or behavioral themes or lessons that the works imparted. The philological emphasis, according to March, was geared to the hope that, as students improved the measure of correctness with which they used the language, they would learn to take pleasure in the challenge of tracing lexical meanings from one author to another. "In this way," he conjectured, students would learn "to rejoice in these noble passages, and remember them forever." A sample research assignment in March's classes called for "an etymological examination of the language of an author, to ascertain what percentage of his words [were] derived from Anglo-Saxon . . . Latin, Greek, and other languages, and to discuss the reason for them" (1895, 77–78). The bulk of required work specifically in English literature at Lafayette by the 1890s concentrated mainly on Anglo-Saxon prosody and grammar. The rationale was that studying Anglo-Saxon provided students with a better understanding and mastery of English as it had been used during and since the time of Chaucer (1895, 81).

In all respects, March taught English philology. Final papers, which called for a general study of some author, were expected to contain extended discussions of the author's "language" (1895, 81). March, in the spirit of the promotion of national culture, which was a central objective of philological studies, advised students preparing for the assignment to choose an author from American literature because the language—American English—was "their own" and his experience indicated that Lafayette's students were "specially drawn" to American writers. The result, he added, was that American periodicals in the library were "worn to tatters, but the English publications, which were the main reading of students of the last generation," were left "in fair covers, looking fresh from the binders" (1895, 81–82). One of his fondest memories, March recalled, was the day in 1877 when William Cullen Bryant publicly presented the senior prize for the best study of his own work to a student named James Wilson Bright. Bright, March proudly added, went on to gain world renown as a professor of English philology at Johns Hopkins University. In 1895, March confidently observed, Bright's torch was "still burning as he runs in the front" (1895, 82). Bright's torch burned ever brighter right into the twentieth century. By 1902, he was the president of the Modern Language Association. Convinced that studying literary content essentially threatened the purity of philology, he would observe in 1903 in a *PMLA* essay titled "Concerning the Unwritten History of the Modern Language Association of America" that "the philological strength and sanity of a nation is the measure of its intellectual and spiritual vitality" (Graff 1987, 114).

The Scottish influence on English literary study in the United States by the 1870s existed only in history. But the impetus for creating the formal study of English literature in the first place was a Scottish, particularly a Scots-Irish, accomplishment. Colonial America went to school on the Scots and, as this study has argued, from the 1740s onward, American schools combined the study of Scottish moral philosophy with courses in rhetoric and oratory, providing the foundation from which English and American literary study emerged. The inception of English and, later, American literary studies, as independent, self-contained academic disciplines, clearly owed much to the Scottish rhetoricians who first introduced literary criticism and vernacular literary selections into their courses of study.

A greater debt, one that actually shaped the pedagogical direction literary study would take as it developed into the nineteenth century, was owed to moral philosophy. Literary study was used principally for something other than just the promotion of taste and the study of the language. It was used "philosophically" and "critically" to promote morality and religion and eventually to improve techniques of persuasive disputation in courses in oratory. The study of literature not only taught students to write well and to dispute; it also contributed, ultimately, to the promotion of a public moral consciousness and to the production of model citizens. As the Virginian George Tucker, who looked admittedly to eighteenth-century Scotland for enlightenment, observed in 1814, "the state of literature in every country depends upon moral causes" (1822, 63). The state of literature and of literary study in the new republic at the time and into the waning years of the nineteenth century bears witness to the historical truth of Tucker's statement.

Appendix

Works Cited

Index

Samuel L. Knapp's 1832 Course in English Literature

The History of the English Language

The History of the Language from Saxon Times to 1066
1135–1180: Layamon
1200–1300: "The Owl and the Nightingale," Robert de Brunne
The 14th Century: The Subjects of the Romance Tradition

The Rise of English Literature to the Elizabethan Age

Chaucer, John Gower, Thomas Occleve, John Lydgate
Reign of Edward IV: John Kay
Reign of Henry VIII: Alexander Barclay, John Skelton, Henry Howard, Earl of
    Surrey
Prose Writers: Sir John Mandeville, Ralph [Ranulf] Higden, John Wycliffe, Regi-
    nald Pecock, Sir John Fortescue, William Caxton, Sir Thomas More, Thomas
    Wilson, William Fullward

The Age of Elizabeth

Edmund Spenser: With Printed Extracts from *Fairy Queen:* "Description of Prince
    Arthur" and "Description of Belphebe"
Michael Drayton: Printed Text of "Description of Lady Geraldine"
Prose Writers: Roger Ascham, John Foxe, Raphael Holinshed, Sir Philip Sidney, Sir
    Walter Raleigh, William Cecil (Lord Burleigh), John Stow, Richard Knolles,
    Richard Hooker
Shakespeare: With a Selection of Lines from His Plays
Sir Francis Bacon

Robert Burton
John Milton: With Printed Excerpt from *Comus*

The Age of Milton

Sir William D'Avenant and Abraham Cowley
John Dryden: With Selected Lines from His Poetry
Christopher Wren, Matthew Prior, Sir Isaac Newton, Daniel Defoe, Joseph Addison, and Robert Steele
Alexander Pope
Poets: Edward Young and John Gay
Jonathan Swift, Lord Bolingbroke (Henry St. John), Sir William Temple
Isaac Watts: With Printed Text of "The Indian Philosopher"

English Literature 1700–1760

Lord George Lyttelton and the Earl of Chesterfield (Philip Dormer Stanhope)
James Thomson: With Excerpts from *Temple of Liberty*
Laurence Sterne
Mark Akenside: With a Selection from *Pleasures of the Imagination*
William Shenstone: With the Full Text of "Jemmy Dawson. A Ballad"
William Collins: With the Full Text of the Ode "To Fear"
Thomas Gray: With the Full Text of the Ode "To Adversity"
Oliver Goldsmith: With a Selection from the *Deserted Village*
Letters, Politics, and Oratory: William Pitt, Earl of Mansfield (William Murray), Edmund Burke, Charles James Fox, Sir Joshua Reynolds
Dr. Samuel Johnson
Poets: James Beattie and George Lord Lyttleton
Satirists: Junius the Unknown Political Satirist, Charles Churchill, Robert Lloyd, and John Wilkes
Literary Scholarship: Thomas and Joseph Warton with the Full Text of Thomas Warton's "The Suicide" and Joseph Warton's "To Superstition"

English Literature from 1764, the Date of the Founding of Johnson's Literary Club, to 1800

William Cowper and Sir William Jones: With a Selection of Poetry from Cowper and the Full Text of Jones's "Solima: An Arabian Eclogue"
The Lake Poets: Robert Southey, Samuel Taylor Coleridge, and William Godwin
Samuel Rogers: With the Full Text of "Verses Written to Be Spoken by Mrs. Siddons"

Thomas Campbell: With Selected Excerpts from His Poetry and the Full Text of "Hohenlinden"

English Literature 1800–1832

George Crabbe: With the Full Text of the Ballad of "Phoebe Dawson"
Histories: John Lingard, Sharon Turner, Sir James Mackintosh, Charles James Fox, George Croly, and William Godwin
Thomas Moore: With the Full Text of "Go Where Glory Waits Thee"
William L. Bowles: With the Full Text of the Sonnet "To Time"
Henry Milman: With the Full Text of "Ode, to the Saviour"
Lord Byron: With the Full Text of "And Thou Art Dead, as Young and Fair"
Percy Bysshe Shelley: With the Text of the "Dedication" from "The Revolt of Islam"
Thomas James Mathias: With an Excerpt of Lines on Mathias from George Canning's Poem, "New Morality"
The Novelists: Godwin, Mrs. Radcliffe, Maria Edgeworth, Sir Walter Scott

Works Cited

Applebee, Arthur. 1974. *Tradition and Reform in the Teaching of English: A History.* Urbana: Univ. of Illinois Press.

Appleton's Cyclopaedia of American Biography. 1887. 1: 340.

Austen, Jessica Tyler. 1911. *Moses Coit Tyler: 1835–1900: Selections from His Letters and Diaries.* New York: Doubleday.

Battle, Kemp P. 1907. *History of the University of North Carolina from Its Beginnings to the Death of President Swain, 1789–1868.* 2 vols. Raleigh, N.C.: Published by the Author.

Bayless, Joy. 1943. *Rufus Wilmot Griswold, Poe's Literary Executor.* Nashville: Vanderbilt Univ. Press.

Bell, Whitfield J., Jr. 1954. "Scottish Emigration to America: A Letter of Dr. Charles Nisbet to Dr. John Witherspoon, 1784." *William and Mary Quarterly* 11 (April): 276–89.

Biddle, Edward W. 1920. *The Founding and Founders of Dickinson College.* Carlisle, Pa.: Dickinson College.

Bishop, Morris. 1962. *A History of Cornell.* Ithaca, N.Y.: Cornell Univ. Press.

Bishop, Robert Hamilton. 1804. *An Apology for Calvinism.* Lexington, Ky.: Bradford.

———. 1823. *An Introduction to a Course of Lectures on History.* Lexington, Ky.: William Tanner.

———. 1839. *Elements of the Science of Government: Being an Outline of a Portion of the Studies of the Senior Class in Miami University.* Oxford, Ohio: R. H. Bishop Jr.

Blair, Hugh. 1965. *Lectures on Rhetoric and Belles Lettres.* Edited by Harold F. Harding. 1783. Reprint. 2 vols. Carbondale: Southern Illinois Univ. Press.

Bright, James Wilson. 1903. "Concerning the Unwritten History of the Modern Language Association of America." *PMLA* 18, appendix I.

Boyd, James Robert. 1844. *Elements of Rhetoric and Literary Criticism, with Copious Practical Exercises and Examples for the Use of Common Schools and Academies, Including, also, a Succinct History of the English Language, and of British*

and American Literature from the Earliest to the Present Times. On the Basis of
... Recent Works by Alexander Reid and Robert Connel. New York: Harper and
Brothers.

———. 1846. *Eclectic Moral Philosophy, Prepared for Literary Institutions.* New
York: Harper and Brothers.

———. 1856. *Elements of Logic: On the Basis of Lectures by William Barron ... Professor of Belles-Lettres and Logic in the University of St. Andrews, with Large Supplementary Additions, Chiefly from Watts, Abercrombie, Brown, Whately, Mills,
and Thomson.* New York: A. S. Barnes.

———. 1860a. *Elements of English Composition, Grammatical, Rhetorical, Logical,
and Practical.* New York: A. S. Barnes.

———. 1860b. *Memoir of the Life, Character, and Writings of Philip Doddridge,
D.D., With a Selection from His Correspondence.* New York: American Tract Society.

Bronson, Walter C. 1971. *The History of Brown University.* 1914. Reprint. New
York: Arno.

Bruce, Philip Alexander. 1920. *History of the University of Virginia, 1819–1919.*
Vol. 1. New York: Macmillan.

Buchanan, Joseph. 1812. *The Philosophy of Human Nature.* Richmond, Ky.: John
A. Grimes.

Burgess, John W. 1934. *Reminiscences of an American Scholar; The Beginnings of
Columbia University.* New York: Columbia Univ. Press.

Caldwell, Wallace E. 1945. "The Humanities at the University of North Carolina,
1795–1945." In *A State University Surveys the Humanities,* edited by L. C.
MacKinney et al., 3–30. Chapel Hill: Univ. of North Carolina Press.

Campbell, George. 1776. *The Philosophy of Rhetoric.* London: W. Strahan.

*Catalogue of the Officers and Students of Lafayette College for the Academical Year,
1841–42.* 1842. Easton, Pa.: Lafayette College.

Chambers, Robert. 1836. *History of English Language and Literature.* Edinburgh:
William and Robert Chambers.

———. 1843–44. *Cyclopaedia of English Literature; Consisting of a Series of Specimens of British Writers in Prose and Verse. Connected by a Historical and Critical
Narrative.* 2 vols. Edinburgh: W. and R. Chambers.

Channing, Edward Tyrell. 1968. *Lectures Read to the Seniors in Harvard College.*
Edited by Dorothy I. Anderson and Waldo Braden. Foreword by David Potter.
1856. Reprint. Edwardsville: Southern Illinois Univ. Press.

———. 1856. *Lectures Read to the Seniors in Harvard College.* With a "Biographical Notice" by Richard H. Dana Jr. Boston: Ticknor and Fields.

Channing, William E. 1899. *Works.* Boston: American Unitarian Society.

Charvat, William. 1968. *The Origins of American Critical Thought 1810–1835.*
1936. Reprint. New York: Russell and Russell.

Cicero, Marcus Tullius. 1942. *De Oratore*. Translated by E. W. Sutton. Can
  Mass: Harvard Univ. Press.

Clark, Gregory, and S. Michael Halloran, eds. 1993. *Oratorical Culture iꞔ ꞁ√ꞔꞔe-
  teenth-Century America: Transformations in the Theory and Practice of Rhetoric*.
  Carbondale: Southern Illinois Univ. Press.

Coleman, Helen Turnbull Waite. 1956. *Banners in the Wilderness: Early Years of
  Washington and Jefferson College*. Pittsburgh: Univ. of Pittsburgh Press.

Collins, Varnum Lansing. 1914. *Princeton*. New York: Oxford Univ. Press.

Connel, Robert. 1831. *A Catechism of English Composition with a Succinct History
  of the English Language and Its Literature*. Edinburgh: Oliver and Boyd.

———. 1834. *Improved System of English Grammar . . . Adapted to Use of Schools*.
  Glasgow: Rutherglen.

Cooper, Anthony Ashley [Lord Shaftesbury]. 1900. *Characteristics of Men, Manners, Opinions, and Times*. Edited by J. M. Robertson. 1711. Reprint. 2 vols.
  London: G. Richards.

Copleston, Frederick, S.J. 1963. *Modern Philosophy: From Descartes to Leibniz. A
  History of Philosophy*. Vol. 4. Garden City, N.J.: Image.

———. 1994. *Modern Philosophy: The British Philosophers from Hobbes to Hume. A
  History of Philosophy*. Vol. 5. New York: Image.

Corbett, Edward P. J. 1965. *Classical Rhetoric for the Modern Student*. New York:
  Oxford Univ. Press.

Court, Franklin E. 1992. *Institutionalizing English Literature: The Culture
  and Politics of Literary Study, 1750–1900*. Stanford, Calif.: Stanford Univ.
  Press.

Craik, George L. 1844–45. *Sketches of the History of Literature and Learning in England*. 6 vols. London: C. Knight and Co.

Crawford, Robert. 1992. *Devolving English Literature*. Oxford: Clarendon.

———, ed. 1998. *The Scottish Invention of English Literature*. Cambridge: Cambridge Univ. Press.

Cuningham, Charles. 1942. *Timothy Dwight 1752–1817: A Biography*. New York:
  Macmillan.

Daiches, David. 1991. "John Witherspoon, James Wilson and the Influence of
  Scottish Rhetoric in America." *Eighteenth-Century Life* 15: 163–80.

Davies, Samuel. 1752. *Miscellaneous Poems Chiefly on Divine Subjects; In Two Books;
  Published for the Religious Entertainment of Christians in General*. Williamsburg, Va.: William Hunter.

———. 1761. *Religion and Public Spirit; a Valedictory Address to the Senior Class,
  Delivered in Nassau Hall, September 21, 1760*. New York: James Parker.

Diamond, Peter J. 1990. "Witherspoon, William Smith and the Scottish Philosophy." In *Scotland and America in the Age of the Enlightenment*, edited by Richard
  B. Sher and Jeffrey R. Smitten, 115–32. Edinburgh: Edinburgh Univ. Press.

Dickinson College, Chartered by the Legislature of Pennsylvania in 1783. 1926. Carlisle, Pa.: Dickinson College.

Dunaway, Wayland F. 1944. *Scotch-Irish of Colonial Pennsylvania.* Chapel Hill: Univ. of North Carolina Press.

Eagleton, Terry. 1995. *Heathcliff and the Great Hunger: Studies in Irish Culture.* London and New York: Verso.

Earnest, Ernest. 1953. *Academic Procession: An Informal History of the American College, 1636–1953.* Indianapolis: Bobbs-Merrill.

Easterby, J. H. 1935. *A History of the College of Charleston, Founded 1770.* Charleston, S.C.: College of Charleston.

Enfield, William. 1774. *The Speaker; or, Miscellaneous Pieces, Selected from the Best English Writers.* London: L. Davis et al.

Ferguson, Adam. 1767. *Essay on the History of Civil Society.* Edinburgh: Kincaid and Bell.

Flower, Milton and Lenore. 1944. *This Is Carlisle, A History of a Pennsylvania Town.* Harrisburg: J. Horace Macfarland.

Gegenheimer, Albert Frank. 1943. *William Smith, Educator and Churchman, 1727–1803.* Philadelphia: Univ. of Pennsylvania Press.

Graff, Gerald. 1987. *Professing Literature: An Institutional History.* Chicago: Univ. of Chicago Press.

Graham, Ian. 1956. *Colonists from Scotland.* Ithaca, N.Y.: Cornell Univ. Press.

Griswold, Rufus. 1842. *Poets and Poetry of America.* Philadelphia: Carey and Hart.

———. 1844. *Gems from American Female Poets.* Philadelphia: H. Hooker.

———. 1845a. *Poets and Poetry of England in the Nineteenth Century.* Philadelphia: Carey and Hart.

———, ed. 1845b. *Poetical Works of James Montgomery. With a Memoir of the Author.* Philadelphia: Sorin and Ball.

———. 1847. *Prose Writers of America with a Survey of the Intellectual History, Condition, and Prospects of the Country.* Philadelphia: Carey and Hart.

———. 1848. *The Female Poets of America.* Philadelphia: Carey and Hart.

———. 1850. "Memoir" in *Works of the Late Edgar Allan Poe with Notices of His Life and Genius.* New York: Redfield.

———. 1898. *Passages from the Correspondence and Other Papers of Rufus W. Griswold.* Cambridge, Mass.: W. M. Griswold.

Guild, Reuben Aldridge. 1897. *Early History of Brown University, Including the Life, Times, and Correspondence of President Manning. 1756–1791.* Providence, R.I.: Snow and Farnham.

Hart, John Seely. 1845a. *Class Book of Poetry: Consisting of Selections from English and American Poets, from Chaucer to the Present Day, with Biographical and Critical Remarks.* Philadelphia: Butler and Co.

———. 1845b. *Class Book of Prose: Consisting of Selections from Distinguished En-*

glish and American Authors, from Chaucer to the Present Day. The Whole Arranged in Chronological Order, with Biographical and Critical Remarks. Philadelphia: Butler and Williams.

————. 1845c. *An English Grammar; or, An Exposition of the Principles and Usages of the English Language.* Philadelphia: E. H. Butler.

————. 1847. *An Essay on the Life and Writings of Edmund Spenser, with a Special Exposition of the Fairy Queen.* New York: Putnam.

————. 1852. *The Female Prose Writers of America. With Portraits, Biographical Notices and Specimens of their Writings.* Philadelphia: E. H. Butler.

————. 1854. *Spenser and the Fairy Queen.* Philadelphia: Hayes and Zell.

————. 1871. *A Manual of Composition and Rhetoric.* Philadelphia: Eldredge.

————. 1872a. *A Manual of American Literature: A Text Book for Schools and Colleges.* Philadelphia: Eldredge.

————. 1872b. *A Manual of English Literature: A Text Book for Schools and Colleges.* Philadelphia: Eldredge.

————. 1873. *A Short Course in Literature, English and American.* Philadelphia: Eldredge.

————. 1874. *Grammar of the English Language, with an Analysis of the Sentence.* Philadelphia: Eldredge.

————. 1888. *The Complete Dramatic and Poetical Works of William Shakespeare. With a Summary Outline of the Life of the Poet . . . Collected from the Latest and Most Reliable Sources, by John S. Hart.* Edited by W. G. Clark and W. A. Wright. Philadelphia: D. McKay.

Havighurst, Walter. 1969. *The Miami Years 1809–1969.* New York: Putnam.

Hobbes, Thomas. 1928. *Elements of Law, Natural and Politic.* Edited by F. Tonnies. 1656. Reprint. Cambridge: The Univ. Press.

————. 1946. *Leviathan.* Edited by M. Oakeshott. 1651. Reprint. Oxford: Basil Blackwell.

Holmes, John and John Sterling. 1788. *A System of Rhetoric.* New York: Hugh Gaine.

Home, Henry [Lord Kames]. 1763. *Elements of Criticism.* 3 vols. Edinburgh: Kincaid and Bell.

————. 1855. *Elements of Criticism.* Edited by James Robert Boyd. 1763. Reprint. New York: A. S. Barnes.

Hook, Andrew. 1975. *Scotland and America: A Study of Cultural Relations 1750–1835.* Glasgow: Blackie.

Hutcheson, Francis. 1725. *Inquiry into the Origin of Our Ideas of Beauty and Virtue; in Two Treatises.* London: J. Darby.

————. 1747. *Philosophiae moralis institutio compendiaria libris tribus ethices et jurisprudentiae naturalis principia conntinens.* Glasgow: R. Foulis.

Ingersoll, Charles J. 1823. *A Discourse Concerning the Influence of America on the*

Mind; Being the Annual Oration Delivered before the American Philosophical Society, at the University of Philadelphia . . . 18th October 1823. Philadelphia: A. Small.

Irving, Washington. 1978. "English Writers on America." In *The Sketch Book of Geoffrey Crayon, Gent,* edited by Haskell Springer. 1819. Reprint. Boston: Twayne.

Jardine, George. 1825. *Outlines of Philosophical Education, Illustrated by the Method of Teaching the Logic Class in the University of Glasgow.* Glasgow: Oliver and Boyd.

Jennings, Walter Wilson. 1955. *Transylvania: Pioneer University of the West.* New York: Pageant.

Kames, Lord [see under Home, Henry].

Kelly, Brooks Mather. 1974. *Yale: A History.* New Haven: Yale Univ. Press.

Kingsley, W. L. 1879. *Yale College, a Sketch of its History.* 2 vols. New York: H. Holt.

Knapp, Samuel Lorenzo. 1821. *Biographical Sketches of Eminent Lawyers, Statesmen, and Men of Letters.* Boston: Richardson and Lord.

———. 1824. *Memoirs of General Lafayette.* Boston: E. G. House.

———. 1829. *Lectures on American Literature with Remarks on Some Passages of American History.* New York: E. Bliss.

———. 1831. *A Memoir of the Life of Daniel Webster.* Boston: Stimpson and Clapp.

———. 1832. *Advice in the Pursuits of Literature: Containing Historical, Biographical, and Critical Remarks.* New York: J. K. Porter.

———. 1834. *Female Biography; Containing, Notices of Distinguished Women in Different Nations and Ages.* New York: J. Carpenter.

———. 1835. *Life of Aaron Burr.* New York: Wiley and Long.

Landsman, Ned C. 1990. "Witherspoon and the Problem of Provincial Identity." In *Scotland and America in the Age of the Enlightenment,* edited by Richard B. Sher and Jeffrey R. Smitten, 29–45. Edinburgh: Edinburgh Univ. Press.

Lehrer, Keith. 1989. *Thomas Reid.* London: Routledge.

Leyburn, James G. 1962. *The Scotch-Irish: A Social History.* Chapel Hill: Univ. of North Carolina Press.

Lowth, Robert. 1762. *A Short Introduction to English Grammar: with Critical Notes.* London: Millar and Dodsley.

March, Francis. 1895. "English at Lafayette College." In *English in American Universities,* edited by William Morton Payne. Boston: D. C. Heath.

Mathias, Thomas James. 1794. *Pursuits of Literature, or, What You Will: a Satirical Poem in Dialogue.* London: J. Owen.

Maxcy, Jonathan. 1844. *The Literary Remains of the Rev. Jonathan Maxcy, D.D., with a Memoir of His Life, by Romeo Elton, D.D.* New York: A. V. Blake.

May, Henry E. 1976. *The Enlightenment in America*. New York: Oxford Univ. Press.

Miller, Perry. 1955. *The Raven and the Whale: The War of Wits and Words in the Era of Poe and Melville*. New York: Harcourt, Brace.

Miller, Thomas P. 1990. "Witherspoon, Blair and the Rhetoric of Civic Humanism." In *Scotland and America in the Age of the Enlightenment*, edited by Richard B. Sher and Jeffrey R. Smitten, 100–14. Edinburgh: Edinburgh Univ. Press.

———. 1994. "John Witherspoon." In *Eighteenth-Century British and American Rhetorics and Rhetoricians*, edited by Michael G. Moran, 268–79. Westport, Conn.: Greenwood.

Montgomery, Thomas Harrison. 1900. *History of the University of Pennsylvania . . . to 1770*. Philadelphia: G. W. Jacobs.

Morgan, James Henry. 1933. *Dickinson College, History of One Hundred and Fifty Years*. Carlisle, Pa.: Dickinson College.

Morison, Samuel Eliot. 1995. *The Founding of Harvard College*. Cambridge, Mass.: Harvard Univ. Press.

Newman, Samuel Phillips. 1995. *A Practical System of Rhetoric; or, the Principles and Rules of Style, Inferred from Examples of Writing*. Introduction by Charlotte Downey. 1827. Reprint. Delmar, N.Y.: Scholars' Reprints.

Norton, David Fare. 1976. "Francis Hutcheson in America." *Studies on Voltaire and the Eighteenth Century* 154: 1562–65.

Ohmann, Richard. 1976. *English in America: A Radical View of the Profession*. New York: Oxford Univ. Press.

Owen, W. B. 1902. *Lafayette College. Some Pages of Its Past; Pictures of Its Present; and Forecasts of Its Future*. Philadelphia: Lafayette College.

Paley, William. 1785. *The Principles of Moral Philosophy and Political Philosophy*. London: Faulder.

———. 1802. *Natural Theology; or, Evidences of the Existence and Attributes of the Deity, Collected from the Appearances of Nature*. London: Faulder.

Parker, William Riley. 1967. "Where Do English Departments Come From?" *College English* 28, no. 5: 339–51.

Pittock, Joan H. 1998. "The Teaching of Literature and Aesthetics at Aberdeen." In *The Scottish Invention of English Literature*, edited by Robert Crawford, 116–33. Cambridge: Cambridge Univ. Press.

Porter, Ebenezer. 1827. *Analysis of the Principles of Rhetorical Delivery as Applied in Reading and Speaking*. New York: J. Leavitt.

Pryde, George. 1957. *The Scottish Universities and the Colleges of Colonial America*. Glasgow: Jackson.

Ramsay, John. 1888. *Scotland and Scotsmen in the Eighteenth Century*. Edited by Alexander Allardyce. 2 vols. Edinburgh: Blackwood's.

Raymond, Andrew Van Vranken. 1907. *Union University: Its History, Influence, Characteristics and Equipment.* 3 vols. New York: Lewis.

Read, Thomas Buchanan. 1848. *Female Poets of America: with Portraits, Biographical Notices, and Specimens of Their Writings.* Philadelphia: E. H. Butler.

Reid, Alexander. 1837. *Rudiments of English Grammar.* Edinburgh: Oliver and Boyd.

———. 1839. *Rudiments of English Composition.* Edinburgh: Oliver and Boyd.

———. 1844. *A Dictionary of English Language, . . .Pronunciation, Etymology and Explanation of All Words Authorized by Eminent Writers.* Edinburgh: Oliver and Boyd.

Reid, Thomas. 1846. *Works.* 2 vols. Edited by W. Hamilton. Edinburgh: Maclachlan and Stewart.

Richardson, C. F., and H. A. Clark, eds. 1878. *The College Book.* Boston: Houghton and Osgood.

Robbins, Caroline. 1954. " 'When It Is That Colonies May Turn Independent:' An Analysis of the Environment and Politics of Francis Hutcheson (1694–1746).' " *William and Mary Quarterly* 11 (April): 200–51.

Rodabaugh, James E. 1935. *Robert Hamilton Bishop.* Columbus: Ohio State Archaeological and Historical Society.

Ross, Ian Simpson. 1995. *The Life of Adam Smith.* Oxford: Clarendon. Quoting Francis Hutcheson, *An Inquiry into the Origin of Our Ideas of Beauty and Virtue; in Two Treatises* (London: J. Darby, 1725).

Ross, James. 1798. *A Plain, Short, Comprehensive Practical Latin Grammar.* Chambersburg, Pa.: Robert Harper.

———. 1844. *A Latin Grammar, Comprising All the Rules and Observations Necessary to an Accurate Knowledge of the Latin Classics.* Philadelphia: Thomas and Cowperthwait.

Rush, Benjamin. 1789. *Essays, Literary, Moral, and Philosophical.* Philadelphia: Bradford.

Scholes, Robert. 1998. *The Rise and Fall of English: Reconstructing English as a Discipline.* New Haven and London: Yale Univ. Press.

Scott, Patrick. 1983. *"Jonathan Maxcy and the Aims of Early Nineteenth-Century Rhetorical Teaching."* College English 45 (January): 21–30.

Scott, William Robert. 1966. *Francis Hutcheson: His Life, Teaching and Position in the History of Philosophy.* New York: A. M. Kelley.

Sellers, Charles Coleman. 1973. *Dickinson College: A History.* Middletown, Conn.: Wesleyan Univ. Press.

Shaw, Thomas B. 1849. *Outlines of English Literature.* London: J. Murray.

———. 1852. *Outlines of English Literature. With a Sketch of American Literature, by H. T. Tuckerman.* Philadelphia: Blanchard and Lea.

———. 1864a. *Choice Specimens of English Literature.* London: J. Murray.

———. 1864b. *History of English Literature*. London: J. Murray.

———. 1867. *Complete Manual of English Literature. With a Sketch of American Literature*, by Henry T. Tuckerman. New York: Sheldon.

———. 1874. *Shaw's New History of English Literature. Prepared on the Basis of "Shaw's Manual."* New York: Sheldon.

Sheridan, Thomas. 1762. *A Course of Lectures on Elocution*. London: Dilly and Longman.

———. 1781. *A Rhetorical Grammar of the English Language*. Dublin: Price and Whitestone.

Skillman, David B. 1932. *The Biography of a College, Being the History of the First Century of Life of Lafayette College*. 2 vols. Easton, Pa.: Lafayette College.

Skinner, Andrew S. 1990. *"Adam Smith and America: The Political Economy of Conflict." In Scotland and America in the Age of Enlightenment*, edited by Richard B. Sher and Jeffrey R. Smitten, 148–62. Edinburgh: Edinburgh Univ. Press.

Sloan, Douglas. 1971. *The Scottish Enlightenment and the American College Ideal*. New York: Teachers College Press.

Smith, Adam. 1963. *Lectures on Rhetoric and Belles Lettres*. Edited by John M. Lothian. London: T. Nelson.

———. 1976. *Theory of Moral Sentiments*. Edited by D. D. Raphael and A. L. Macfie. 1759. Reprint. Oxford: Clarendon.

———. 1983. *Lectures on Rhetoric and Belles Lettres*. Edited by J. C. Bryce. Oxford: Clarendon.

Smith, Horace Wemyss. 1880. *Life and Correspondence of Rev. William Smith, D.D.* Philadelphia: Ferguson Brothers.

Smith, J. H., and E. W. Parks, eds. 1951. *The Great Critics: An Anthology of Literary Criticism*. New York: Norton.

Smith, Joseph. 1857. *History of Jefferson College: Including an Account of the Early "Log-Cabin" Schools, and the Canonsburg Academy*. Pittsburgh: Shryock.

Snider, William B. 1992. *Light on the Hill: A History of the University of North Carolina at Chapel Hill*. Chapel Hill and London: Univ. of North Carolina Press.

Snow, Louis Franklin. 1907. *The College Curriculum in the United States*. New York: Printed for the Author.

Spalding, William. 1853. *History of English Literature: With an Outline of the Origin and Growth of the English Language*. Edinburgh: Oliver and Boyd.

Spiller, Robert A. 1963. *Literary History of the United States*. New York: Macmillan.

Stewart, Dugald. 1792–1827. *Elements of the Philosophy of the Human Mind*. 3 vols. London: A. Strahan.

Stille, Charles Janeway. 1869. *A Memoir of the Rev. William Smith*. Philadelphia: Moore and Sons.

Stocking, George. 1987. *Victorian Anthropology*. New York: Free Press.

Sullivan, Dolores P. 1994. *William Holmes McGuffey: Schoolmaster to the Nation*. London and Ontario: Associated University Presses.

Sweet, William. 1936. *The Presbyterians*. Vol. 2. of Religion on the American Frontier. New York: Harper and Brothers.

Tarver, J. 1996. *"Abridged Editions of Blair's* Lectures on Rhetoric and Belles Lettres *in America: What Nineteenth-Century College Students Really Learned about Blair on Rhetoric."* The Bibliotheck: A Journal of Scottish Bibliography 21: 54–67.

Thacher, Thomas A. 1852. *A Discourse Commemorative of Professor James L. Kingsley*. New York: Baker and Godwin.

Tilson, Alistair. 1991. *"Who Now Reads Spalding?"* English Studies in Canada 17 (December): 469–78.

Trinterud, Leonard J. 1949. *Forming of an American Tradition*. Philadelphia: Westminster.

Tucker, Abraham. 1805. *The Light of Nature Pursued*. 7 vols. Edited by H. P. St. John Mildmay. London: R. Faulder.

Tucker, George. 1822. *Essays on Various Subjects of Taste, Morals, and National Policy*. Georgetown, D.C.: J. Milligan.

———. 1837. *The Law of Wages, Profits, and Rent Investigated*. Philadelphia: Carey and Hart.

———. 1839. *The Theory of Money and Banks Investigated*. Boston: Little, Brown.

———. 1859. *Political Economy for the People*. Philadelphia: Sherman.

Tuman, Myron. 1986. *"From Astor Place to Kenyon Road."* College English 48 (April): 339–49.

Tyler, Moses Coit. 1949. *History of American Literature, 1607–1765*. 1878. Reprint. Ithaca, N.Y.: Cornell Univ. Press.

Tyler, William Seymour. 1873. *History of Amherst College During Its First Half Century, 1821–1871*. Springfield, Mass: C. W. Bryan.

Vanderbilt, Kermit. 1986. *American Literature and the Academy: The Roots, Growth, and Maturity of a Profession*. Philadelphia: Univ. of Pennsylvania Press.

Ward, John. 1759. *A System of Oratory, Delivered in a Course of Lectures Publicly Read at Gresham College, London*. 2 vols. London: J. Ward.

Wayland, Francis. 1842. *Thoughts on the Present Collegiate System in the United States*. Boston: Gould, Kendall, and Lincoln.

———. 1854. *The Education Demanded by the People of the United States*. Introduction by Theodore R. Crane. Boston: Phillips and Sampson.

———. 1864. *Memoir of the Christian Labors . . . of Thomas Chalmers*. Boston: Gould and Lincoln.

Webster, Noah. 1787. *An American Selection of Lessons in Reading and Speaking. Calculated to Improve the Minds and Refine the Taste of Youth. And also to Instruct Them in the Geography, History, and Politics of the United States.* Philadelphia: Young and M'Culloch.

Wellek, René. 1963. *Concepts of Criticism.* Edited by Stephen G. Nichols Jr. New Haven and London: Yale Univ. Press.

Whately, Richard. 1826. *Elements of Logic. Comprising the Substance of the Article in the Encyclopaedia Metropolitana: With Additions, etc.* London: J. Mawman.

———. 1828. *Elements of Rhetoric. Comprising the Substance of the Article in the Encyclopaedia Metropolitana: With additions, etc.* London: J. Murray.

Williamson, Harold, and Payson S. Wild. 1976. *Northwestern University: A History, 1850–1975.* Evanston, Ill.: Northwestern Univ. Press.

Wills, Gary. 1978. *Inventing America: Jefferson's Declaration of Independence.* Garden City, N.Y.: Doubleday.

Witherspoon, John. 1765–1815. *"Eloquence."* In Works, vol. 7. London: E. and C. Dilly.

———. 1800. *Lectures on Moral Philosophy.* Philadelphia: Woodward.

Wright, John D. 1975. *Transylvania: Tutor to the West.* Lexington, Ky.: Transylvania Univ.

Index